KNOTT'S

HANDBOOK FOR VEGETABLE GROWERS

THIRD EDITION

KNOTT'S

HANDBOOK FOR VEGETABLE GROWERS

THIRD EDITION

OSCAR A. LORENZ

Professor Emeritus of Vegetable Crops
University of California, Davis

DONALD N. MAYNARD

Professor of Vegetable Crops
Gulf Coast Research and Education Center
University of Florida
Bradenton, Florida

A Wiley-Interscience Publication
JOHN WILEY & SONS
New York / Chichester / Brisbane / Toronto / Singapore

Library of Congress Cataloging-in-Publication Data:

Knott, James Edward, 1897–
Knott's handbook for vegetable growers.

"A Wiley-Interscience publication."
Includes index.
1. Truck farming—Handbooks, manuals, etc. 2. Vegetables—Handbooks, manuals, etc. 3. Vegetable gardening—Handbooks, manuals, etc. I. Lorenz, Oscar Anthony, 1914– . II. Maynard, Donald N., 1932– . III. Title. IV. Title: Handbook for vegetable growers.

SB321.K49 1988 635 87-25224
ISBN 0-471-85240-6

Printed in the United States of America

10 9 8 7 6 5 4 3

PREFACE

Third edition

Technological advances, new nomenclature, and changes in governmental regulations that have occurred since 1980 are reflected in the third edition of *Handbook for Vegetable Growers*. Whenever possible and appropriate, information in the second edition has been made current.

The general format of the second edition has been retained. Part 2 has been expanded to include plant growing and greenhouse vegetable production. Where appropriate, information on strawberry has been added because it is herbaceous, is cultured as an annual in the major producing states, and for the most part is grown by vegetable growers rather than fruit growers.

Much new technical information has been included. For example, sections on integrated pest management, soil solarization, row covers, polyethylene mulches, gel seeding, seed priming, vegetable quality, compatibility of produce in mixed loads, and vegetable marketing alternatives have been added. Every effort has been made to include the most practical and current information.

Again we express gratitude to our colleagues who have provided materials and suggestions, and who have encouraged us in this revision. We hope that *Handbook for Vegeta-*

ble Growers will continue to be a ready reference for those concerned with vegetable crops as envisaged by Dr. Knott when the *Handbook* was first published in 1956.

O. A. LORENZ
D. N. MAYNARD

Davis, California
Bradenton, Florida
February 1988

CONTENTS

PART 1

VEGETABLES AND THE VEGETABLE INDUSTRY

BOTANICAL NAMES, COMMON NAMES, AND EDIBLE PARTS OF VEGETABLES

Botanical Name	Common Name	Edible Plant Part
Monocotyledoneae		
Alismataceae	Water-plantain family	
Sagittaria sagittifolia L.	Chinese arrowhead	Corm
Amaryllidaceae	Amaryllis family	
Allium ampeloprasum L. Porrum group	Leek	Leaf base
Allium cepa L. Cepa group	Onion	Bulb, leaf
Allium cepa L. Aggregatum group	Shallot, multiplier onion, potato onion	Bulb
Allium cepa L. Proliferum group	Egyptian onion, top onion	Bulb
Allium chinense G. Don.	Rakkyo	Bulb
Allium fistulosum L.	Welsh onion, Japanese bunching onion	Leaf
Allium sativum L.	Garlic	Bulb
Allium schoenoprasum L.	Chive	Leaf
Allium tuberosum Rottl. ex K. Spreng	Chinese chive	Leaf
Araceae	Arum family	
Colocasia esculenta (L.) Schott.	Taro, dasheen	Corm
Xanthosoma sagittofolium (L.) Schott.	Malanga, yautia	Corm
Cyperaceae	Sedge family	
Eleocharis dulcis (Burm. f.) Trin. ex Henschel	Water chestnut	Corm

Dioscoreaceae	Yam family	
Dioscorea alata L.	Greater yam	Tuber
Dioscorea batatas Decne.	Chinese yam	Tuber
Dioscorea rotundata Poir.	White yam	Tuber
Gramineae	Grass family	
Zea mays var. *praecox* Bonaf.	Popcorn	Mature seed
Zea mays var. *rugosa* Bonaf.	Sweet corn	Immature seed
Liliaceae	Lily family	
Asparagus officinalis L.	Asparagus	Shoot
Zingiberaceae	Ginger family	
Zingiber officinale Roscoe	Ginger	Rhizome
Dicotyledoneae		
Amaranthaceae	Amaranth family	
Amaranthus tricolor L.	Tampala, Chinese spinach	Leaf
Araliaceae	Ginseng family	
Aralia cordata Thunb.	Udo	Shoot
Panax quinquefolius L.	American ginseng	Root
Basellaceae	Basella family	
Basella alba L.	Malabar spinach	Leaf
Chenopodiaceae	Goosefoot family	
Atriplex hortensis L.	Orach	Leaf
Beta vulgaris L. Cicla group	Swiss chard	Leaf
Beta vulgaris L. Crassa group	Beet	Root, leaf
Spinacia oleracea L.	Spinach	Leaf
Compositae	Sunflower family	
Articum lappa L.	Burdock	Root
Chrysanthemum coronarium L.	Garland chrysanthemum	Shoot

BOTANICAL NAMES, COMMON NAMES, AND EDIBLE PARTS OF VEGETABLES—Continued

Botanical Name	Common Name	Edible Plant Part
Cichorium endiva L.	Endive, escarole	Leaf
Cichorium intybus L.	Witloof chicory, radicchio	Leaf
Cynara cardunculus L.	Cardoon	Petiole
Cynara scolymus L.	Globe artichoke	Immature flower
Helianthus tuberosus L.	Jerusalem artichoke	Tuber
Lactuca sativa L.	Lettuce	Leaf
Petasites japonicus (Siebold & Zucc.) Maxim.	Fuki	Petiole
Scolymus hispanicus L.	Spanish oyster plant	Root
Scorzonera hispanica L.	Black salsify	Root
Taraxacum officinale Wiggers	Dandelion	Leaf
Tragopogon porrifolius L.	Salsify	Root
Convolvulaceae	Morning-glory family	
Ipomoea aquatica Forsk.	Water spinach	Leaf
Ipomoea batatas (L.) Lam.	Sweet potato	Root, leaf
Cruciferae	Mustard family	
Armoracia rusticana P. Gaertn., B. Mey & Scherb.	Horseradish	Root
Barbarea verna (Mill.) Asch.	Upland cress	Leaf
Brassica juncea (L.) Czerniak.	Mustard greens	Leaf
Brassica napus L. Napobrassica group	Rutabaga	Root
Brassica napus L. Pabularia group	Siberian kale, Hanover salad	Leaf
Brassica oleracea L. Acephala group	Kale, collard	Leaf
Brassica oleracea L. Alboglabra group	Chinese kale	Leaf

Brassica oleracea L. Botrytis group	Cauliflower	Immature flower
Brassica oleracea L. Capitata group	Cabbage	Leaf
Brassica oleracea L. Gemmifera group	Brussels sprouts	Axillary bud
Brassica oleracea L. Gongylodes group	Kohlrabi	Stem
Brassica oleracea L. Italica group	Broccoli	Immature flower
Brassica rapa L. Chinensis group	Pak-choi, Chinese mustard	Leaf
Brassica rapa L. Pekinensis group	Pe-tsai, Chinese cabbage	Leaf
Brassica rapa L. Perviridis group	Spinach mustard	Leaf
Brassica rapa L. Rapifera group	Turnip	Root, leaf
Brassica rapa L. Ruvo group	Broccoli raab	Leaf
Crambe maritima L.	Sea kale	Leaf
Eruca vesicaria sativa (Mill.) Thell.	Rocket salad	Leaf
Lepidium sativum L.	Garden cress	Leaf
Nasturtium officinale R. Br.	Watercress	Leaf
Raphanus sativus L.	Radish	Root
Raphanus sativus L. Longipinnatus group	Daikon	Root
Cucurbitaceae	Gourd family	
Benincasa hispida (Thunb.) Cogn.	Chinese winter melon, wax gourd	Fruit
Citrullus lanatus (Thunb.) Matsum. & Nakai	Watermelon	Fruit
Citrullus lanatus var. *citroides* (L. H. Bailey) Mansf.	Citron	Fruit
Cucumis anquira L.	West Indian gherkin	Fruit
Cucumis melo L. Inodorus group	Honeydew melon, casaba melon	Fruit
Cucumis melo L. Reticulatus group	Muskmelon, Persian melon	Fruit
Cucumis sativus L.	Cucumber	Fruit
Cucurbita maxima Duchesne	Winter squash	Fruit
Cucurbita mixta Pang.	Cushaw squash	Fruit

BOTANICAL NAMES, COMMON NAMES, AND EDIBLE PARTS OF VEGETABLES—Continued

Botanical Name	Common Name	Edible Plant Part
Cucurbita moschata (Duchesne) Poir.	Winter crookneck squash	Fruit
Cucurbita pepo L. var. *pepo*	Pumpkin, acorn squash	Fruit
Cucurbita pepo var. *melopepo* (L.) Alef.	Bush summer squash	Fruit
Lagenaria siceraria (Mol.) Standl.	Calabash gourd, zucca melon	Fruit
Luffa acutangula (L.) Roxb.	Chinese okra	Fruit
Luffa aegyptiaca Mill.	Sponge gourd	Fruit
Momordica charantia L.	Bitter melon	Fruit
Sechium edule (Jacq.) Swartz	Chayote	Fruit
Trichosanthes anguina L.	Snake gourd	Fruit
Euphorbiaceae	Spurge family	
Manihot esculenta Crantz	Cassava, yuca	Root
Leguminosae	Pea family	
Glycine max (L.) Merrill	Soybean	Seed
Pachyrhizus erosus (L.) Urb.	Jicama, yam bean	Root
Pachyrhizus tuberosus (Lam.) A. Spreng.	Potato bean	Root
Phaseolus acutifolius var. *latifolius* G. Freem.	Tepary bean	Seed
Phaseolus coccineus L.	Scarlet runner bean	Fruit
Phaseolus limensis Macfady.	Lima bean	Seed
Phaseolus limensis var. *limenanus* L. H. Bailey	Bush lima bean	Seed
Phaseolus lunatus L.	Sieva bean	Seed
Phaseolus vulgaris L.	Snap bean	Fruit, seed
Phaseolus vulgaris var. *humilis* Alef.	Bush snap bean	Fruit, seed
Pisum sativum L.	Pea	Seed

Pisum sativum var. *arvense* (L.) Poir.	Field pea	Seed
Pisum sativum var. *macrocarpon* Ser.	Edible-podded pea	Fruit
Psophocarpus tetragonolobus (L.) DC	Winged bean	All
Trigonella foenum-gracecum L.	Fenugreek	Leaf
Vicia faba L.	Broad bean, fava bean, horse bean	Seed
Vigna aconitifolia (Jacq.) Marechal	Moth bean	Seed
Vigna angularis (Willd.) Ohwi & Ohashi	Adzuki bean	Fruit, seed
Vigna mungo (L.) Hepper	Urd, black bean	Fruit, seed
Vigna radiata (L.) R. Wilcz.	Mung bean	Fruit, sprouts
Vigna umbellata (Thunb.) Ohwi & Ohashi	Rice bean	Fruit
Vigna unguiculata (L.) Walp.	Southern pea	Fruit, seed
Vigna unguiculata cylindrica (L.) Van Eselt. ex Verdc.	Catjang	Seed
Vigna unguiculata sesquipedalis (L.) Verdc.	Yard-long bean	Fruit
Malvaceae	Cotton family	
Abelmoschus esculentus (L.) Moench	Okra	Fruit
Hibiscus sabdariffa L.	Roselle	Flower
Martyniaceae	Martynia family	
Proboscidea louisianica (Mill.) Thell.	Martynia	Fruit
Nymphaceae	Water-lily family	
Nelumbo nucifera Gaertn.	Lotus	Root
Polygonaceae	Buckwheat family	
Rheum rhabarbarum L.	Rhubarb	Petiole
Rumex acetosa L.	Garden sorrel	Leaf
Rumex patientia L.	Patience dock	Leaf
Rumex scutatus L.	French sorrel	Leaf
Rosaceae	Rose family	
Fragaria × *ananassa* Duchesne.	Strawberry	Fruit

BOTANICAL NAMES, COMMON NAMES, AND EDIBLE PARTS OF VEGETABLES—Continued

Botanical Name	Common Name	Edible Plant Part
Solanaceae	Potato family	
Capsicum annuum var. *annuum* L.	Pepper: Bell, cayenne, chili, cone, red cluster	Fruit
Capsicum frutescens L.	Tabasco pepper	Fruit
Cyphomandra betacea (Cav.) Sendtn.	Tree tomato	Fruit
Lycopersicon esculentum Mill.	Tomato	Fruit
Lycopersicon esculentum var. *cerasiforme* (Dunal) Alef.	Cherry tomato	Fruit
Lycopersicon esculentum var. *pyriforme* (Dunal) Alef.	Pear tomato	Fruit
Lycopersicon pimpinellifolium (Jusl.)	Currant tomato	Fruit
Physalis ixocarpa Brot.	Tomatillo	Fruit
Physalis pruinosa L.	Husk tomato	Fruit
Solanum melongena L.	Eggplant	Fruit
Solanum muricatum Ait.	Pepino	Fruit
Solanum tuberosum L.	Potato	Tuber
Tetragoniaceae	Carpetweed family	
Tetragonia tetragoniodes (Pall.) O. Kuntze	New Zealand spinach	Leaf
Umbelliferae	Parsley family	
Anthriscus cerefolium (L.) Hoffm.	Chervil	Leaf
Apium graveolens L. var. *dulce* (Mill.) Pers.	Celery	Petiole
Apium graveolens L. var. *rapaceum* (Mill.) Gaud-Beaup.	Celeriac	Root
Coriandrum sativum L.	Chinese parsley, cilantro	Leaf

Daucus carota L.	Carrot	Root
Foeniculum vulgare Mill.	Fennel	Leaf
Foeniculum vulgare var. *azoricum* (Mill.) Thell.	Florence fennel	Leaf
Pastinaca sativa L.	Parsnip	Root
Petroselinum crispum (Mill.) Nyman ex A. W. Hill	Parsley	Leaf
Petroselinum crispum var. *neapolitanum* Danert	Italian parsley	Leaf
Petroselinum crispum var. *tuberosum* (Bernh.) Crov.	Turnip-rooted parsley	Root
Valerianaceae	Valerian family	
Valerianella locusta (L.) Betcke	Corn salad	Leaf

Botanical names conform to *Hortus Third*, Macmillan, New York (1976). Families are alphabetized within Monocotyledoneae and Dicotyledoneae and genera are alphabetized within families for convenience.

English	French	Dutch	German	Danish	Spanish	Italian
Artichoke	artischaut	artisjok	Artischocke	artiskok	alcachofa	carciofo
Asparagus	asperge	asperge	Spargel	asparges	espárrago	sparago
Broad bean	féve	tuinboon	Puffbohne	hestebønne	haba	fava
Snap bean	haricot	boon	Bohne	bønne	ejote	fagiolino
Beet	betterave rouge	kroot	rote Rübe	rødbede	betabol	bietola da orta
Broccoli	chou-brocoli	broccoli	Brokkoli	broccoli	brocoli	broccolo
Brussels sprouts	chou de Bruxelles	spruitkool	Rosenkohl	rosenkål	col de Bruselas	cavolo di Bruxells
Cabbage	chou	kool	Kohl	kål	col, repollo	cavolo
Carrot	carotte	peen	Karotte	karot	zanahoria	carota
Cauliflower	chou-fleur	bloemkool	Blumenkohl	blomkål	coliflor	cavolfiore
Celery	céleri	selderij	Sellerie	selleri	apio	sedano
Celeriac	céleri-rave	knolselderij	Knollensellerie	knoldselleri	apio nabo	sedano rapa
Chicory	chicorée	cichorei	Zichorien-wurzel	cikorie	achicoria raíz	cicoria
Chinese cabbage	chou de Chine	Chinese kool	Chinakohl	kinesisk kål	col de China	cavolo cinese
Sweet corn	mais sucré	suikermais	Zuckermais	sukkermajs	elate	mais dolce
Cucumber	concombre	komkommer	Gurke	agurk	pepino	cetriolo
Eggplant	aubergine	eierplant	Eierfrucht	aegplante	berenjena	melanzana
Endive	chicorée frisée	andijvie	Endivie	endivie	escarola	indivia
Horseradish	raifort	mierikswortel	Meerrettich	peberrod	rábano rusticana	ramolaccio
Kale	chou vert	groene kool	Grünkohl	grønkål	sin cabeza	cavolo verza

Kohlrabi	chou-rave	koolrabi	Kohlrabi	knudekål	colirábano	cavolo rapa
Leek	poireau	prei	Breitlauch	porre	puerro	porro
Lettuce	laitue	sla	Salat	salat	lechuga	lattuga
Muskmelon	melon	meloen	Melone	melon	melón	popone
Onion	ognon	ui	Zwiebel	løg	cebolla	cipolla
Parsley	persil	peterselie	Petersilie	persille	perejil	prezzemolo
Parsnip	panais	pastinaak	Pastinake	pastinak	pastinaca	pastinaca
Pea	pois	erwt	Erbse	haveaert	guisante	cece
Pepper	piment	Spaanse peper	Spanischer Pfeffer	spansk peber	chile	pepezone
Potato	pomme de terre	aardappel	Kartoffel	kartoffel	patata	patata
Pumpkin	potiron	pompoen	Zentnerkürbis	centnergraeskar	calabaza grande	zucca invernale
Radish	radis	radijs	Radies	radis	rábano	ravanello
Rhubarb	rhubarbe	rabarber	Rhabarber	rabarber	ruibarbo	rabarbaro
Rutabaga	chou-navet	koolraap	Kohlrübe	kalrabi	colinabo	cavolo rapa
Spinach	épinard	spinazie	Spinat	spinat	espinaca	spinaci
New Zealand spinach	tétragone	Nieuwzeelandshe spinazie	neuseeländisher Spinat	Nyzeelandsk spinat	espinaca Nueva Zelandia	spinacio di Nuova Zelanda
Strawberry	fraise	aardbei	Erdbeere	jordbaer	fresa	fragola
Summer squash	courge	pompoen	Kürbis	mandelgraeskar	calabacita	zucchina
Swiss chard	poirée	snijbiet	Mangold	bladbede	acelga	bietola de costa
Tomato	tomate	tomaat	Tomate	tomat	tomate	pomodoro
Turnip	navet	raap	Weissrübe	majroe	nabo	cavolo rapa
Watermelon	melon d'eau	watermeloen	Wassermelone	vandmelon	sandia	cocomero

Adapted from J. Nijdan and A. DeJong (eds.), *Elsevier's Dictionary of Horticulture*, Elsevier, New York (1970).

U.S. VEGETABLE PRODUCTION STATISTICS: LEADING FRESH MARKET VEGETABLE STATES, 1986[1]

	Harvested Acreage		Production		Value	
Rank	State	% of Total	State	% of Total	State	% of Total
1	California	45.6	California	50.7	California	48.6
2	Florida	12.8	Florida	12.6	Florida	20.5
3	Arizona	5.1	Arizona	6.1	Arizona	5.3
4	Texas	5.0	Texas	4.6	Texas	3.8
5	Michigan	4.7	Oregon	3.5	New York	3.5

Adapted from Vegetables, USDA Vg 1–2 (1986).

[1]Includes data for asparagus, broccoli, carrot, cauliflower, celery, sweet corn, lettuce, honeydew melon, onion, and tomato only.

IMPORTANT STATES IN THE PRODUCTION OF U.S. FRESH MARKET VEGETABLES BY CROP VALUE, 1986

Crop	First	Second	Third
Artichoke[1,2]	California	–	–
Asparagus	California	Washington	Michigan
Bean, snap[2]	Florida	California	New York
Broccoli	California	Arizona	–
Brussels sprouts[1,2]	California	–	–
Cabbage[2]	Texas	Florida	New York
Carrot	California	Texas	Florida
Cauliflower	California	Arizona	–
Celery	California	Florida	Michigan
Corn, sweet	Florida	New York	California
Cucumber[2]	Florida	California	Texas
Eggplant[2]	Florida	New Jersey	–
Escarole[2]	Florida	New Jersey	Ohio
Garlic[2]	California	–	–
Honeydew melon	California	Texas	Arizona
Lettuce	California	Arizona	Florida
Muskmelon[2]	California	Texas	Arizona
Onion[1]	California	Texas	New York
Pepper, green[1,2]	Florida	California	Texas
Spinach[2]	Texas	California	Colorado
Strawberry	California	Florida	New York
Tomato	Florida	California	Tennessee
Watermelon[2]	Florida	Texas	California

Adapted from Vegetables, estimates by seasonal groups and states, 1978–82, USDA Statistical Bulletin 728 (1985) and Vegetables, USDA Vg 1–2 (1986).

[1]Includes fresh market and processing.

[2]1981 data. The USDA discontinued data collection after the 1981 crop.

HARVESTED ACREAGE, PRODUCTION, AND VALUE OF U.S. FRESH MARKET VEGETABLES, 1984–1986 AVERAGE

Crop	Acres	Production (1000 cwt)	Value ($1000)
Artichoke[1,2]	9,767	927	29,122
Asparagus	92,520[1]	1,194	88,728
Bean, snap[2]	89,930	2,966	83,226
Broccoli	108,300[1]	7,354	174,048
Brussels sprouts[1,2]	5,467	747	15,943
Cabbage[2]	83,347	19,343	149,247
Carrot	89,913[1]	15,503	203,359
Cauliflower	62,467[1]	5,170	155,137
Celery	34,183	18,214	210,068
Corn, sweet	188,900	15,371	203,941
Cucumber[2]	52,077	6,034	87,769
Eggplant[2]	3,750	699	10,734
Escarole[2]	7,913	1,029	17,965
Garlic[1,2]	14,200	1,824	32,579
Honeydew melon	25,900	4,756	61,139
Lettuce	218,847	61,636	700,206
Muskmelon[2]	88,823	12,670	164,906
Onion[1]	122,417	43,884	380,399
Pepper, green[1,2]	57,667	5,729	126,739
Spinach[2]	15,523	1,226	31,292
Strawberry	43,900[1]	7,457	395,431
Tomato	124,757	29,830	759,869
Watermelon[2]	197,800	24,307	139,522

Adapted from Vegetables, estimates by seasonal groups and states, 1978–82, USDA Statistical Bulletin 728 (1985) and Vegetables, USDA Vg 1-2 (1986).

[1]Includes fresh market and processing.

[2]1979–1981 average. The USDA discontinued data collection after the 1981 crop.

AVERAGE U.S. YIELDS OF FRESH MARKET VEGETABLES, 1984–1986

Crop	Yield (cwt/acre)
Artichoke[1,2]	95
Asparagus[1]	22
Bean, snap[2]	33
Broccoli[1]	97
Brussels sprouts	137
Cabbage[2]	232
Carrot[1]	257
Cauliflower[1]	110
Celery[1]	533
Corn, sweet	81
Cucumber[2]	116
Eggplant[2]	186
Escarole[2]	130
Garlic[1,2]	128
Honeydew melon	183
Lettuce	282
Muskmelon[2]	143
Onion[1]	359
Pepper, green[1,2]	100
Spinach[2]	79
Strawberry	230
Tomato	239
Watermelon[2]	123

Adapted from Vegetables, estimates by seasonal groups and states, 1978–82, USDA Statistical Bulletin 728 (1985) and Vegetables, USDA Vg 1-2 (1986).

[1]Includes fresh market and processing.

[2]1979–1981 average. The USDA discontinued data collection after the 1981 crops.

LEADING PROCESSING VEGETABLE STATES, 1986[1]

	Harvested Acreage		Production		Value	
Rank	State	% of Total	State	% of Total	State	% of Total
1	Wisconsin	22.5	California	56.7	California	45.5
2	California	18.0	Wisconsin	9.3	Wisconsin	11.4
3	Minnesota	16.3	Minnesota	7.4	Minnesota	7.0
4	Oregon	7.1	Oregon	4.5	Oregon	6.0
5	Washington	6.9	Ohio	2.8	Washington	4.5

Adapted from Vegetables, USDA Vg 1-2 (1986).

[1]Includes data for snap bean, sweet corn, pea, processing cucumber, and tomato only.

HARVESTED ACREAGE, PRODUCTION, AND VALUE OF U.S. PROCESSING VEGETABLES, 1984–1986 Average

Crop	Acres	Production (tons)	Value ($1000)
Asparagus	92,520[1]	44,660	41,575
Bean, lima[2]	55,290	71,817	28,856
Bean, snap	209,787	659,333	109,999
Beet[2]	13,590	203, 597	9,190
Broccoli	108,300[1]	159,477	60,776
Cabbage[2]	9,700	230,977	7,897
Carrot	89,913[1]	383,850	24,084
Cauliflower	62,467[1]	84,110	22,395
Corn, sweet	425,160	2,574,263	159,432
Cucumber	109,697	650,037	113,461
Pea, green	318,837	496,010	116,512
Spinach[2]	20,763	157,316	13,857
Strawberry	43,900[1]	132,000	60,473
Tomato	269,810	7,417,193	488,578

Adapted from Vegetables, estimates by seasonal groups and states, 1978–82, USDA Statistical Bulletin 728 (1985) and Vegetables, USDA Vg 1-2 (1986).

[1]Includes fresh market and processing.

[2]1979–1981 average. The USDA discontinued data collection after the 1981 crop.

IMPORTANT STATES IN THE PRODUCTION OF U.S. PROCESSING VEGETABLES BY CROP VALUE, 1986

Crop	First	Second	Third
Asparagus	Washington	Michigan	California
Bean, lima[1]	California	Delaware	Wisconsin
Bean, snap	Wisconsin	Oregon	New York
Beet[1]	New York	Wisconsin	—
Broccoli	California	—	—
Cabbage[1]	New York	Wisconsin	Ohio
Carrot	California	Washington	Oregon
Cauliflower	California	—	—
Corn, sweet	Minnesota	Wisconsin	Oregon
Cucumber	Michigan	North Carolina	California
Pea, green	Wisconsin	Minnesota	Washington
Spinach[1]	California	—	—
Strawberry	California	Oregon	Washington
Tomato	California	Ohio	Indiana

Adapted from Vegetables, estimates by seasonal groups and states, 1978–82, USDA Statistical Bulletin 728 (1985) and Vegetables, USDA Vg 1–2 (1986).

[1] 1981 data. The USDA discontinued data collection after the 1981 crop.

AVERAGE U.S. YIELDS OF PROCESSING VEGETABLES, 1984–1986

Crop	Yield (tons/acre)
Bean, lima[1]	1.29
Bean, snap	3.14
Beet[1]	15.10
Cabbage[1]	23.79
Corn, sweet	6.05
Cucumber	5.93
Pea, green	1.55
Spinach[1]	7.58
Tomato	27.56

Adapted from Vegetables, estimates by seasonal groups and states, 1979–1982, USDA Statistical Bulletin 728 (1985) and Vegetables, USDA Vg 1–2 (1986).

[1] 1979–1981 average. The USDA discontinued data collection after the 1981 crop.

POTATO AND SWEET POTATO PRODUCTION STATISTICS: HARVESTED ACREAGE, YIELD, PRODUCTION, AND VALUE

Crop	Acres	Yield (cwt/acre)	Production (1000 cwt)	Value ($1000)
Potato[1]	1,331,050	239	384,860	1,604,862
Sweet potato[2]	108,900	124	13,458	145,505

Adapted from Potatoes, USDA Agricultural Statistics Board Pot 6 (9-86) (1986) and Vegetable outlook and situation report, USDA TVS-234 (1984).

[1] 1984–1985 average.
[2] 1982–1983 average.

IMPORTANT STATES IN POTATO AND SWEET POTATO PRODUCTION BY CROP VALUE

Rank	Potato[1]	Sweet Potato[2]
1	Idaho	North Carolina
2	Washington	Louisiana
3	California	California
4	Oregon	Texas
5	Wisconsin	Georgia

Adapted from Potatoes, USDA Agricultural Statistics Board Pot 6 (9-86) (1986) and Vegetable outlook and situation report, USDA TVS-234 (1984).

[1] 1984–1985 data.
[2] 1982–1983 data.

UTILIZATION OF THE POTATO CROP, 1983–1985 AVERAGE

Item	Amount			
	1000 cwt	% of Total		
A. Sales	325,424	88		
1. Table stock	115,785		31	
2. Processing	183,017		50	
a. Chips and shoestrings	42,662			12
b. Dehydration	28,186			8
c. Frozen french fries	85,480			23
d. Other frozen products	19,278			5
e. Canned potatoes	2,293			<1
f. Other canned products	1,812			<1
g. Starch and flour	3,306			<1
3. Other sales	26,622		7	
a. Livestock feed	5,506			1
b. Seed	21,116			6
B. Nonsales	42,454	12		
1. Seed used on farms where grown	4,693			1
2. Household and feed used on farms where grown	1,910			<1
3. Shrinkage	38,850			11
Total production	367,877			

Adapted from Potatoes, USDA Agricultural Statistics Board Pot 6 (9-86) (1986).

CONSUMPTION OF VEGETABLES: TRENDS IN PER CAPITA CONSUMPTION OF FRESH, CANNED, AND FROZEN VEGETABLES[1] (FRESH WEIGHT BASIS)

	Amount (lb)			
Period	Fresh	Canned	Frozen	Total
1947–1949 average	121	72	7	200
1957–1959 average	104	81	15	200
1965	98	85	18	201
1970	99	94	21	214
1975	98	101	20	219
1980	108	89	21	218
1981[2]	105	87	23	215

Adapted from Vegetable outlook and situation report, USDA TVS-233 (1984).

[1] Excluding melon and potato.

[2] USDA discontinued data collection on many vegetables after the 1981 crop.

PER CAPITA CONSUMPTION OF COMMERCIALLY PRODUCED VEGETABLES, 1985

Vegetable	Amount (lb)			
	Fresh	Canned	Frozen	Total
Artichoke[4]	0.50	—	—	0.50
Asparagus	0.50	0.28	0.10	0.88
Bean, lima[1]	—	0.20	0.40	0.60
Bean, snap	1.40[2]	4.53	1.87	7.80
Beet[1]	—	1.10	—	1.10
Broccoli	2.88	—	1.55	3.98
Brussels sprouts[2]	—	—	0.20	0.20
Cabbage	8.60[4]	1.40[2]	—	10.00
Carrot	7.64	0.88	2.37	10.89
Cauliflower	2.22	—	0.86	3.08
Celery	7.40	—	—	7.40
Corn, sweet	7.70	11.54	9.23	28.47
Cucumber	4.40[4]	5.72	—	10.12
Eggplant[4]	0.60	—	—	0.60
Garlic[4]	0.70	—	—	0.70
Honeydew melon	2.10	—	—	2.10
Lettuce	25.50	—	—	25.50
Muskmelon[4]	19.20	—	—	19.20
Onion[5]	19.40	—	—	19.40
Pea, green	—	3.03	1.64	4.67
Pepper[4]	3.50	—	—	3.50
Pumpkin and squash[4]	—	0.40	—	0.40
Spinach	0.90[4]	0.50[4]	0.60[2]	2.00
Tomato	15.77	61.96	—	77.73
Watermelon[4]	12.30	—	—	12.30
Other vegetables	9.90[4]	2.50[3]	1.50[2]	13.90

Adapted from Vegetable situation and outlook report, USDA TVS-239 (1986); Vegetable outlook and situation report, USDA TVS-237 (1985); Vegetable outlook and situation report, USDA TVS-233 (1984); and Vegetable outlook and situation, USDA TVS-229 (1983).

[1] 1984 data. [2] 1983 data. [3] 1982 data. [4] 1981 data. [5] Includes fresh and processed onion.

TRENDS IN PER CAPITA CONSUMPTION OF POTATO, SWEET POTATO, DRY BEAN, AND DRY PEA

	Amount (lb)			
Period	Potato[1]	Sweet Potato[2]	Dry Bean	Dry Pea
1947–1949 average	114	13	6.7	0.6
1957–1959 average	107	8	7.7	0.6
1965	108	6	6.6	0.4
1970	118	6	5.9	0.3
1975	122	5	6.5	0.4
1980	116	5	5.4	0.4
1981	115	5	5.4	0.4
1982	120	6	7.4	0.4
1983	119	5	6.2	0.4

Adapted from Vegetable outlook and situation report, USDA TVS-233 (1984).

[1] Includes table stock and processed potato.

[2] Includes canned sweet potato.

COMPOSITION OF THE EDIBLE PORTIONS OF FRESH, RAW VEGETABLES

Vegetable	Amount/100 g Edible Portion										
	Water (%)	Energy (kcal)	Protein (g)	Fat (g)	Carbo-hydrate (g)	Fiber (g)	Ca (mg)	P (mg)	Fe (mg)	Na (mg)	K (mg)
Artichoke	84	51	2.7	0.2	11.9	1.1	48	77	1.6	80	339
Asparagus	92	22	3.1	0.2	3.7	0.8	22	52	0.7	2	302
Bean, green	90	31	1.8	0.1	7.1	1.1	37	38	1.0	6	209
Bean, lima	70	113	6.8	0.9	20.2	1.9	34	136	3.1	8	467
Beet greens	92	19	1.8	0.1	4.0	1.3	119	40	3.3	201	547
Beet roots	87	44	1.5	0.1	10.0	0.8	16	48	0.9	72	324
Broccoli	91	28	3.0	0.4	5.2	1.1	48	66	0.9	27	325
Brussels sprouts	86	43	3.4	0.3	9.0	1.5	42	69	1.4	25	389
Cabbage, common	93	24	1.2	0.2	5.4	0.8	47	23	0.6	18	246
Cabbage, red	92	27	1.4	0.3	6.1	1.0	51	42	0.5	11	206
Cabbage, savoy	91	27	2.0	0.1	6.1	0.8	35	42	0.4	28	230
Carrot	88	43	1.0	0.2	10.1	1.0	27	44	0.5	35	323
Cauliflower	92	24	2.0	0.2	4.9	0.9	29	46	0.6	15	355
Celery	95	16	0.7	0.1	3.6	0.7	36	26	0.5	88	284
Chicory, witloof	95	15	1.0	0.1	3.2	—	—	21	0.5	7	182
Chinese cabbage	94	16	1.2	0.2	3.2	0.6	77	29	0.3	9	238
Collard	94	19	1.6	0.2	3.8	0.6	117	16	0.6	28	148
Cucumber	96	13	0.5	0.1	2.9	0.6	14	17	0.3	2	149
Eggplant	92	26	1.1	0.1	6.3	1.0	36	33	0.6	4	219
Endive	94	17	1.3	0.2	3.4	0.9	52	28	0.8	22	314

COMPOSITION OF THE EDIBLE PORTIONS OF FRESH, RAW VEGETABLES—Continued

Vegetable	Amount/100 g Edible Portion										
	Water (%)	Energy (kcal)	Protein (g)	Fat (g)	Carbo-hydrate (g)	Fiber (g)	Ca (mg)	P (mg)	Fe (mg)	Na (mg)	K (mg)
Garlic	59	149	6.4	0.5	33.1	1.5	181	153	1.7	17	401
Kale	85	50	3.3	0.7	10.0	1.5	135	56	1.7	43	447
Kohlrabi	91	27	1.7	0.1	6.2	1.0	24	46	0.4	20	350
Leek	83	61	1.5	0.3	14.1	1.5	59	35	2.1	20	180
Lettuce, butterhead	96	13	1.3	0.2	2.3	—	—	—	0.3	5	257
Lettuce, crisphead	96	13	1.0	0.2	2.1	0.5	19	20	0.5	9	158
Lettuce, loose leaf	94	18	1.3	0.3	3.5	0.7	68	25	1.4	9	264
Lettuce, romaine	95	16	1.6	0.2	2.4	0.7	36	45	1.1	8	290
Melon, casaba	92	26	0.9	0.1	6.2	0.5	5	7	0.4	12	210
Melon, honeydew	90	35	0.5	0.1	9.2	0.6	6	10	0.1	10	271
Melon, other netted	90	35	0.9	0.3	8.4	0.4	11	17	0.2	9	309
Mushroom	92	25	2.1	0.4	4.7	0.8	5	104	1.2	4	370
Mustard greens	91	26	2.7	0.2	4.9	1.1	103	43	1.5	25	354
Okra	90	38	2.0	0.1	7.6	0.9	81	63	0.8	8	303
Onion, bunching	92	25	1.7	0.1	5.6	0.8	60	33	1.9	4	257
Onion, dry	91	34	1.2	0.3	7.3	0.4	25	29	0.4	2	155
Parsley	88	33	2.2	0.3	6.9	1.2	130	41	6.2	39	536
Parsnip	80	75	1.2	0.3	18.0	2.0	36	71	0.6	10	375
Pea, edible-podded	89	42	2.8	0.2	7.6	2.5	43	53	2.1	4	200
Pea, green	79	81	5.4	0.4	14.5	2.2	25	108	1.5	5	244

Pepper, hot, chili	88	40	2.0	0.2	9.5	1.8	18	46	1.2	7	340
Pepper, sweet	93	25	0.9	0.5	5.3	1.2	6	22	1.3	3	195
Potato	79	79	2.1	0.1	18.0	0.4	7	46	0.8	6	543
Pumpkin	92	26	1.0	0.1	6.5	1.1	21	44	0.8	1	340
Radish	95	17	0.6	0.5	3.6	0.5	21	18	0.3	24	232
Rhubarb	94	21	0.9	0.2	4.6	0.7	86	14	0.2	4	288
Rutabaga	90	36	1.2	0.2	8.1	1.1	47	58	0.5	20	337
Salsify	77	82	3.3	0.2	18.6	1.8	60	75	0.7	20	380
Southern pea	67	127	9.0	0.8	21.8	1.8	26	53	1.1	4	432
Spinach	92	22	2.9	0.4	3.5	0.9	99	49	2.7	79	558
Squash, butternut	86	45	1.0	0.1	11.7	1.4	48	33	0.7	4	352
Squash, Hubbard	88	40	2.0	0.5	8.7	1.4	14	21	0.4	7	320
Squash, scallop	94	18	1.2	0.2	3.8	0.6	19	36	0.4	1	182
Squash, summer	94	20	1.2	0.2	4.4	0.6	20	35	0.5	2	195
Squash, winter	89	37	1.5	0.2	8.8	1.4	31	32	0.6	4	350
Squash, zucchini	96	14	1.2	0.1	2.9	0.5	15	32	0.4	3	248
Strawberry	92	30	0.6	0.4	7.0	0.5	14	19	0.4	1	166
Sweet corn	76	86	3.2	1.2	19.0	0.7	2	89	0.5	15	270
Sweet potato	73	105	1.7	0.3	24.3	0.9	22	28	0.6	13	204
Swiss chard	93	19	1.8	0.2	3.7	0.8	51	46	1.8	213	379
Tomato, green	93	24	1.2	0.2	5.1	0.5	13	28	0.5	13	204
Tomato, ripe	94	19	0.9	0.2	4.3	0.5	7	23	0.5	8	207
Turnip greens	91	27	1.5	0.3	5.7	0.8	190	42	1.1	40	296
Turnip roots	92	27	0.9	0.1	6.2	0.9	30	27	0.3	67	191
Watermelon	93	26	0.5	0.2	6.4	—	7	10	0.5	1	100

Adapted from D. B. Haytowitz and R. H. Matthews, *Composition of Foods, Vegetables and Vegetable Products—Raw, Processed, Prepared*, USDA Agricultural Handbook 8-11 (1984) and S. E. Gebhardt, R. Cutrufelli, and R. H. Matthews, *Composition of Foods, Fruits and Fruit Juices—Raw, Processed, Prepared*, USDA Agricultural Handbook 8-9 (1982).

VITAMIN CONTENT OF FRESH RAW VEGETABLES

Vegetable	Amount/100 g Edible Portion					
	Vitamin A (IU)	Thiamine (mg)	Riboflavin (mg)	Niacin (mg)	Ascorbic Acid (mg)	Vitamin B_6 (mg)
Artichoke	185	0.08	0.06	0.76	10.8	0.11
Asparagus	897	0.11	0.12	1.14	33.0	0.15
Bean, green	668	0.08	0.11	0.75	16.3	0.07
Bean, lima	303	0.22	0.10	1.47	23.4	0.20
Beet greens	6,100	0.10	0.22	0.40	30.0	0.11
Beet roots	20	0.05	0.02	0.40	11.0	0.05
Broccoli	1,542	0.07	0.12	0.64	93.2	0.16
Brussels sprouts	883	0.14	0.09	0.75	85.0	0.22
Cabbage, common	126	0.05	0.03	0.30	47.3	0.10
Cabbage, red	40	0.05	0.03	0.30	57.0	0.21
Cabbage, savoy	1,000	0.07	0.03	0.30	31.0	0.19
Carrot	28,129	0.10	0.06	0.93	9.3	0.15
Cauliflower	16	0.08	0.06	0.63	71.5	0.23
Celery	127	0.03	0.03	0.30	6.3	0.03
Chicory, witloof	0	0.07	0.14	0.50	10.0	0.05
Chinese cabbage	1,200	0.04	0.05	0.40	27.0	0.23
Collard	3,330	0.03	0.06	0.37	23.3	0.07
Cucumber	45	0.03	0.02	0.30	4.7	0.05
Eggplant	70	0.09	0.02	0.60	1.6	0.09

Endive	2,050	0.08	0.08	0.40	6.5	0.02
Garlic	0	0.20	0.11	0.70	31.2	—
Kale	8,900	0.11	0.13	1.00	120.0	0.27
Kohlrabi	36	0.05	0.02	0.40	62.0	0.15
Leek	95	0.06	0.03	0.40	12.0	—
Lettuce, butterhead	970	0.06	0.06	0.30	8.0	—
Lettuce, crisphead	330	0.05	0.03	0.19	3.9	0.04
Lettuce, loose leaf	1,900	0.05	0.08	0.40	18.0	0.06
Lettuce, romaine	2,600	0.10	0.10	0.50	24.0	—
Melon, casaba	30	0.06	0.02	0.40	16.0	—
Melon, honeydew	40	0.08	0.02	0.60	24.8	0.06
Melon, other netted	3,224	0.04	0.02	0.57	42.2	0.12
Mushroom	0	0.10	0.45	4.12	3.5	0.10
Mustard greens	5,300	0.08	0.11	0.80	70.0	—
Okra	660	0.20	0.06	1.00	21.1	0.22
Onion, bunching	5,000	0.07	0.14	0.20	45.0	—
Onion, dry	0	0.06	0.01	0.10	8.4	0.16
Parsley	5,200	0.08	0.11	0.70	90.0	0.16
Parsnip	0	0.09	0.05	0.70	17.0	0.09
Pea, edible-podded	145	0.15	0.08	0.60	60.0	0.16
Pea, green	640	0.27	0.13	2.09	40.0	0.17
Pepper, hot, chili	770	0.09	0.09	0.95	242.5	0.28
Pepper, sweet, green	530	0.09	0.05	0.55	128.0	0.16
Potato	—	0.09	0.04	1.48	19.7	0.26
Pumpkin	1,600	0.05	0.11	0.60	9.0	—
Radish	8	0.01	0.05	0.30	22.8	0.07
Rhubarb	100	0.02	0.03	0.30	8.0	0.09
Rutabaga	0	0.09	0.04	0.70	25.0	0.10
Salsify	0	0.08	0.22	0.50	8.0	—

VITAMIN CONTENT OF FRESH RAW VEGETABLES—Continued

Vegetable	Amount/100 g Edible Portion					
	Vitamin A (IU)	Thiamine (mg)	Riboflavin (mg)	Niacin (mg)	Ascorbic Acid (mg)	Vitamin B_6 (mg)
Southern pea	817	0.11	0.15	1.45	2.5	0.07
Spinach	6,715	0.08	0.19	0.72	28.1	0.20
Squash, butternut	7,800	0.10	0.02	1.20	21.0	0.15
Squash, Hubbard	5,400	0.07	0.04	0.50	11.0	0.15
Squash, scallop	110	0.07	0.03	0.60	18.0	0.11
Squash, summer	196	0.06	0.04	0.55	14.8	0.11
Squash, winter	4,060	0.10	0.03	0.80	12.3	0.08
Squash, zucchini	340	0.07	0.03	0.40	9.0	0.09
Strawberry	27	0.02	0.07	0.23	56.7	0.06
Sweet corn	281	0.20	0.06	1.70	6.8	0.06
Sweet potato	20,063	0.07	0.15	0.67	22.7	0.26
Swiss chard	3,300	0.04	0.09	0.40	30.0	—
Tomato, green	642	0.06	0.04	0.50	23.4	—
Tomato, ripe	1,133	0.06	0.05	0.60	17.6	0.05
Turnip greens	7,600	0.07	0.10	0.60	60.0	0.38
Turnip roots	0	0.04	0.03	0.40	21.0	0.09
Watermelon	590	0.03	0.03	0.20	7	—

Adapted from D. B. Haytowitz and R. H. Matthews, *Composition of Foods, Vegetables and Vegetable Products—Raw, Processed, Prepared*, USDA Agricultural Handbook 8–11 (1984) and S. E. Gebhardt, R. Cutrufelli, and R. H. Matthews, *Composition of Foods, Fruits and Fruit Juices—Raw, Processed, Prepared*, USDA Agricultural Handbook 8–9 (1982).

SELECTION OF VEGETABLE VARIETIES

Selection of the variety (technically, *cultivar*) to plant is one of the most important decisions the commercial vegetable grower must make each season. Each year seed companies and experiment stations release dozens of new varieties to compete with those already available. Glowing descriptions, tempting photographs, and sometimes exaggerated claims accompany the release of each new variety. Growers should evaluate some new varieties each year on a trial basis to observe performance on their own farms. A limited number of new varieties should be evaluated so that observations on plant performance and characteristics and yields can be noted and recorded. It is relatively easy to establish a trial but very time-consuming to make all the observations necessary to make a decision on adoption of a new variety. Some factors to consider before adopting a variety follow:

Yield: The variety should have the potential to produce crops at least equivalent to those already grown. Harvested yield is usually much less than potential yield because of market restraints.

Disease Resistance: The most economical and effective means of pest management is through the use of varieties with genetic resistance to disease. When all other factors are about equal, it would be prudent to select a variety with the needed disease resistance.

Horticultural Quality: Characteristics of the plant habit as related to climate and production practices and of the marketed plant product must be acceptable.

Adaptability: Successful varieties must perform well under the range of environmental conditions usually encountered on the individual farm.

Market Acceptability: The harvested plant product must have characteristics desired by the packer, shipper, wholesaler, retailer, and consumer. Included among these qualities are pack out, size, shape, color, flavor, and nutritional quality.

During the past few years there has been a decided shift to hybrid varieties in an effort by growers to achieve earliness, higher yields, better quality, and greater uniformity. Seed costs for hybrids are higher than for open-pollinated varieties.

Variety selection is a very dynamic process. Some varieties retain favor for many years, whereas others might be used only a few seasons if some special situation, such as plant disease or marketing change, develops. If a variety was released by the USDA or a university, many seed companies may have it available. Varieties developed by a seed company may be available only from that source, or may be distributed through many sources.

The Cooperative Extension Service in most states publishes annual or periodic lists of recommended varieties. These lists are usually available in county extension offices.

Adapted from D. N. Maynard, Commercial vegetable varieties for Florida, Florida Cooperative Extension Service Circular 530B (1986).

PART 2

PLANT GROWING AND GREENHOUSE VEGETABLE PRODUCTION

TRANSPLANT PRODUCTION

Vegetable crops are established in the field by direct seeding or by use of vegetative propagules (see Part 3) or transplants. Transplants are produced in containers of various sorts in greenhouses, protected beds, and open fields. Either containerized or field-grown transplants can be used successfully. Generally containerized transplants get off to a faster start, but are more expensive.

Transplant production is a very specialized segment of the vegetable business which demands suitable facilities and careful attention to detail. For these reasons, many vegetable growers choose to purchase containerized or field-grown transplants from production specialists rather than grow them themselves.

ADVANTAGES AND DISADVANTAGES OF VARIOUS PLANT GROWING CONTAINERS

Container	Advantages	Disadvantages
Clay pot	Long life	Slow to work with Pots dry out Pots are heavy
Fiber block	Easily handled	May have slow root penetration
Fiber tray	Allows maximum use of space	Hard to handle when wet
Single peat pellet	No media preparation Low storage requirement	Requires individual handling in setup Limited sizes
Prespaced peat pellet	No media preparation Can be handled as a unit of 50	Limited to rather small sizes

ADVANTAGES AND DISADVANTAGES OF VARIOUS PLANT GROWING CONTAINERS—Continued

Container	Advantages	Disadvantages
Single peat pot	Good root penetration Easy to handle in field Available in large sizes	Difficult to separate Master container is required Dries out easily May act as a wick in the field if not properly covered
Strip peat pots	Good root penetration Easy to handle in field Available in large sizes Saves setup and filling time	May be slow to separate in the field Dries out easily
Plastic flat with unit	Easily handled Reusable Good root penetration	Requires storage during off season May be limited in sizes
Plastic pack	Easily handled	Roots may grow out of container causing handling problems Limited in sizes Requires some setup labor
Plastic pot	Reusable Good root penetration	Requires handling as single plant
Polyurethane foam flat	Easily handled Requires less medium than similar sizes of other containers Comes in many sizes Reusable	Requires regular fertilization Plants grow slowly at first because cultural systems use low levels of nitrogen
Soil band	Good root penetration	Requires extensive labor to setup
Soil block	Excellent root penetration	Expensive machinery

Adapted from D. C. Sanders and G. R. Hughes (eds.), Production of commerical vegetable transplants, North Carolina Agricultural Extension Service AG-337 (1984).

COMMON CONTAINER SIZES FOR VEGETABLE TRANSPLANTS

Vegetable	Container Diameter (in.)[1]
Asparagus	1.5–3.0
Broccoli	1.0–3.0
Cabbage	1.0–2.5
Cauliflower	1.0–3.0
Cucumber	1.5–4.0
Eggplant	1.5–4.0
Endive, escarole	1.0–2.5
Lettuce	1.0–2.5
Muskmelon	1.5–4.0
Okra	1.0–3.0
Pepper	1.0–4.0
Tomato	1.5–6.0
Watermelon	1.5–4.0

Adapted from D. C. Sanders and G. R. Hughes (eds.), Production of commercial vegetable transplants, North Carolina Agricultural Extension Service AG-337 (1984).

[1]The largest sizes listed are used for early crops in some areas.

1. *Media.* Field soil alone usually is not a desirable seeding medium, because it may crust or drain poorly under greenhouse conditions. Adding sand or sand and peat (see page 38) may produce a very good seeding mixture. Many growers use artificial mixes (see page 39) because of the difficulty of obtaining field soil that is free from pests and contaminating chemicals.

   A desirable seeding mix should provide good drainage but retain moisture well enough to prevent rapid fluctuations, have good aeration, be low in soluble salts, and be free from insects, diseases, and weed seeds.
2. *Seeding.* Adjust seeding rates to account for the stated germination percentages and variations in soil temperatures. Excessively thick stands result in spindly seedlings and poor stands are wasteful of valuable bench or bed space.

   Seeding depth should be carefully controlled; most seeds should be planted from 1/4 to 1/2 in. deep. Exceptions are celery, which should only be 1/8 in. deep, and the vine crops, sweet corn, and beans, which can be seeded 1 in. or deeper.
3. *Moisture.* Maintain soil moisture in the desirable range by thorough watering after seeding and careful periodic watering as necessary. A combination of "spot watering" of dry areas and overall watering is usually necessary. Do not overwater.
4. *Temperature.* Be certain to maintain the desired temperature. Cooler than optimum temperatures may encourage disease and warmer temperatures result in spindly seedlings.
5. *Disease control.* Use diseasefree or treated seed to prevent early disease problems. Containers should be new or diseasefree. A diseasefree seeding medium is essential. Maintain a strict sanitation program to prevent introduction of diseases. Carefully control watering and relative humidity. Use approved fungicides as drenches or sprays when necessary.
6. *Transplanting.* Start transplanting when seedlings show the first true leaves so that transplanting can be completed before the seedlings become large and overcrowded.

APPROXIMATE SEED REQUIREMENTS FOR PLANT GROWING

Vegetable	Plants/oz of Seed	Seed Required to Produce 10,000 Transplants
Asparagus	550	$1\frac{1}{4}$ lb
Broccoli	5,000	2 oz
Brussels sprouts	5,000	2 oz
Cabbage	5,000	2 oz
Cauliflower	5,000	2 oz
Celery	15,000	1 oz
Sweet corn	100	$6\frac{1}{4}$ lb
Cucumber	500	$1\frac{1}{4}$ lb
Eggplant	2,500	4 oz
Lettuce	10,000	1 oz
Muskmelon	500	$1\frac{1}{4}$ lb
Onion	4,000	3 oz
Pepper	1,500	7 oz
Summer squash	200	$3\frac{1}{4}$ lb
Tomato	4,000	3 oz
Watermelon	200	$3\frac{1}{4}$ lb

To determine seed requirements per acre:

$$\frac{\text{Desired plant population}}{10{,}000} \times \text{seed required for 10,000 plants}$$

Example 1: To grow enough broccoli for a population of 20,000 plants/acre:

$$\frac{20{,}000}{10{,}000} \times 2 = 4 \text{ oz seed}$$

Example 2: To grow enough summer squash for a population of 3600 plants/acre:

$$\frac{3600}{10{,}000} \times 3^1/_4 \text{ lb} = 1^1/_4 \text{ lb approximately}$$

TEMPERATURES AND TIMES REQUIRED FOR GROWING PLANTS FOR FIELD TRANSPLANTING[1]

Vegetable	Day[2] (°F)	Night (°F)	Time (weeks)
Asparagus	70–80	65–70	8–10
Broccoli	60–70	50–60	5–7
Brussels sprouts	60–70	50–60	5–7
Cabbage	60–70	50–60	5–7
Cauliflower	60–70	50–60	5–7
Celery	65–75	60–65	10–12
Corn, sweet	70–75	60–65	3–4
Cucumber	70–75	60–65	3–4
Eggplant	70–80	65–70	6–8
Lettuce	55–65	50–55	5–7
Muskmelon	70–75	60–65	3–4
Onion	60–65	55–60	10–12
Pepper	65–75	60–65	6–8
Summer squash	70–75	60–65	3–4
Tomato	65–75	60–65	5–7
Watermelon	70–80	65–70	3–4

[1]Adjust temperatures slightly to alter growth rates.
[2]Select the lower temperature on cloudy days.

SOIL AND ARTIFICIAL MIXES FOR PLANT GROWING: JOHN INNES COMPOSTS

Constituent	Seeding Mixture	Growing Mixture
	Parts by Volume	
Composted medium loam	2	7
Peat	1	3
Coarse sand	1	2
	(lb/cu yd)	
Ground limestone	1½	1½
Superphosphate—20% P_2O_5	3	—
Base fertilizer[1]	—	8½
or		
5–10–10	—	12

Adapted from W. J. C. Lawrence and J. Newell, *Seed and Potting Composts*, 4th ed., Allen and Unwin, London (1950).

[1]2 hoof and horn : 2 superphosphate : 1 sulfate of potash (w : w : w).

PENN STATE UNIVERSITY SOIL MIXES[1]

Soil Type	Parts by Volume: Soil	Sphagnum Peat	Perlite
Clay loam	1	2	2
Sandy clay loam	1	1	1
Sandy loam	2	2	0

Adapted from J. W. Mastalerz, *The Greenhouse Environment*, Wiley, New York (1977).

[1]12–17 lb limestone and 17–21 lb 20% superphosphate are added to each cubic yard.

GLASSHOUSE CROPS RESEARCH INSTITUTE MIXES

Constituent	Seeding Mixture	Growing Mixture
	Parts by Volume	
Sphagnum peat	1	3
Sand	1	1
	Amounts/cu yd	
Ground limestone	5¼ lb	4 lb
Dolomitic limestone	—	4 lb
Superphosphate—20%	1¼ lb	2 lb 10 oz
Potassium nitrate	10 oz	1 lb 5 oz
Ammonium nitrate	—	10 oz
Fritted trace elements	—	10 oz

Adapted from A. C. Bunt, Loamless composts, *Glasshouse Crops Research Institute Annual Report* (1965).

THE UC MIXES

	% by Volume	
Mix	Fine Sand	Peat Moss
A	100	0
B	75	25
C[1]	50	50
D	25	75
E	0	100

Adapted from K. F. Baker (ed), The UC system for producing healthy container grown plants, California Agricultural Experiment Station Manual 23 (1972).

[1]Fertilizers for each cubic yard of mix C: 4 oz potassium nitrate, 4 oz potassium sulfate, 2½ lb 20% superphosphate, 7½ lb dolomitic limestone, and 2½ lb ground limestone.

CORNELL PEAT–LITE MIXES

Component	Amount (cu yd)
Sphagnum peat	0.5
Horticultural vermiculite	0.5

Additions for Specific Uses (amount/cu yd)

		Greenhouse Tomatoes	
Addition	Seedlings or Bedding Plants	Liquid Feed	Slow-Release Feed
Ground limestone (lb)	5	10	10
20% superphosphate (lb)	1–2	2.5	2.5
Calcium or potassium nitrate (lb)	1	1.5	1.5
Fritted trace elements (oz)	2	2	2
Osmocote (lb)	0	0	10
Mag Amp (lb)	0	0	5
Wetting agent (oz)[1]	3	3	3

Adapted from J. W. Boodley and R. Sheldrake, Jr., Cornell peat–lite mixes for commercial plant growing, New York Agricultural Experiment Station Agricultural Information Bulletin 43 (1982).

[1]Some commercial wetting agents are Aqua Gro, Ethomid 0/15, Hydro-Wet, Surf-Side, Tetronic 908, and Triton B-1956.

RELATIVE EASE OF TRANSPLANTING VEGETABLES

Easy	Moderate	Require Special Care[1]
Beet	Celery	Sweet corn
Broccoli	Eggplant	Cucumber
Brussels sprouts	Onion	Muskmelon
Cabbage	Pepper	Summer squash
Cauliflower		Watermelon
Chard		
Lettuce		
Tomato		

[1]Containerized transplants are recommended.

TEMPERATURES REQUIRED TO DESTROY PESTS IN COMPOST SOIL

Pests	30-min Temperature (°F)
Nematodes	120
Damping-off organisms	130
Most pathogenic bacteria and fungi	150
Soil insects and most viruses	160
Most weed seeds	175
Resistant weeds and resistant viruses	212

Adapted from K. F. Baker (ed), The UC system for producing healthy container grown plants, California Agricultural Experiment Station Manual 23 (1972).

Agent	Method	Recommendation
Heat	Steam	30 min at 180°F
	Aerated steam	30 min at 160°F
	Electric	30 min at 180°F
Chemical	Formalin (37–40%)	Dilute 1 part formalin to 50 parts water and apply 2 qt of this mixture as a drench to each sq ft of soil. Cover for 14–36 hr. Aerate for 14 days or until no odor is detected before using
	Chloropicrin	3–5 cc/cu ft of soil. Cover for 1–3 days. Aerate for 14 days or until no odor is detected before using
	Vapam	1 qt/100 sq ft. Allow 7–14 days before use
	Methyl bromide	1 lb/cu yd of soil or 2 lb/100 sq ft. Cover with gasproof cover for 24–48 hr. Aerate for 24–48 hr before use

General suggestions: Methyl bromide is effective for soils in flats and containers; chloropicrin or methyl bromide for bulk soils; chloropicrin, methyl bromide, or Vapam for other situations.

Caution: Chemical fumigants are highly toxic. Follow manufacturer's recommendations on the label.

Soluble salts, manganese, and ammonium usually increase after heat sterilization. Delay using heat-sterilized soil for at least 2 weeks to avoid problems with these toxic materials.

Adapted from K. F. Baker (ed), The UC system for producing healthy container grown plants, California Agricultural Experiment Station Manual 23 (1972).

PREVENTING CONTAMINATION OF STERILIZED SOIL

Most diseases of vegetable plants in greenhouses or seedbeds are caused by soilborne organisms. An effective sterilization of soils, containers, tools, and surroundings can largely overcome problems caused by these organisms. The advantage of sterilization can be lost if faulty sanitation allows the reintroduction of disease organisms. The following suggestions will help to maintain soils in a diseasefree condition:

1. Sterilize an entire greenhouse or bed area at the same time to reduce the chance for contamination.
2. Disinfect floors, bins, or benches before dumping sterilized soil. Disinfect all surfaces that come in contact with sterilized soil, containers, or tools.
3. Do not transplant infected seedlings or plants from out-of-doors in sterilized soil.
4. Do not handle sterilized soil with dirty hands or tools.
5. Do not walk on sterilized soil piles.
6. Keep the nozzle of watering hoses off the floor and out of contact with soil at all times.

Maintenance of "kitchen clean" sanitation is a good rule to follow in seeding and plant growing areas.

Adapted from A. G. Gentile et al., *Insect, disease and weed control for vegetable crops in Massachusetts*, Massachusetts Agricultural Extension Service (1978).

SOLUBLE SALTS LEVELS FOR GREENHOUSE CROPS

Soluble Salts[1] EC × 10^{-5} mhos			
Mineral Soil[1]	Peat–lite Mix[1]	Level	Interpretation
0–50[2]	0–100[2]	Low	Frequency and/or rate of fertilization may need adjustment
51–125	101–175	Medium	Satisfactory for plant growth; excellent for crops with daily fertigation
126–175	176–225	High	Satisfactory for established plants. Upper level may be too high for seedlings
176–200	226–350	Very high	Approaching toxicity, injury may occur if media is allowed to dry out
Above 201	Above 350	Excessive	Plants may be severely injured

Adapted from Cornell recommendations for commerical floriculture crops, New York Cooperative Extension Service (1981).

[1]Measured on one volume of medium extracted with two volumes water.
[2]Electrical conductivity.

FERTILIZERS FOR FERTIGATION (CONSTANT FEED) OF TRANSPLANTS[1]

Fertilizer Materials	oz/100 gal Water
1. Ammonium nitrate	3
Potassium nitrate	4
2. Sodium nitrate	5⅓
Potassium nitrate	4
3. Calcium nitrate	5⅓
Potassium nitrate	4
4. Urea	2
Potassium nitrate	4
5. 12–4–8[2]	8½
Potassium nitrate	2
6. 12–12–12[2]	10½
7. 15–30–15[2]	8½
8. 15–15–15[2]	8½
9. 15–0–15[2]	8½

Adapted from J. W. Mastalerz (ed.), *Bedding Plants*, 2nd ed., Pennsylvania Flower Growers, University Park, PA (1976).

[1]Each combination will provide 100 ppm nitrogen and 100 ppm potassium.

[2]Water-soluble fertilizers.

SUGGESTED MEDIA NUTRIENT LEVELS FOR TRANSPLANTS

Characteristic	Form	Approximate Level
Nitrogen	NO_3-N	50–250 ppm
Phosphorus	P	125–450 ppm
Potassium	K	0.75–1.5 meq/100 g 3–7.5% of CEC
Calcium	Ca	8–13 meq/100 g 52–85% of CEC
Magnesium	Mg	1.2–3.5 meq/100 g 7.5–21% of CEC
pH		5–7
Soluble salts	EC $\times 10^{-5}$ mhos	40–140

Adapted from J. W. Mastalerz (ed.), *Bedding Plants*, 2nd ed., Pennsylvania Flower Growers, University Park, PA (1976).

EC = electrical conductivity; CEC = cation exchange capacity.

DIAGNOSIS AND CORRECTION OF TRANSPLANT DISORDERS

Symptoms	Possible Causes	Corrective Measures
1. Spindly growth	Shade, cloudy weather, excessive watering, excessive temperature	Provide full sun, reduce temperature, restrict watering, ventilate or reduce night temperature, fertilize less frequently, provide adequate space
2. Dwarf plants	Low fertility	Apply fertilizer frequently in low concentration
A. Purple leaves	Phosphorus deficiency	Apply a soluble, phosphorus-rich fertilizer such as 10–55–10 or 15–30–15 (1 oz/gal of water to each 6–12 sq ft of bench area)
B. Yellow leaves	Nitrogen deficiency	Apply KNO_3 (1 oz/3 gal of water for 6–12 sq ft of bench area). Wash the foliage with water after application
C. Discolored roots	High soluble salts from overfertilization.	Leach the soil by excess watering
	High soluble salts from poor soil sterilization	Do not sterilize at temperatures above 160°F. Leach soils before planting when soil tests indicate high amounts of soluble salts
D. Normal roots	Low temperature	Maintain suitable day and night temperature
3. Tough, woody plants	Overhardening	Apply starter solution (10–55–10 or 15–30–15 at 1 oz/gal to each 6–12 sq ft of bench area) 3–4 days before transplanting

DIAGNOSIS AND CORRECTION OF TRANSPLANT DISORDERS—Continued

Symptoms	Possible Causes	Corrective Measures
4. Water-soaked and decayed stems near the soil surface	Damping-off	Use a sterile, well-drained medium. Adjust watering and ventilation practices to provide a less moist environment. Use approved fungicidal drenches
5. Poor root growth	Poor soil aeration. Poor soil drainage. Low soil fertility. Excess soluble salts. Low temperature. Residue from chemical sterilization. Herbicide residue	Determine the cause and take corrective measures
6. Green algae or mosses growing on soil surface	High soil moisture, especially in shade or during cloudy periods	Adjust watering and ventilation practices to provide a less moist environment. Use a better drained medium

Adapted from J. W. Mastalerz (ed.), *Bedding Plants*, 2nd ed., Pennsylvania Flower Growers, University Park, PA (1976).

Objective: To prepare plants to withstand stress conditions in the field. These may be low temperatures, high temperatures, drying winds, low soil moisture, or injury to the roots in transplanting. Growth rates decrease during hardening, and the energy otherwise used in growth is stored in the plant to aid in resumption of growth after transplanting.

Methods: Any treatment that restricts growth will increase hardiness. Cool-season crops generally develop hardiness in proportion to the severity of the treatment and length of exposure, and will when well-hardened withstand subfreezing temperatures. Warm-season crops, even when hardened, will not withstand temperatures much below freezing.

1. *Water supply.* Gradually reduce water by watering lightly at less frequent intervals. Do not allow the plants to dry out suddenly with severe wilting.
2. *Temperature.* Expose plants to lower temperatures (5–10°F) than those used for optimum growth. High day temperatures may reverse the effects of cool nights, making temperature management difficult. Do not expose biennials to prolonged cool temperatures, for this induces bolting. (See page 382.)
3. *Fertility.* Do not fertilize, particularly with nitrogen, immediately before or during the initial stages of hardening. Apply a starter solution or liquid fertilizer 1 or 2 days before field setting and/or with the transplanting water. (See page 49.)
4. *Combinations.* Restricting water and lowering temperatures and fertility, used in combination, are perhaps more effective than any single approach.

Duration: Seven to ten days is usually sufficient to effect the hardening process. Do not impose conditions so severe that plants will be overhardened in case of delayed planting because of poor weather.

Overhardened plants require too much time to resume growth, and early yields may be lower.

STARTER SOLUTIONS[1]

Materials	Quantity to Use in Transplanter Tank
Readily Soluble Commercial Mixtures	
8–24–8, 11–48–0 23–21–17, 13–26–13 6–25–15, 10–52–17	(Follow manufacturer's directions) Usually 3 lb/50 gal of water
Straight Nitrogen Chemicals	
Ammonium sulfate, calcium nitrate, or sodium nitrate	2½ lb/50 gal of water
Ammonium nitrate	1½ lb/50 gal of water
Commercial Solutions	
30% nitrogen solution	1½ pt/50 gal of water
8–24–0 solution (N and P_2O_5)	2 qt/50 gal of water
Regular Commercial Fertilizer Grades	
4–8–12, 5–10–5, 5–10–10, etc.:	
1 lb/gal for stock solution; stir well and let settle	5 gal of stock solution with 45 gal of water

[1]Apply at a rate of about ½ pt/plant.

CULTURAL MANAGEMENT OF GREENHOUSE VEGETABLES

Although most vegetables can be grown successfully in greenhouses, only a very few are grown commercially. Tomato, cucumber, and lettuce are the three most commonly grown vegetables in commercial greenhouses. Some general cultural management principles are discussed here.

Sanitation

There is no substitute for good sanitation for preventing insect and disease outbreaks in greenhouse crops.

To keep greenhouses clean, remove and destroy all dead plants, unnecessary mulch material, flats, weeds, and so on. Burn or bury all plant refuse. Do not contaminate streams or water supplies with plant refuse. Weeds growing in and near the greenhouse after the cropping period should be destroyed. Do not attempt to overwinter garden or house plants in the greenhouses. Pests will also be maintained, for an early invasion of vegetable crops. To prevent disease organisms from carrying over on the structure of the greenhouse and on the heating pipes and walks, spray with formaldehyde (3 gal of 37% formalin in 100 gal of water). Immediately after spraying, close up the greenhouse for 4–5 days, then ventilate. CAUTION: Wear a respirator when spraying with formaldehyde.

A 15- to 20-ft strip of carefully maintained lawn or bare ground around the greenhouse will help decrease trouble from two-spotted mite or other pests. To reduce entry of whiteflies, leafhoppers, and aphids from weeds and other plants near the greenhouses, spray such growth occasionally with a labeled insecticide.

Monitoring Pests

Insects such as greenhouse whiteflies, thrips, and leaf miners are attracted to shades of yellow and will fly toward that color. Thus insect traps can be made by painting pieces of board with the correct shade of yellow pigment and then covering the paint with a sticky substance. Similar traps are available commercially from several sources. By placing a number of traps within the greenhouse range it is possible to check infestations daily and be aware of early infestations. Control programs can then be commenced while populations are low.

Two-spotted mites cannot be trapped in this way, but infestations usually begin in localized areas first. Check cucumber leaves daily and begin control measures as soon as the first infested areas are noted.

Spacing

Good-quality container-grown transplants should be set in arrangements to allow about 4 sq ft/plant for tomato, 5 sq ft/plant for American-type cucumber, and 7–9 sq ft/plant for European-type cucumber. Lettuce requires 36–81 sq in./plant.

Temperature

Greenhouse tomato varieties may vary in their temperature requirements, but most varieties perform well at a day temperature of 70–75°F and a night temperature of 62–64°F. Temperatures for cucumber seedlings should be 72–76°F day and 68°F night. In a few weeks, night temperature can be gradually lowered to 62–64°F. Night temperatures for lettuce can be somewhat lower than those used for tomato and cucumber.

In northern areas, provisions should be made to heat water to be used in greenhouses to about 70°F.

Pruning and Tieing

Greenhouse tomatoes and cucumbers are usually pruned to a single stem by frequent removal of axillary shoots or suckers. Other pruning systems are possible and are sometimes used. Various tieing methods are used; a common method is to train the pruned plant around a string suspended from an overhead wire.

Pollination

Greenhouse tomatoes must be hand pollinated to assure a good set of fruit. This involves tapping or vibrating each flower cluster to transfer the pollen grains from the anther to the stigma. This should be done daily as long as there are open blossoms on the flower cluster. The pollen is transferred most readily during sunny periods and with the most difficulty during dark, cloudy days. The electric or battery-operated hand vibrator is the most widely accepted tool for vibrating tomato flower clusters. Most red-fruited varieties pollinate more easily than pinks and can often be pollinated satisfactorily by "tapping" the overhead support wires, or by shaking flowers by air stream from a motor-driven backpack duster.

Pollination of European seedless cucumbers causes off-shape fruit, so bees must be prevented from entering the greenhouse. To help overcome this, gynoecious cultivars have been developed that bear almost 100% female flowers. Only gynoecious cultivars are now recommended for commercial production.

American-type cucumbers require bees for pollination. One colony of honeybees per house should be provided. It is advisable to shade colonies from the afternoon sun, and to avoid excessively high temperatures and humidities. Honeybees fly well in glass and polyethylene plastic houses, but fail to work under certain other types of plastic. Under these conditions, crop failures may occur through lack of pollination.

Adapted from Ontario Ministry of Agriculture Publication 356 (1985–1986).

CARBON DIOXIDE ENRICHMENT OF GREENHOUSE ATMOSPHERES

The beneficial effects of adding carbon dioxide (CO_2) to the greenhouse environment are well established. The crops that respond most consistently to supplemental CO_2 are cucumber, lettuce, and tomato, although almost all other greenhouse crops will also benefit.

Outside air contains about 340 parts per million (ppm) of CO_2 by volume. Most plants grow well at this level, but if levels are higher, the plants will respond by producing more sugars. During the day, in a closed greenhouse, the plants use the CO_2 in the air and reduce the level below the normal 340 ppm. This is the point at which CO_2 addition is most important. Most crops respond to CO_2 additions up to about 1300 ppm. Somewhat lower concentrations are adequate for seedlings or when growing conditions are less than ideal.

Carbon dioxide can be obtained by burning natural gas, propane, or kerosene, and also directly from containers of pure CO_2. Each source has potential advantages and disadvantages. When natural gas, propane, or kerosene is burned, not only is CO_2 produced, but also heat, which can supplement the normal heating system. Incomplete combustion or contaminated fuels may cause plant damage. Most sources of natural gas and propane have sufficiently low levels of impurities, but you should notify your supplier of your intention to use the fuel for CO_2 addition. Sulfur levels in the fuel should not exceed 0.02% by weight.

A number of commercial companies have burners available for natural gas, propane, and liquid fuels. The most important feature of a burner should be that it burns the fuel completely.

Because photosynthesis occurs only during daylight hours, CO_2 addition is not required at night, but supplementation is recommended during dull days. Supplementation should start approximately one hour before sunrise and the system should be shut off one hour before sunset. If supplemental lighting is used at night, intermittent addition of CO_2 or the use of a CO_2 controller may be helpful.

When ventilators are opened, it is not possible to maintain high CO_2 levels. However, it is often during these hours (high light intensity and temperature) that CO_2 supplementation is beneficial. Because it is impossible to maintain optimal levels, it is suggested to maintain at least ambient. A CO_2 controller, whereby the CO_2 concentration can be maintained at any level above ambient is therefore very useful.

One very important factor is an adequate distribution system. The distribution of CO_2 mainly depends on the air movement in the greenhouse(s), for CO_2 does not travel very far by diffusion. For instance, if a single source of CO_2 is used for a large surface area or several connecting greenhouses, a distribution system must be installed. Air circulation (horizontal fans or fanjet system) that moves a large volume of air will provide uniform distribution within the greenhouse.

Adapted from Ontario Ministry of Agriculture and Food AGDEX 290/27 (1984).

Well-managed field soils supply crops with sufficient water and appropriate concentrations of the 13 essential inorganic elements. A combination of desirable soil chemical, physical, and biotic characteristics provide conditions for extensive rooting, which results in anchorage, the third general quality provided to crops by soil.

When field soils are used in the greenhouse for repeated intensive crop culture, desirable soil characteristics deteriorate rapidly. Diminishing concentrations of essential elements and impaired physical properties are restored as in the field by applications of lime, fertilizer, and organic matter. Deterioration of the biotic quality of the soil by increased pathogenic microorganism and nematode populations has been restricted mostly by steam sterilization.

Even with the best management, soils may deteriorate in quality over time. In addition, the costs—particularly of steam sterilization—of maintaining greenhouse soils in good condition have escalated so that soilless culture methods are competitive, or perhaps more economically favorable than soil culture. Accordingly, there has been a considerable shift from soil culture to soilless culture in greenhouses in recent years. Liquid and media systems are used.

Liquid Soilless Culture

The nutrient-film technique (NFT) is the most commonly used liquid system.

NFT growing systems consist of a series of narrow channels through which nutrient solution is recirculated from a supply tank. A plumbing system of plastic tubing and a submersible pump in the tank are the basic components. The channels are generally constructed of opaque plastic film or plastic pipe; asphalt-coated wood and fiberglass also have been used. The basic characteristic of all NFT systems is the shallow depth of solution that is maintained in the channels. Flow is usually continuous, but sometimes systems are operated intermittently by supplying solution a few minutes every hour. The purpose of intermittent flow is to assure adequate aeration of the root systems. This also reduces the energy required; but under rapid growth conditions, plants could experience water stress if the flow period is too short or infrequent. Therefore, intermittent flow management seems better adapted to mild temperature periods or to plantings during the early stages of development. Capillary matting is sometimes used in the bottom of NFT channels, principally to avoid the side-to-side meandering of the solution stream around young root systems, but it also acts as a reservoir by retaining nutrients and water during periods when flow ceases.

NFT channels are frequently designed for a single row of plants with a channel width of 6–8 inches. Wider channels of 12–15 inches have been used to accommodate two rows of plants, but meandering of the shallow solution stream becomes a greater problem with greater width. To minimize this problem, small dams can be created at intervals down the channel by placing thin wooden sticks crossways in the stream, or the channel may be lined with capillary matting. The channels should be sloped 4–6 inches per 100 feet to maintain gravity flow of the solution. Flow rate into the channels should be in the range of 1–2 qt/min. Channel length should be limited to a maximum of 100 ft in order to minimize increased solution temperature on bright days. The ideal solution temperature for tomato is 68–77°F. Temperatures below 59° or above 86°F decrease plant growth and tomato yield. Channels of black plastic film increase solution temperature on sunny days. During cloudy weather, it may be necessary to heat the solution to the recommended temperature. Solution temperatures in black plastic channels can be decreased by shading or painting the surfaces white or silver. As an alternative to channels lined with black polyethylene, 4- to 6-in. PVC pipe may be used. Plant holes are spaced appropriately along the pipe. The PVC system is permanent once it is constructed compared to the polyethylene-lined channels, which must be replaced for each crop. Initial costs are higher for the PVC and sanitation between crops may be more difficult.

Solid Soilless Culture

Lightweight media in containers or bags and rock-wool mats are the most commonly used media culture systems.

Media Culture

Soilless culture in bags, pots, or troughs with a lightweight medium is the simplest, most economical, and easiest to manage of all soilless systems. The most common media used in containerized systems of soilless culture are peat–lite or a mixture of bark and wood chips. Container types range from long wooden troughs in which one or two rows of plants are grown, to polyethylene bags or rigid plastic pots containing one to three plants. Bag or pot systems using bark chips or peat–lite are in common use throughout the United States and offer some major advantages over other types of soilless culture: (1) these materials have excellent retention qualities for nutrients and water; (2) containers of medium are readily moved in or out of the greenhouse whenever necessary or desirable; (3) they are lightweight and easily handled; (4) the medium is useful for several successive crops; (5) the containers are significantly less expensive and less time-consuming to install; and (6) in comparison with recirculated hydroponic systems, the nutrient-solution system is less complicated and less expensive to manage. From a plant nutrition standpoint, the latter advantage is of significant importance. In a recirculated system the solution is continuously changing in its concentration and its nutrient balance because of differential plant uptake. In the bag or pot system, the solution is not recirculated. Nutrient solution is supplied from a fertilizer proportioner or large supply tank to the surface of the medium in a sufficient quantity to wet the medium. Any excess is drained away from the system through drain holes in the base of the containers. Thus the concentration and balance of nutrients in solution fed to the plants is the same at each application. This eliminates the need to sample and analyze the solution periodically to determine the kind of necessary adjustments and avoids the possibility of solution excess or deficiencies.

In the bag or pot system, the volume of medium per container varies from about ½ cu ft in vertical polyethylene bags or pots to 2 cu ft in lay-flat bags. In the vertical bag system, 4-mil black polyethylene bags with prepunched drain holes at the bottom are common. One, but sometimes two, tomato or cucumber plants are grown in each bag. Lay-flat bags accommodate two or three plants. In either case, the bags are aligned in rows with spacing appropriate to the type of crop being grown. It is good practice to place vertical bags or pots on a narrow sheet of plastic film to prevent root contact or penetration into the underlying soil. Plants in lay-flat bags, which have drainage slits (or overflow ports) cut along the sides an inch or so above the base, would also benefit from a protective plastic sheet beneath them.

Nutrient solution is delivered to the containers by supply lines of black polyethylene tubing, spaghetti tubing, spray sticks, or ring drippers in the containers. The choice of application system is important in order to provide proper wetting of the medium at each irrigation. Texture and porosity of the growing medium and the surface area to be wetted are important considerations in making the choice. Spaghetti tubing provides a point-source wetting pattern, which might be appropriate for fine-textured media that allow water to be conducted laterally with ease. In lay-flat bags, single spaghetti tubes at individual plant holes will provide good wetting of peat–lite. In a vertical bag containing a porous medium, a spray stick with a 90-degree spray pattern will do a good job of irrigation if it is located to wet the majority of the surface. Ring drippers are also a good choice for vertical bags although somewhat more expensive. When choosing an application system for bag or container culture, remember that the objective of irrigation is to distribute nutrient solution uniformly so that all of the medium is wet.

Rock-wool Culture

Rock wool is made by melting various types of rocks at very high temperatures. The resulting particles are formed into growing blocks or mats that are sterile and free of organic matter. The growing mats have a very high water-holding capacity, no buffering capacity, and an initial pH of 7–8.5, which is lowered quickly with application of slightly acidic nutrient solutions. Uncovered mats, which are covered with polyethylene during setup, or polyethylene enclosed mats can be purchased. The mats are 8–12 in. wide, 36 in. long, and 3 in. thick.

The greenhouse floor should be carefully leveled, and covered with 3-mil black/white polyethylene which will restrict weed growth and act as a light reflector with the white side up. The mats are placed end-to-end to form a row; single or double rows are spaced for the crop and greenhouse configuration.

A complete nutrient solution made with good-quality water is used for initial soaking of the mats. Large volumes are necessary because of the high water-holding capacity of the mats. Drip-irrigation tubing or spaghetti tubing arranged along the plant row are used for initial soaking and later for fertigation. After soaking, uncovered mats are covered with polyethylene and drainage holes are made in the bagged mats.

Cross-slits, corresponding in size to the propagating blocks, are made in the polyethylene mat cover at desired in-row plant spacings; usually two plants are grown in each 30-in.-long mat. The propagating blocks containing the transplant are placed on the mat, and the excess polyethylene from the cross-slit is arranged around the block. Frequent irrigation is required until plant roots are established in the mat; thereafter fertigation is applied 4–10 times a day depending upon the growing conditions and stage of crop growth. The mats are leached with good-quality water when samples taken from the mats with a syringe have increased conductivity readings.

Some growers use rock-wool mats for more than one crop.

Adapted in part from H. Johnson, Jr., G. J. Hochmuth, and D. N. Maynard, Soilless culture of greenhouse vegetables, Florida Cooperative Extension Bulletin 218 (1985).

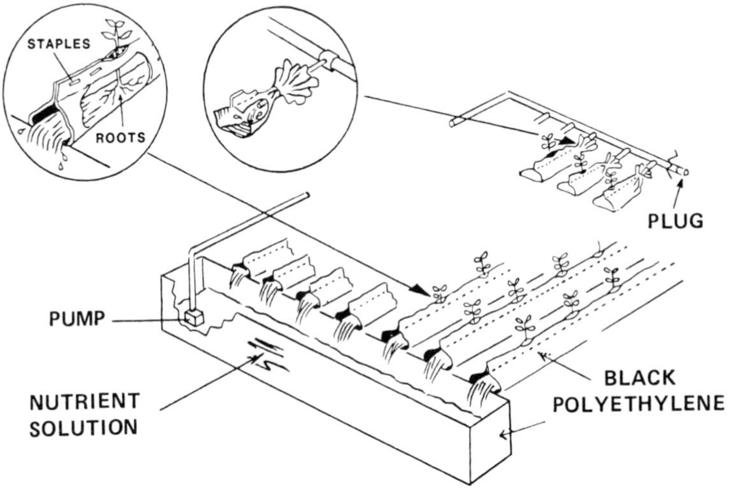

NFT culture system using polyethylene film to hold plants and supply nutrient solution through a recirculation system (From Florida Cooperative Extension Bulletin 218).

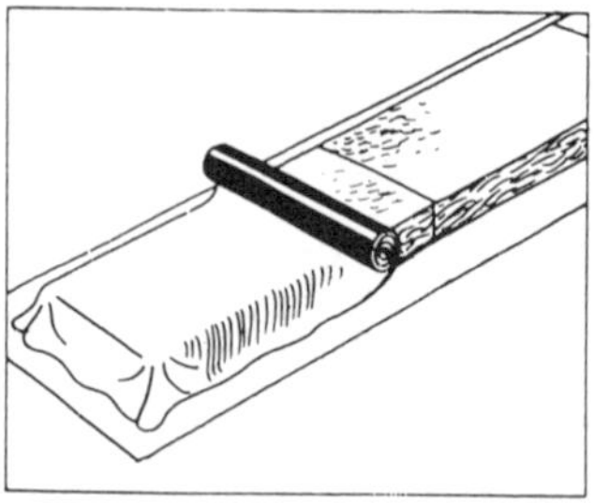

Arranged mats are covered with white/ black polyethylene.

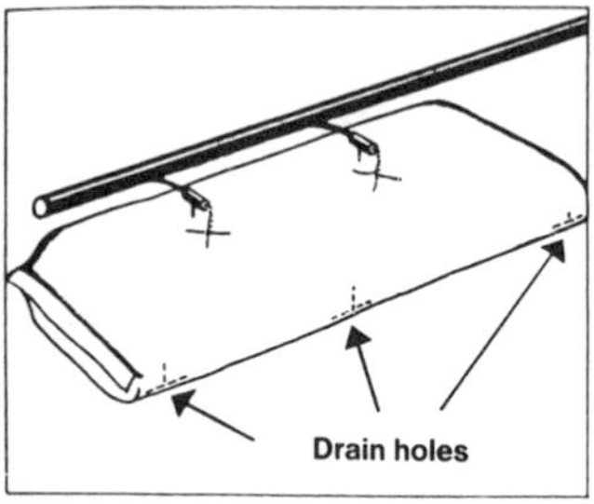

Irrigation system and drainage holes for rock-wool mats enclosed in a polyethylene bag.

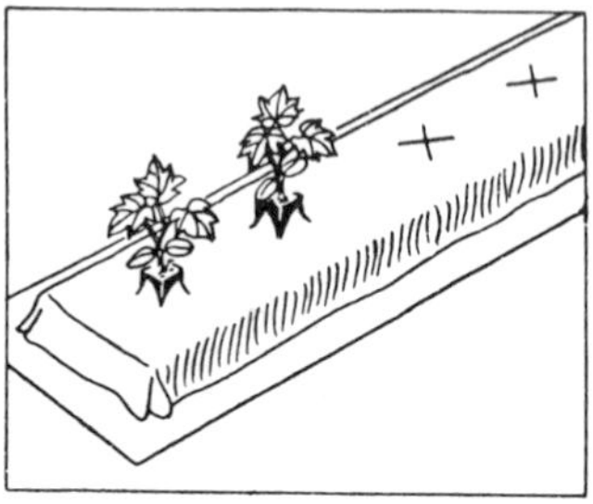

Cross-slits are made to accommodate transplants in propagation blocks.

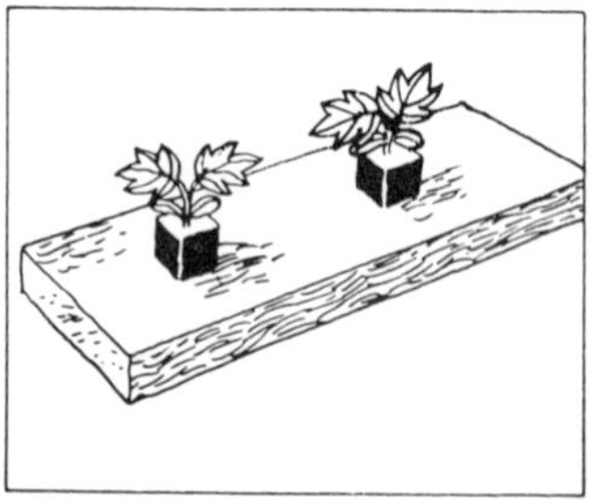

Ordinarily, two plants are placed in each 30-in.-long mat.

Fertigation supplied by spaghetti tubing to each plant.

Fertigation supplied by drip irrigation tubing.

Removal of sample from rock-wool mat with a syringe for conductivity determination.

Adapted from GRODAN® Instructions for cultivation—cucumbers, Grodania A/S, Denmark and used with permission.

NUTRIENT SOLUTIONS FOR SOILLESS CULTURE

Because the water and/or media used for soilless culture of greenhouse vegetables is devoid of essential elements, they must be supplied in a nutrient solution.

Commercially available fertilizer mixtures may be used, or nutrient solutions can be prepared from individual chemical salts. The most widely used and generally successful nutrient solution is one developed by D. R. Hoagland and D. I. Arnon at the University of California. Many commercial mixtures are based on their formula.

Detailed directions for preparation of Hoagland's nutrient solutions, which are suitable for experimental or commercial use, and the formulas for several nutrient solutions that are suitable for commercial use follow.

HOAGLAND'S NUTRIENT SOLUTIONS

Salt	Stock Solution (g to make 1 liter)	Final Solution (ml to make 1 liter)
	Solution 1	
$Ca(NO_3)_2 \cdot 4H_2O$	236.2	5
KNO_3	101.1	5
KH_2PO_4	136.1	1
$MgSO_4 \cdot 7H_2O$	246.5	2
	Solution 2	
$Ca(NO_3)_2 \cdot 4H_2O$	236.2	4
KNO_3	101.1	6
$NH_4H_2PO_4$	115.0	1
$MgSO_4 \cdot 7H_2O$	246.5	2

Micronutrient Solution

Compound	Amount (g) Dissolved in 1 Liter of Water
H_3BO_3	2.86
$MnCl_2 \cdot 4H_2O$	1.81
$ZnSO_4 \cdot 7H_2O$	0.22
$CuSO_4 \cdot 5H_2O$	0.08
$H_2MoO_4 \cdot H_2O$	0.02

Iron Solution

Iron chelate, such as Sequestrene 330, made to stock solution containing 1 g actual iron/liter. Sequestrene 330 is 10% iron; thus 10 g/liter are required. The amounts of other chelates will have to be adjusted on the basis of their iron content.

Procedure: To make 1 liter of Solution 1, add 5 ml $Ca(NO_3)_2 \cdot 4H_2O$ stock solution, 5 ml KNO_3, 1 ml KH_2PO_4, 2 ml $MgSO_4 \cdot 7H_2O$, 1 ml micronutrient solution, and 1 ml iron solution to 800 ml distilled water. Make up to 1 liter. Some plants grow better on Solution 2, which is prepared in the same way.

Adapted from D. R. Hoagland and D. I. Arnon, The water-culture method for growing plants without soil, California Agricultural Experiment Station Circular 347 (1950).

SOME NUTRIENT SOLUTIONS FOR COMMERCIAL GREENHOUSE VEGETABLE PRODUCTION

These solutions are designed to be supplied directly to greenhouse vegetable crops.

JOHNSON'S SOLUTION

Compound	Amount (g/100 gal of water)
Potassium nitrate	95
Monopotassium phosphate	54
Magnesium sulfate	95
Calcium nitrate	173
Chelated iron (FeDTPA)	9
Boric acid	0.5
Manganese sulfate	0.3
Zinc sulfate	0.04
Copper sulfate	0.01
Molybdic acid	0.005

	N	P	K	Ca	Mg	S	Fe	B	Mn	Zn	Cu	Mo
ppm	105	33	138	85	25	33	2.3	0.23	0.26	0.024	0.01	0.007

JENSEN'S SOLUTION

Compound	Amount (g/100 gal of water)
Magnesium sulfate	187
Monopotassium phosphate	103
Potassium nitrate	77
Calcium nitrate	189
Chelated iron (FeDTPA)	9.6
Boric acid	1.0
Manganese chloride	0.9
Cupric chloride	0.05
Molybdic acid	0.02
Zinc sulfate	0.15

	N	P	K	Ca	Mg	S	Fe	B	Mn	Zn	Cu	Mo
ppm	106	62	156	93	48	64	3.8	0.46	0.81	0.09	0.05	0.03

LARSEN'S SOLUTION

Compound	Amount (g/100 gal of water)
Potassium nitrate	67
Calcium nitrate	360
Potassium magnesium sulfate	167
Potassium sulfate	130
Chelated iron (FeDTPA)	12
Phosphoric acid (75%)	(40 ml)
Manganese sulfate	1.5
Boric acid	2.2
Zinc sulfate	0.5
Copper sulfate	0.5
Molybdic acid	0.04

	N	P	K	Ca	Mg	S	Fe	B	Mn	Zn	Cu	Mo
ppm	172	41	300	180	48	158	3	1.0	1.3	0.3	0.3	0.07

COOPER'S SOLUTION

Compound	Amount (g/100 gal of water)
Potassium nitrate	221
Magnesium sulfate	194
Calcium nitrate	380
Monopotassium phosphate	99
Iron chelate (FeEDTA)	30
Manganese sulfate	2.3
Boric acid	0.6
Copper sulfate	0.15
Zinc sulfate	0.17
Ammonium molybdate	0.14

	N	P	K	Ca	Mg	S	Fe	B	Mn	Zn	Cu	Mo
ppm	236	60	300	185	50	68	12	0.3	2.0	0.1	0.1	0.2

Adapted from H. Johnson, Jr., G. J. Hochmuth, and D. N. Maynard, Soilless culture of greenhouse vegetables, Florida Cooperative Extension Bulletin 218 (1985).

APPROXIMATE NORMAL TISSUE COMPOSITION OF HYDROPONICALLY GROWN GREENHOUSE VEGETABLES[1]

Element	Tomato	Cucumber
K	5–8%	8–15%
Ca	2–3%	1–3%
Mg	0.4–1.0%	0.3–0.7%
NO_3-N	14,000–20,000 ppm	10,000–20,000 ppm
PO_4-P	6000–8000 ppm	8000–10,000 ppm
Fe	40–100 ppm	90–120 ppm
Zn	15–25 ppm	40–50 ppm
Cu	4–6 ppm	5–10 ppm
Mn	25–50 ppm	50–150 ppm
Mo	1–3 ppm	1–3 ppm
B	20–60 ppm	40–60 ppm

Adapted from H. Johnson, Hydroponics: A guide to soilless culture systems, University of California Division of Agricultural Science Leaflet 2947 (1977).

[1]Values are for recently expanded leaves, 5th or 6th from the growing tip, petiole analysis for macronutrients, leaf blade analysis for micronutrients. Expressed on a dry weight basis.

PART 3
FIELD PLANTING

COOL-SEASON AND WARM-SEASON VEGETABLES

Vegetables generally can be divided into two broad groups. Cool-season vegetables develop edible vegetative parts, that is, roots, stems, leaves, and buds or immature flower parts. Exceptions to this rule are the sweet potato and other tropical root crops (root used) and New Zealand spinach (leaf and stem used). Warm-season vegetables develop edible immature and mature fruits. Pea and broad bean are exceptions, being cool-season crops.

Cool-season crops generally differ from warm-season crops in the following respects:

1. They are hardy or frost tolerant.
2. Seeds germinate at cooler soil temperatures.
3. Root systems are shallower.
4. Plant size is smaller.
5. They respond more to nitrogen and phosphorus application.
6. Some, the biennials, are susceptible to premature seed stalk development from exposure to prolonged cool weather (see page 382).
7. They are stored near 32°F, except for the white potato. Sweet corn is the only warm-season crop held at 32°F after harvest.
8. The harvested product is not subject to chilling injury at temperatures between 32 and 50°F, as is the case with some of the warm-season vegetables.

CLASSIFICATION OF VEGETABLE CROPS ACCORDING TO THEIR ADAPTATION TO FIELD TEMPERATURES

Cool-season Crops

Hardy[1]		Half-hardy[1]
Asparagus	Kohlrabi	Beet
Broad bean	Leek	Carrot
Broccoli	Mustard	Cauliflower
Brussels sprouts	Onion	Celery
Cabbage	Parsley	Chard
Chive	Pea	Chicory
Collard	Radish	Chinese cabbage
Garlic	Rhubarb	Globe artichoke
Horseradish	Spinach	Endive
Kale	Turnip	Lettuce
		Parsnip
		Potato
		Salsify

Warm-season Crops

Tender[1]	Very Tender[1]
Cowpea	Cucumber
New Zealand spinach	Eggplant
Snap bean	Lima bean
Soybean	Muskmelon
Sweet corn	Okra
Tomato	Pepper, hot
	Pepper, sweet
	Pumpkin
	Squash
	Sweet potato
	Watermelon

Adapted from A. A. Kader, J. M. Lyons, and L. L. Morris, Postharvest responses of vegetables to preharvest field temperatures, *HortScience* 9:523–529 (1974).

[1]Relative resistance to frost and light freezes.

APPROXIMATE MONTHLY TEMPERATURES FOR BEST GROWTH AND QUALITY OF VEGETABLE CROPS

Some crops can be planted as temperatures approach the proper range. Cool-season crops grown in the spring must have time to mature before warm weather. Fall crops can be started in hot weather to ensure a sufficient period of cool temperature to reach maturity. Within a crop, varieties may differ in temperature requirements; hence this listing provides general rather than specific guidelines.

Temperatures (°F)			
Optimum	Minimum	Maximum	Vegetable
55–75	45[1]	85	Chicory, chive, garlic, leek, onion, salsify, scolymus, scorzonera, shallot
60–65	40[1]	75	Beet, broad bean, broccoli, Brussels sprouts, cabbage, chard, collard, horseradish, kale, kohlrabi, parsnip, radish, rutabaga, sorrel, spinach, turnip
60–65	45[1]	75	Artichoke, cardoon, carrot, cauliflower, celeriac, celery, Chinese cabbage, endive, Florence fennel, lettuce, mustard, parsley, pea, potato
60–70	50	80	Lima bean, snap bean
60–75	50	95	Sweet corn, Southern pea, New Zealand spinach
65–75	50	90	Chayote, pumpkin, squash
65–75	60	90	Cucumber, muskmelon
70–75	65	80	Sweet pepper, tomato
70–85	65	95	Eggplant, hot pepper, martynia, okra, roselle, sweet potato, watermelon

[1]See page 382 for effect of prolonged exposure to temperatures less than 40°F on bolting of certain vegetables in this group.

SOIL TEMPERATURE CONDITIONS FOR VEGETABLE SEED GERMINATION[1]

Vegetable	Minimum (°F)	Optimum Range (°F)	Optimum (°F)	Maximum (°F)
Asparagus	50	60–85	75	95
Bean	60	60–85	80	95
Bean, Lima	60	65–85	85	85
Beet	40	50–85	85	95
Cabbage	40	45–95	85	100
Carrot	40	45–85	80	95
Cauliflower	40	45–85	80	100
Celery	40	60–70	70[2]	85[2]
Chard, Swiss	40	50–85	85	95
Corn	50	60–95	95	105
Cucumber	60	60–95	95	105
Eggplant	60	75–90	85	95
Lettuce	35	40–80	75	85
Muskmelon	60	75–95	90	100
Okra	60	70–95	95	105
Onion	35	50–95	75	95
Parsley	40	50–85	75	90
Parsnip	35	50–70	65	85
Pea	40	40–75	75	85
Pepper	60	65–95	85	95
Pumpkin	60	70–90	90	100
Radish	40	45–90	85	95
Spinach	35	45–75	70	85
Squash	60	70–95	95	100
Tomato	50	60–85	85	95
Turnip	40	60–105	85	105
Watermelon	60	70–95	95	105

[1]Compiled by J. F. Harrington, Department of Vegetable Crops, University of California, Davis.
[2]Daily fluctuation to 60°F or lower at night is essential.

SCHEDULING SUCCESSIVE PLANTINGS

Successive plantings are necessary to ensure a continuous supply of produce. This seemingly easy goal is in fact extremely difficult to achieve because of interrupted planting schedules, poor stands, and variable weather.

Maturity can be predicted in part by use of "days to harvest" or "heat units." Additional flexibility is provided by using varieties that differ in time and heat units to reach maturity. Production for fresh market entails the use of days to harvest while some processing crops may be scheduled using the heat unit concept.

Fresh Market Crops

Sweet corn is used as an example, since it is an important fresh market crop in many parts of the country and requires several plantings to obtain a season-long supply.

Step 1. Select varieties suitable for your area which mature over a period of time. We have chosen five sample varieties maturing in 68–84 days from planting with 4-day intervals between varieties.

Step 2. Make the first planting as early as possible in your area.

Step 3. Construct a table like the one following and calculate the time of the next planting, so that the earliest variety used matures 4 days after 'Capitan' in the first planting. We chose to use 'Merit' as the earliest variety in the second planting; thus 88 days − 80 days = 8 days elasped time before the second and subsequent plantings.

Step 4. As sometimes happens, the third planting was delayed 4 days by rain. To compensate for this delay, 'Mevak' is selected as the earliest variety in the third planting to provide corn 96 days after the first planting.

EXAMPLES OF SWEET CORN PLANTINGS

		Time (days)		
Planting	Variety	To Maturity	From First Planting	To Next Planting
First	Aztec	68	68	
	Comanche	72	72	
	Mevak	76	76	
	Merit	80	80	
	Capitan	84	84	
				8
Second	Merit	80	88	
	Capitan	84	92	
				12
Third	Mevak	76	96	
	Merit	80	100	
	Capitan	84	104	

Adapted from H. Tiessen, Scheduled planting of vegetable crops, Ontario Ministry of Agriculture and Food AGDEX 250/22 (1980).

Processing Crops

The heat unit system is used to schedule plantings and harvests for some processing crops, most notably pea and sweet corn. The use of this system implies that accumulated temperatures over a selected base temperature are a more accurate means of measuring growth than a time unit such as days.

In its simplest form heat units are calculated as follows:

$$\frac{\text{Maximum} + \text{minimum daily temperature}}{2} - \text{base temperature}$$

The base temperature is 40°F for pea and 50°F for sweet corn. A number of variations to this basic formula have been proposed to further extend its usefulness.

Heat unit requirements to reach maturity have been determined for most processing pea and sweet corn varieties and many snap bean varieties. Processors using the heat unit system assist growers in scheduling plantings to coincide with plant operating capacity.

DAYS REQUIRED FOR SEEDLING EMERGENCE AT VARIOUS SOIL TEMPERATURES FROM SEED PLANTED ½ IN. DEEP

The days from planting to emergence constitute the time interval when a preemergence weed control treatment can be used safely and effectively. More days are required with deeper seeding because of cooler temperatures and the greater distance of growth.

	Soil Temperature (°F)								
Vegetable	32	41	50	59	68	77	86	95	104
Asparagus	NG	NG	53	24	15	10	12	20	28
Bean, Lima	—	—	NG	31	18	7	7	NG	—
Bean, snap	NG	NG	NG	16	11	8	6	6	NG
Beet	—	42	17	10	6	5	5	5	—
Cabbage	—	—	15	9	6	5	4	—	—
Carrot	NG	51	17	10	7	6	6	9	NG
Cauliflower	—	—	20	10	6	5	5	—	—

Celery	NG	41	16	12	7	NG	NG	NG	—
Corn, sweet	NG	NG	22	12	7	4	4	3	NG
Cucumber	NG	NG	NG	13	6	4	3	3	—
Eggplant	—	—	—	—	13	8	5	—	—
Lettuce	49	15	7	4	3	2	3	NG	NG
Muskmelon	—	—	—	—	8	4	3	—	—
Okra	NG	NG	NG	27	17	13	7	6	7
Onion	136	31	13	7	5	4	4	13	NG
Parsley	—	—	29	17	14	13	12	—	—
Parsnip	172	57	27	19	14	15	32	NG	NG
Pea	—	36	14	9	8	6	6	—	—
Pepper	NG	NG	NG	25	13	8	8	9	NG
Radish	NG	29	11	6	4	4	3	—	—
Spinach	63	23	12	7	6	5	6	NG	NG
Tomato	NG	NG	43	14	8	6	6	9	NG
Turnip	NG	NG	5	3	2	1	1	1	3
Watermelon	—	NG	—	—	12	5	4	3	—

Adapted from J. F. Harrington and P. A. Minges, Vegetable seed germination, California Agricultural Extension Mimeo Leaflet (1954).

NG = No germination, — = not tested.

APPROXIMATE NUMBER OF SEEDS PER OUNCE AND PER GRAM AND FIELD SEEDING RATES FOR TRADITIONAL PLANT DENSITIES

	Number of Seeds		Field Seeding[1]	
Vegetable	oz	g	lb/acre	kg/ha
Asparagus	1,200	40	2–3	2–3
Bean, bush Lima	25–75	1–3	40–60	40–70
Bean, pole Lima	25–75	1–3	30–40	30–45
Bean, bush snap	100–125	4–5	70–90	75–100
Bean, pole snap	100–125	4–5	20–40	20–45
Beet	1,600	55	10–15	10–16
Broad bean	20–50	1–2	60–80	65–90
Broccoli	9,000	320	½–1½	½–1½
Brussels sprouts	9,000	320	½–1½	½–1½
Cabbage	9,000	320	½–1½	½–1½
Cardoon	700	25	4–5	4–6
Carrot	23,000	820	2–4	2–4
Cauliflower	9,000	320	½–1½	½–1½
Celeriac	72,000	2,500	1–2	1–2
Celery	72,000	2,500	1–2	1–2
Chicory	27,000	95	3–5	3–6
Chinese cabbage	9,000	320	1–2	1–2
Collard	9,000	320	2–4	2–5
Corn salad	13,000	465	10	10
Cucumber	1,100	40	3–5	3–6
Dandelion	35,000	1,250	2	2
Eggplant	6,500	230	2	2
Endive	27,000	965	3–4	3–5
Florence fennel	7,000	250	3	3
Kale	9,000	320	2–4	2–5
Kohlrabi	9,000	320	3–5	3–6
Leek	11,000	395	4	4–5
Lettuce	25,000	900	1–3	1–3
Muskmelon	1,300	45	2–4	2–5
Mustard	15,000	535	3–5	3–6
New Zealand spinach	350	12	15	17
Okra	500	20	6–8	6–9
Onion	8,500	305	3–4	3–5
Parsley	18,500	660	3–4	3–5
Parsnip	12,000	430	3–5	3–5
Pea	90–175	3–6	90–220	100–250

APPROXIMATE NUMBER OF SEEDS PER OUNCE AND PER GRAM AND FIELD SEEDING RATES FOR TRADITIONAL PLANT DENSITIES—Continued

	Number of Seeds		Field Seeding[1]	
Vegetable	oz	g	lb/acre	kg/ha
Pepper	4,500	160	2–4	2–5
Pumpkin	100–300	4–11	4	4–5
Radish	2,500	90	10–20	10–25
Roselle	950	35	3–5	3–6
Rutabaga	12,000	430	1–2	1–2
Salsify	1,900	70	8–10	10
Sorrel	30,000	1,070	2–3	2–3
Southern pea	225	8	20–40	20–50
Soybean	175–350	6–12	20–40	20–50
Spinach	2,800	100	10–15	10–17
Squash	120–400	4–14	2–6	2–7
Swiss chard	1,600	57	6–8	7–9
Sweet corn	120–180	4–6	10–15	10–17
Tomato	7,000–12,000	250–430	½–1	½–1
Turnip	15,000	500	1–2	1–2
Watermelon	300–600	10–20	1–3	1–3

[1]Actual seeding rates are adjusted to desired plant populations, germination of the seed lot, and weather conditions that influence germination.

Weigh out a 1-oz sample of the seed lot and count the number of seeds.

The following table gives the approximate pounds of seed per acre for certain between-row and in-row spacings of lima bean, pea, snap bean, and sweet corn. These are based on 100% germination. If the seed germinates only 90%, for example, then divide the pounds of seed by 0.90 to get the planting rate. Do the same with other germination percentages.

Example: 30 seeds/oz to be planted in 22-in. rows at 1-in. spacing between seeds.

$$\frac{595}{0.90} = 661 \text{ lb/acre}$$

Only precision planting equipment would begin to approach as exact a job of spacing as this table indicates. Moreover, field conditions such as soil structure, temperature, and moisture will affect germination and final stand.

PLANTING RATES FOR LARGE SEEDS

No. of Seeds/oz	Spacing between Rows (in.): 18						20						22					
	Spacing between Seeds in Row (in.): 1	2	3	4	5	6	1	2	3	4	5	6	1	2	3	4	5	6
	Seed Needed (lb/acre)																	
30	726	364	242	182	146	121	655	328	218	164	131	109	595	298	198	149	119	98
40	545	273	182	136	110	90	491	246	163	123	99	82	446	223	148	112	90	74
50	440	220	146	110	88	74	396	198	132	99	79	66	361	180	120	90	72	60
60	354	178	118	90	76	59	318	159	106	80	64	53	289	145	97	73	58	48
70	312	156	104	78	62	56	281	140	94	70	56	47	256	128	85	64	51	43
80	272	136	90	68	54	46	245	123	82	62	49	41	223	112	74	56	45	37
90	242	120	82	60	48	40	218	109	73	55	44	37	198	99	66	50	40	33
100	216	108	72	54	42	38	198	99	66	50	39	33	181	90	60	45	35	30
110	198	99	66	50	40	34	173	89	59	44	35	30	161	80	54	40	32	27
120	180	90	60	45	36	30	162	81	54	40	33	27	148	74	49	37	30	25
130	168	84	56	42	34	28	152	76	51	38	31	25	138	69	46	34	28	23
140	156	78	52	38	30	26	141	70	47	35	28	24	128	64	43	32	25	22
150	146	73	49	36	28	24	131	66	44	33	26	22	119	60	40	30	24	20

PLANTING RATES FOR LARGE SEEDS—Continued

	Spacing between Rows (in.): 24						30						36					
	Spacing between Seeds in Row (in.):																	
No. of Seeds/oz	1	2	3	4	5	6	1	2	3	4	5	6	1	2	3	4	5	6
	Seed Needed (lb/acre)																	
30	545	273	182	136	109	91	437	219	146	109	88	73	363	182	121	91	73	61
40	408	204	136	102	82	68	328	164	106	82	66	54	272	136	91	68	55	45
50	330	165	110	82	66	55	265	132	88	66	53	44	220	110	73	55	44	37
60	265	133	88	67	57	44	212	106	71	59	43	35	177	89	59	45	38	29
70	234	117	78	59	47	39	188	94	63	47	38	31	156	78	52	39	31	26
80	204	102	68	51	41	34	164	82	53	41	33	27	136	68	45	34	27	23
90	181	90	61	45	36	30	146	73	49	37	29	25	121	60	41	30	24	20
100	162	81	55	40	32	28	131	67	44	33	27	22	108	54	37	27	21	19
110	148	74	49	37	30	25	119	60	40	30	24	20	99	49	33	25	20	17
120	135	68	45	34	27	23	108	54	36	27	22	18	90	45	30	23	18	15
130	126	63	42	32	25	21	101	51	34	25	20	17	84	42	28	21	17	14
140	117	58	39	29	23	20	94	47	32	23	19	16	78	39	26	19	15	13
150	109	55	38	27	22	18	88	44	29	22	18	15	73	37	24	18	14	12

SPACING OF VEGETABLES AND PLANT POPULATIONS

Spacing for vegetables is determined by the equipment used to plant, maintain, and harvest the crop as well as by the area required for growth of the plant without undue competition from neighboring plants. Previously row spacings were dictated almost entirely by the space requirement of cultivating equipment. Many of the traditional row spacings can be traced back to the horse cultivator.

Modern herbicides have largely eliminated the need for extensive cultivation in many crops; thus row spacings need not be related to cultivation equipment. Instead the plant's space requirement can be used as the determining factor.

Invariably, plant populations increase when this approach is used. A more uniform product with a higher proportion of marketable vegetables as well as higher total yields result from the closer plant spacings. The term "high-density production" has been developed to describe vegetable spacings designed to satisfy the plants space requirement.

HIGH-DENSITY SPACING OF VEGETABLES

Vegetable	Spacing (in.)	Plant Population (plants/acre)
Snap bean	3 × 12	174,000
Beet	2 × 12	261,000
Carrot	1½ × 12	349,000
Cauliflower	12 × 18	29,000
Cabbage	12 × 18	29,000
Cucumber (processing)	3 × 20	104,000
Lettuce	12 × 18	29,000
Onion	1 × 12	523,000

TRADITIONAL PLANT AND ROW SPACINGS FOR VEGETABLES

Vegetable	Between Plants in Row (in.)	Between Rows (in.)
Artichoke	48–72	84–96
Asparagus	9–15	48–72
Bean, broad	8–10	20–48
Bean, bush	2–4	18–36
Bean, Lima, bush	3–6	18–36
Bean, Lima, pole	8–12	36–48
Bean, pole	6–9	36–48
Beet	2–4	12–30
Broccoli	12–24	18–36
Broccoli raab	3–4	24–36
Brussels sprouts	18–24	24–40
Cabbage	12–24	24–36
Cardoon	12–18	30–42
Carrot	1–3	16–30
Cauliflower	14–24	24–36
Celeriac	4–6	24–36
Celery	6–12	18–40
Chard, Swiss	12–15	24–36
Chervil	6–10	12–18
Chicory	4–10	18–24
Chinese cabbage	10–18	18–36
Chive	12–18	24–36
Collard	12–24	24–36
Corn	8–12	30–42
Cress	2–4	12–18
Cucumber	8–12	36–72
Dandelion	3–6	14–24
Dasheen (taro)	24–30	42–48
Eggplant	18–30	24–48
Endive	8–12	18–24
Florence fennel	4–12	24–42
Garlic	1–3	12–24
Horseradish	12–18	30–36
Jerusalem artichoke	15–18	42–48
Kale	18–24	24–36
Kohlrabi	3–6	12–36
Leek	2–6	12–36
Lettuce, cos	10–14	16–24

TRADITIONAL PLANT AND ROW SPACINGS FOR VEGETABLES—Continued

Vegetable	Between Plants in Row (in.)	Between Rows (in.)
Lettuce, head	10–15	16–24
Lettuce, leaf	8–12	12–24
Muskmelon and other melons	12	60–84
Mustard	5–10	12–36
New Zealand spinach	10–20	36–60
Okra	8–24	42–60
Onion	1–4	16–24
Parsley	4–12	12–36
Parsley, Hamburg	1–3	18–36
Parsnip	2–4	18–36
Pea	1–3	24–48
Pepper	12–24	18–36
Potato	6–12	30–42
Pumpkin	36–60	72–96
Radish	½–1	8–18
Radish, storage type	4–6	18–36
Rhubarb	24–48	36–60
Roselle	24–46	60–72
Rutabaga	5–8	18–36
Salsify	2–4	18–36
Scolymus	2–4	18–36
Scorzonera	2–4	18–36
Shallot	4–8	36–48
Sorrel	½–1	12–18
Southern pea	3–6	18–42
Spinach	2–6	12–36
Squash, bush	24–48	36–60
Squash, vining	36–96	72–96
Strawberry	10–24	24–64
Sweet potato	10–18	36–48
Tomato, flat	18–48	36–60
Tomato, staked	12–24	36–48
Tomato, processing	2–10	42–60
Turnip	2–6	12–36
Turnip greens	1–4	6–12
Watercress	1–3	6–12
Watermelon	24–36	72–96

LENGTH OF ROW PER ACRE AT VARIOUS ROW SPACINGS

Distance Between Rows (in.)	Row Length (ft/acre)	Distance Between Rows (in.)	Row Length (ft/acre)
6	87,120	40	13,068
12	43,560	42	12,445
15	34,848	48	10,890
18	29,040	60	8,712
20	26,136	72	7,260
21	24,891	84	6,223
24	21,780	96	5,445
30	17,424	108	4,840
36	14,520	120	4,356

NUMBER OF PLANTS PER ACRE AT VARIOUS SPACINGS

In order to obtain other spacings, divide 43,560, the number of square feet per acre, by the product of the between-rows and in-the-row spacings, each expressed as feet; that is, 43,560 divided by 0.75 (36 × 3 in. or 3 × 0.25 ft) = 58,080.

Spacing (in.)	Plants	Spacing (in.)	Plants	Spacing (ft)	Plants
12 × 1	522,720	30 × 3	69,696	6 × 1	7260
12 × 3	174,240	30 × 6	34,848	6 × 2	3630
12 × 6	87,120	30 × 12	17,424	6 × 3	2420
12 × 12	43,560	30 × 15	13,939	6 × 4	1815
		30 × 18	11,616	6 × 5	1452
15[1] × 1	418,176	30 × 24	8,712	6 × 6	1210
15 × 3	139,392				
15 × 6	69,696	36 × 3	58,080	7 × 1	6223
15 × 12	34,848	36 × 6	29,040	7 × 2	3111
		36 × 12	14,520	7 × 3	2074

NUMBER OF PLANTS PER ACRE AT VARIOUS SPACINGS—Continued

Spacing (in.)	Plants	Spacing (in.)	Plants	Spacing (ft)	Plants
18[1] × 3	116,160	36 × 18	9,680	7 × 4	1556
18 × 6	58,080	36 × 24	7,260	7 × 5	1244
18 × 12	29,040	36 × 36	4,840	7 × 6	1037
18 × 14	24,891			7 × 7	889
18 × 18	19,360	40 × 6	26,136		
		40 × 12	13,068	8 × 1	5445
20[1] × 3	104,544	40 × 18	8,712	8 × 2	2722
20 × 6	52,272	40 × 24	6,534	8 × 3	1815
20 × 12	26,136			8 × 4	1361
20 × 14	22,402	42 × 6	24,891	8 × 5	1089
20 × 18	17,424	42 × 12	12,445	8 × 6	907
		42 × 18	8,297	8 × 8	680
21[1] × 3	99,564	42 × 24	6,223		
21 × 6	49,782	42 × 36	4,148	10 × 2	2178
21 × 12	24,891			10 × 4	1089
21 × 14	21,336	48 × 6	21,780	10 × 6	726
21 × 18	16,594	48 × 12	10,890	10 × 8	544
		48 × 18	7,260	10 × 10	435
24 × 3	87,120	48 × 24	5,445		
24 × 6	43,560	48 × 36	3,630		
24 × 12	21,780	48 × 48	2,722		
24 × 18	14,520				
24 × 24	10,890	60 × 12	8,712		
		60 × 18	5,808		
		60 × 24	4,356		
		60 × 36	2,904		
		60 × 48	2,178		
		60 × 60	1,742		

[1]Equivalent to double rows on beds at 30, 36, 40, and 42 in. centers, respectively.

High-density plantings, high costs of hand thinning, and erratic performance of mechanical thinners have resulted in the development of precision seeding techniques. The success of precision seeding depends on exact placement of each seed and nearly 100% germination.

Some precautions must be taken to ensure the proper performance of precision seeding equipment:

1. A fine, smooth seedbed is required for uniform seeding depth.
2. Seed must have high germination.
3. Seed must be uniform in size; this can be achieved by seed sizing or seed coating.
4. Seed must be of regular shape; irregular seeds such as carrot, lettuce, and onion must be coated for satisfactory precision seeding. Seed size is increased two to five times with clay or proprietary coatings.

Several types of equipment are available for precision seeding of vegetables:

1. *Belt.* Holes or notches in an endless belt match the seed diameter and shape to the desired spacing. Seeds gravity-feed onto the holes or notches in the belt and drop into the open furrow. Two or three parallel seed lines may be seeded simultaneously with the hole-design belt.
2. *Plate.* Holes in a seed plate select seeds from the bottom of the hopper and deliver them down a tube to the furrow.
3. *Pneumatic.* Seeds flow to the bottom of a revolving drum that is under constant air pressure. Individual seeds are held in place by air escaping through holes in the seed pockets. Seeds drop from the top of the drum into tubes and are carried by air pressure to the furrow.
4. *Seed wheel.* Seeds fall into slots on the meter wheel and are delivered to a slotted frame that drops the seeds in the furrow.
5. *Gel seeding.* Normal or pregerminated seeds are suspended in a gel that is forced from an orifice into the furrow (see page 89).

Guidelines for Operation and Maintenance of Equipment

1. Check the planter for proper operation and replace worn parts during the off-season.
2. Thoroughly understand the contents of the manufacturer's manual.
3. Make certain that the operator is trained to use the equipment and check its performance.

4. Double check your settings to be sure that you have the desired spacing and depth.
5. Make a trial run before moving to the field.
6. Operate the equipment at the recommended tractor speed.
7. Check the seed drop of each unit periodically during the planting operation.

Adapted in part from Precision Planting Program, Asgrow Seed Co., Kalamazoo, MI.

NUMBER OF SEEDS PLANTED PER MINUTE AT VARIOUS SPEEDS AND SPACINGS[1]

Planter Speed (mph)	In-row Spacing (in.)			
	2	3	4	6
2.5	1320	880	660	440
3.0	1584	1056	792	528
4.0	2112	1408	1056	704
5.0	2640	1760	1320	880

Adapted from Precision Planting Program, Asgrow Seed Co., Kalamazoo, MI.

[1]For most conditions, a planter speed of 2–3 mph will result in the greatest precision.

SEED PRIMING

With increasing mechanization, strong demands have arisen for sure, rapid, and uniform establishment of crops. A promising method of increasing the rate of uniformity of seedling establishment is seed priming, or osmoconditioning. Priming involves the hydration of seeds in an osmotic solution that permits the preliminary processes of germination but not the final phase of radicle emergence. Seed priming is essentially a process of controlled hydration of seeds, usually followed by dehydration to the original moisture content. Some materials and conditions that have been found beneficial in seed priming are given.

SUGGESTED PRIMING CONDITIONS FOR SELECTED VEGETABLE SEEDS

Vegetable	Material	Concentration (g/liter)	Temperature (°F)	Duration (days)
Beet	PEG	302	59	7
Brussels sprouts	PEG	250	59	7
Cabbage	PEG	250	59	7
Carrot	PEG	273	59	14
Celery	PEG	273	59	14
Lettuce	K_3PO_4	10	59	9 hr
Onion	PEG	307	68	17
Pea	PEG	250	59	8
Pepper	PEG	240	59	5
Spinach	PEG	298	50	14
Sweet corn	PEG	250	59	8
Tomato	$KNO_3 + K_3PO_4$	10 (each)	75	6
Tomato	PEG	92	59	7
Watermelon	KNO_3	30	68	6

Adapted from K. J. Bradford, Seed priming, *Oregon Horticultural Society* 25:227–233 (1984).
PEG = polyethylene glycol.

GEL SEEDING OF VEGETABLES

Gel seeding is a new technique for planting pregerminated seeds. The gel acts as a carrier and protects the small root from mechanical damage. Small-seeded vegetables such as tomato, carrot, onion, and celery are more appropriate for gel seeding than are large-seeded vegetables such as pea, bean, and sweet corn, because there is currently no planting equipment that singulates large seeds. The four basic steps in gel seeding are pregerminating the seed, preparing the gel, mixing the seed and gel, and planting the gel–seed mixture with appropriate equipment. Compared with planting regular seed, pregerminating seed in water at optimum temperature and oxygen levels makes plants emerge in the field sooner. The simplest way to pregerminate is to place the seeds loosely in cheesecloth, pantyhose, or other similar material and immerse them in a fish tank or other container filled with water. A thermostatically controlled heater and airstone hooked up to an air pump in the tank enables the temperature to be maintained at 80°F with good aeration. This allows germination and root emergence to be completed within 24–96 hr, depending on the vegetable seeds. The root should not be longer than 0.06 in. before being placed in the gel to plant. If the planting of germinated seed must be delayed, store seeds in moistened cheesecloth or a similar material at 36–38°F for up to 3 days.

GERMINATION TIME REQUIRED FOR SEED PREGERMINATION AT 80°F WATER TEMPERATURE AND WITH VIGOROUS AERATION[1]

Vegetable Seed	Germination Period
Asparagus	3 days
Cabbage	2–4 hr
Carrot	24–30 hr
Celeriac	3 days
Celery	4 days
Cress	20–24 hr
Cucumber	12–18 hr
Eggplant	60 hr
Endive	24 hr
Lettuce	16 hr
Melon	12–18 hr
Onion	2 days
Parsnip	3–4 days
Pepper	3 days
Spinach	20 hr
Tomato	40–48 hr

[1]When germinating seeds for longer than 24 hr, change the water in the germinating tank every 24 hr.

Gel used for planting vegetable seeds must be easy to prepare, have a good flow characteristic, be noninjurious to the seeds, be nonsuppressive to plant growth and development, and be inert. Because large volumes of gel may be mixed by the grower at one time, the gel should dissolve readily and quickly form a complete, uniform suspension in water. Several commercial gels are available. Gels will not store after initial mixing for more than 2–3 weeks. Gels that are less dense are used for continuous bead; more dense gels are used for clump planting.

Adding the pregerminated seed to the gel of optimum consistency is a critical operation. Stirring or agitating too vigorously can mechanically damage the roots, resulting in seed that will not emerge when planted. In addition, poor distribution of seeds within the gel may result in erratic plant stands in the row. A large tank or container and a large wooden paddle are ideal for mixing the pregerminated seed with the gel.

Several gel-seeding planters are commercially available. The gel is generally extruded from the planters by one of two basic methods. Either the gel is forced through a squeeze pump flowing from the gel–seed tank through plastic tubing into the furrow, or the gel–seed mixture flows by gravity out of the tank and into the furrow, and the flow is controlled by a solenoid valve. As a result, there are two patterns that can be used in the field. If the crop is planted in hills (e.g., tomato, pepper, or melon), the gel is extruded in globs at predetermined intervals, with two to five seeds per glob of gel. If the crop is planted in a continuous row (e.g., carrot, onion, or spinach), a solid bead or strip of gel is extruded down the row with a predetermined number of seeds per linear foot of row. If planting in dry soil, rainfall or irrigation is necessary within 2 days to prevent seed dehydration and lack of emergence.

SUGGESTED RATES FOR COMMERCIAL FIELD GELS

Gel	Rate (oz/gal water)
Laponite 445 and 508 (445 is to be used with additives)	2
Liqua-gel	0.1–0.5
N-Gel	2

Adapted from The Pennsylvania vegetable production guide, Pennsylvania State University Cooperative Extension Service (1987).

STORAGE OF PLANT PARTS USED FOR VEGETATIVE PROPAGATION

Plant Part	Temperature (°F)	Relative Humidity (%)	Comments
Asparagus crowns	30–32	85–90	Roots may be trimmed to 8 in. Prevent heating and excessive drying
Garlic bulbs	50	50–65	Fumigate for mites, if present. Hot-water-treat (120°F for 20 min) for control of stem and bulb nematode immediately before planting
Horseradish roots	32	85–90	Pit storage is used in cold climates
Onion sets	32	70–75	Sets may be cured naturally in the field, in trays, or artificially with warm, dry air
Potato tubers	36–40 (extended storage) 40–50 (short storage)	90	Cure at 60–65°F and 90–95% relative humidity for 10–14 days. Move to 60–65°F 10–14 days before planting
Sweet potato roots	55–60	85–90	Cure roots at 85°F and 85–90% relative humidity for 6–8 days before storage
Rhubarb crowns	32–35	80–85	Field storage is satisfactory in cold climates
Strawberry plants	30–32	85–90	Store in crates lined with 1.5-mil polyethylene
Witloof chicory roots	32	90–95	Prevent excessive drying

FIELD REQUIREMENTS FOR VEGETATIVELY PROPAGATED CROPS

Vegetable	Plant Parts	Quantity/acre[1]
Artichoke	Root sections	807–1,261
Asparagus	Crowns	5,808–10,890
Dasheen	Corms (2–5 oz)	9–18 cwt
Garlic	Cloves	8–20 cwt
Jerusalem artichoke	Tubers (2 oz)	10–12 cwt
Horseradish	Root cuttings	9,000–11,000
Onion	Sets	5–10 cwt
Rhubarb	Crown divisions	4,000–5,000
Strawberry	Plants	6,000–50,000
Sweet potato	Roots for bedding	5–6 cwt
Potato	Tubers or tuber sections	13–26 cwt

[1]Varies with field spacing, size of individual units, and vigor of stock.

SEED POTATOES REQUIRED PER ACRE, WITH VARIOUS PLANTING DISTANCES AND SIZES OF SEED PIECE

Spacing of Rows and Seed Pieces	Pounds of Seed/Acre with Various Seed Piece Weights				
	1 oz	1¼ oz	1½ oz	1¾ oz	2 oz
Rows 30 in. Apart					
8-in. spacing	1632	2040	2448	2856	3270
10-in. spacing	1308	1638	1956	2286	2614
12-in. spacing	1089	1361	1632	1908	2178
14-in. spacing	936	1164	1398	1632	1868
16-in. spacing	816	1020	1224	1428	1632
Rows 32 in. Apart					
8-in. spacing	1530	1914	2298	2682	3066
10-in. spacing	1224	1530	1836	2142	2448
12-in. spacing	1020	1278	1536	1788	2040

SEED POTATOES REQUIRED PER ACRE, WITH VARIOUS PLANTING DISTANCES AND SIZES OF SEED PIECE—Continued

Spacing of Rows and Seed Pieces	Pounds of Seed/Acre with Various Seed Piece Weights				
	1 oz	$1\frac{1}{4}$ oz	$1\frac{1}{2}$ oz	$1\frac{3}{4}$ oz	2 oz
Rows 32 in. Apart					
14-in. spacing	876	1092	1314	1530	1752
16-in. spacing	768	960	1152	1344	1536
Rows 34 in. Apart					
8-in. spacing	1440	1800	2160	2520	2880
10-in. spacing	1152	1440	1728	2016	2304
12-in. spacing	960	1200	1440	1680	1920
14-in. spacing	822	1026	1236	1440	1644
16-in. spacing	720	900	1080	1260	1440
Rows 36 in. Apart					
8-in. spacing	1362	1704	2040	2382	2724
10-in. spacing	1086	1362	1632	1902	2178
12-in. spacing	906	1134	1362	1590	1812
14-in. spacing	780	972	1164	1362	1554
16-in. spacing	678	852	1020	1188	1362
18-in. spacing	606	756	906	1056	1212
Rows 42 in. Apart					
18-in. spacing	516	648	780	906	1038
24-in. spacing	390	486	582	678	780
30-in. spacing	312	390	468	546	624
36-in. spacing	258	324	390	456	516
Rows 48 in. Apart					
18-in. spacing	456	570	678	792	906
24-in. spacing	342	426	510	594	678
30-in. spacing	270	342	408	474	546
36-in. spacing	228	282	342	396	456

POLYETHYLENE MULCHES

Mulches of black, white, or clear polyethylene are used widely in vegetable production. More than 100,000 acres of polyethylene-mulched vegetables are grown in Florida alone.

Some of the potential benefits of use of polyethylene mulches for vegetable production are as follows:

1. Soil temperature modification
2. Reduction of leaching of fertilizer
3. Reduction of evaporation from the soil surface
4. Control of weeds with black polyethylene
5. Retention of fumigants after application.

The benefits derived from polyethylene mulching usually result in higher early and total yields than those obtained from unmulched vegetables.

Polyethylene film, 1 to 1½ mils thick, is applied over moist and fertilized soil or previously formed beds. In most cases, the soil is fumigated before the mulch is applied. Many commercial mulch applicators are available; often bed preparation, fertilization, fumigation, and mulch application are combined into a single operation. Fumigation may necessitate a delay before planting—follow label instructions.

Polyethylene mulches are used most commonly with transplanted vegetables. Several commercial transplanters that operate through mulches are available. Likewise, plug-mix planters and various seeders that plant through polyethylene mulch are commercially available.

The polyethylene mulch must be disposed of after cropping. Follow local environmental regulations for proper disposal.

Row covers have been used for many years for early growth enhancement of certain vegetables in a few production areas such as San Diego County, California. New materials and methods have been developed recently which make the use of row covers a viable production practice wherever vegetables are seeded or transplanted when temperatures are below optimum and early production is desired. Row covers, when properly used, will result in earlier harvest and perhaps greater total production. There are two general types of row covers—supported and floating; many variations of the row cover concept are possible, depending on the needs of the individual grower. Row covers generally work best when used in conjunction with black polyethylene-mulched rows or beds.

Supported Row Covers

Clear polyethylene, 5–6 ft wide and 1 to 1½ mils thick, is the most convenient material to use and is generally used just once. Slitted row covers have slits 5 in. long and ¾ in. apart in two rows. The slits, arranged at the upper sides of the constructed supported row cover, provide ventilation; otherwise the cover would have to be manually opened and closed each day. Hoops, of No. 8 or No. 9 wire, are cut 63 in. long for 5-ft wide polyethylene.

Hoops are installed over the polyethylene-mulched crop so that the center of the hoop is 14–16 in. above the row. The slitted row cover can be mechanically applied over the hoops with a high-clearance tractor and a modified mulch applicator.

Floating Row Covers

Floating row covers are made of spun-bonded polyester and polypropylene. The material appears very similar to the fabrics used in the clothing industry for interlining, interfacing, and other uses. It is white or off-white, porous to air and water, very lightweight (0.6 oz/sq yd) and transmits about 80% of the light. The material comes in rolls 67 in. wide and 250–2500 ft long. One-piece blankets are also available. With care, the spun-bonded fabrics can be used two to three or more times.

Immediately after planting (seeds or transplants) the spun-bonded fabric is laid directly over the row, and the edges are secured with soil, boards, bricks, or wire pins. Because the material is of such light weight, the plants will push up the fabric as the plants grow. Accordingly, enough slack should be provided to allow for the plants to reach maximum size during the time the material is left over the plants. For bean or tomato, about 12 in. of slack should be left. For a crop such as cucumber, 8 in. is sufficient.

Floating covers can be left over vegetables for 3–8 weeks, depending on the crop and the weather. For tomato and pepper, it can be left on for about

1 month but should be removed (at least partially) when the temperature under the covers reaches 86°F and is likely to remain that high for several hours.

The blossoms of muskmelon can withstand very high temperatures, but the cover must be removed when the first female flowers appear so that bees can begin pollination.

Frost Protection

Frost protection with slitted and floating covers is not as good as with solid plastic covers. A maximum of 3–4°F is all that can be expected, whereas with solid covers, frost protection of 5–7°F has been attained. Row covers should not be viewed merely as a frost-protection system but as a growth-intensifying system during cool spring weather. Therefore, do not attempt to plant very early and hope to be protected against heavy frosts. An earlier planting date of 10 days to 2 weeks would be more reasonable. The purpose of row covers is to increase productivity through an economical increase of early and perhaps total production per unit area.

Adapted from O. S. Wells and J. B. Loy, Row covers for intensive vegetable production, New Hampshire Cooperative Extension Service (1985).

PART 4

SOILS AND FERTILIZERS

Rapid decomposition of fresh organic matter contributes most effectively to the physical condition of a soil. Plenty of moisture, nitrogen, and a warm temperature speed up the rate of decomposition.

Organic matter serves as a source of energy for soil microorganisms and as a source of plant nutrients.

Organic matter holds the minerals absorbed from the soil against loss by leaching until they are released by the action of microorganisms.

Bacteria thriving on the organic matter produce complex carbohydrates that cement soil particles together into aggregates.

Acids produced in the decomposition of organic matter may make available mineral nutrients of the soil to crop plants.

The entrance and percolation of water into and through the soil are facilitated. This reduces losses of soil by erosion.

Penetration of roots through the soil is improved by good structure brought about by the decomposition of organic matter.

The water-holding capacity of sands and sandy soils may be increased by the incorporation of organic matter. Aggregation in heavy soils may improve drainage.

It is seldom possible to make a large permanent increase in the organic-matter content of a soil.

TYPICAL COMPOSITION OF MANURES

Manures vary greatly in their nutrient content. The kind of feed used, the percentage and type of litter or bedding, the moisture content, and the age and degree of rotting or drying all modify the composition. In the case of the commercially dried pulverized manures, some nitrogen is lost in the process. The following data are representative analyses from widely scattered reports.

		Approximate Composition (% dry weight)		
Source	Dry Matter (%)	N	P_2O_5	K_2O
Dairy	15–25	0.6–2.1	0.7–1.1	2.4–3.6
Feedlot	20–40	1.0–2.5	0.9–1.6	2.4–3.6
Horse	15–25	1.7–3.0	0.7–1.2	1.2–2.2
Poultry	20–30	2.0–4.5	4.5–6.0	1.2–2.4
Sheep	25–35	3.0–4.0	1.2–1.6	3.0–4.0
Swine	20–30	3.0–4.0	0.4–0.6	0.5–1.0

TYPICAL COMPOSITION OF SOME ORGANIC FERTILIZER MATERIALS

The nitrogen in organic materials becomes available to plants slowly. There is considerable variation among samples. The guarantee on the bag should be read carefully. These data are representative of many noted in the literature and in reports of state control departments.

	Percentage on a Dry Weight Basis		
Organic Materials	N	P_2O_5	K_2O
Bat guano	10.0	4.0	2.0
Blood	13.0	2.0	1.0
Bone meal, raw	3.0	22.0	—
Bone meal, steamed	1.0	15.0	—
Castor bean meal	5.5	2.0	1.0
Cottonseed meal	6.0	3.0	1.5
Fish meal	10.0	6.0	—
Garbage tankage	2.5	2.0	1.0
Peanut meal	7.0	1.5	1.2
Sewage sludge	1.5	1.3	0.4
Sewage sludge, activated	6.0	3.0	0.2
Soybean meal	7.0	1.2	1.5
Tankage	7.0	10.0	1.5

COMPOSITION OF ORGANIC MATERIALS

		Approximate Pounds per Ton of Dry Material		
Materials	Moisture (%)	N	P_2O_5	K_2O
Alfalfa hay	10	50	11	50
Alfalfa straw	7	28	7	36
Barley hay	9	23	11	33
Barley straw	10	12	5	32

Materials	Moisture (%)	Approximate Pounds per Ton of Dry Material N	P_2O_5	K_2O
Bean straw	11	20	6	25
Beggarweed hay	9	50	12	56
Buckwheat straw	11	14	2	48
Clover hay				
Alyce	11	35	—	—
Bur	8	60	21	70
Crimson	11	45	11	67
Ladino	12	60	13	67
Sweet	8	60	12	38
Cowpea hay	10	60	13	36
Cowpea straw	9	20	5	38
Field pea hay	11	28	11	30
Field pea straw	10	20	5	26
Horse bean hay	9	43	—	—
Lezpedeza hay	11	41	8	22
Lezpedeza straw	10	21	—	—
Oat hay	12	26	9	20
Oat straw	10	13	5	33
Ryegrass hay	11	26	11	25
Rye hay	9	21	8	25
Rye straw	7	11	4	22
Sorghum stover, Hegari	13	18	4	—
Soybean hay	12	46	11	20
Soybean straw	11	13	6	15
Sudan grass hay	11	28	12	31
Sweet corn fodder	12	30	8	24
Velvet bean hay	7	50	11	53
Vetch hay				
Common	11	43	15	53
Hairy	12	62	15	47
Wheat hay	10	20	8	35
Wheat straw	8	12	3	19

Adapted from *Morrison Feeds and Feeding,* Morrison Publishing Co., Ithaca, NY (1948).

SEED REQUIREMENTS OF SOIL-IMPROVING CROPS AND AREAS OF ADAPTATION

Soil-Improving Crops	Seed (lb/acre)	U.S. Area to Which Crop is Adapted
Winter Cover Crops		
Legumes		
Berseem (*Trifolium alexandrinum*)	15	West and southeast
Black medic (*Medicago lupulina*)	15	All
Black lupine (*Lupinus hirsutus*)	70	All
Clover		
Crimson (*Trifolium incarnatum*)	15	South and southeast
Bur, California (*Medicago hispida*)	25	South
Southern (*M. arabica*) unhulled	100	Southeast
Tifton (*M. rigidula*) unhulled	100	Southeast
Sour (*Melilotus indica*)	20	South
Sweet, hubam (*Melilotus alba*)	20	All
Fenugreek (*Trigonella foenum graecum*)	30	Southwest
Field pea (*Pisum sativum*)		
Canada	80	All
Austrian winter	70	All
Horse bean (*Vicia faba*)	100	Southwest and southeast
Rough pea (*Lathyrus hirsutus*)	60	Southwest and southeast
Vetch		
Bitter (*Vicia ervilia*)	30	West and southeast
Common (*V. sativa*)	50	West and southeast
Hairy (*V. villosa*)	30	All
Hungarian (*V. pannonica*)	50	West and southeast
Monantha (*V. articulata*)	40	West and southeast
Purple (*V. bengalensis*)	40	West and southeast
Smooth (*V. villosa* var. *glabrescens*)	30	All
Woollypod (*V. dasycarpa*)	30	Southeast
Nonlegumes		
Barley (*Hordeum vulgare*)	75	All
Mustard (*Brassica nigra*)	20	All
Oat (*Avena sativa*)	75	All
Rape (*Brassica napus*)	20	All

SEED REQUIREMENTS OF SOIL-IMPROVING CROPS AND AREAS OF ADAPTATION—Continued

Soil-Improving Crops	Seed (lb/acre)	U.S. Area to Which Crop is Adapted
	Winter Cover Crops	
Nonlegumes		
Rye (*Secale cereale*)	75	All
Wheat (*Triticum sativum*)	75	All
	Summer Cover Crops	
Legumes		
Alfalfa (*Medicago sativa*)	20	All
Beggarweed (*Desmodium purpureum*)	10	Southeast
Clover		
Alyce (*Alysicarpus vaginalis*)	20	Southeast
Crimson (*Trifolium incartum*)	15	Southeast
Red (*T. pratense*)	10	All
Cowpea (*Vigna sinensis*)	90	South and southwest
Hairy indigo (*Indigofera hirsuta*)	10	Southern tier
Lezpedeza		
Common (*Lezpedeza striata*)	25	Southeast
Korean (*L. stipulacea*)	20	Southeast
Sesbania (*Sesbania exaltata*)	30	Southwest
Soybean (*Glycine max*)	75	All
Sweet clover, white (*Melilotus alba*)	20	All
Sweet clover, (*M. officinalis*)	20	All
Velvet bean (*Stizolobium deeringianum*)	100	Southeast
Nonlegumes		
Buckwheat (*Fagopyrum esculentum*)	75	All
Pearl millet (*Pennisetum glaucum*)	25	Southern and southeast
Sorghum, Hegari (*Sorghum vulgare*)	40	Western half
Sudan grass (*Sorghum vulgare* var. *sudanese*)	25	All

Adapted from Growing summer cover crops, USDA Farmers' Bulletin 2182 (1967); P. R. Henson and E. A. Hollowell, Winter annual legumes for the south, USDA Farmers' Bulletin 2146 (1960); B. A. Madson, Winter cover crops, California Agricultural Extension Service Circular 174 (1951).

DECOMPOSITION OF SOIL-IMPROVING CROPS

The normal carbon:nitrogen (C:N) ratio in soils is about 10:1. Turning under organic matter upsets this ratio because most organic matter is richer in carbon than in nitrogen. Unless the residue contains at least 1.5% nitrogen, the decomposing organisms will utilize soil nitrogen. Soil organisms will tie up about 25 lb of nitrogen per acre from the soil in the process of decomposition of carbon-rich organic matter.

A soil-improving crop should be fertilized adequately with nitrogen. This fertilization will increase the nitrogen content somewhat and improve later decomposition. Nitrogen may have to be added as the soil-improving crop is incorporated into the soil. This speeds the decomposition and prevents a temporary shortage of nitrogen for the succeeding vegetable crop.

As a general rule about 20 lb of nitrogen should be added for each ton of dry matter for a nonlegume green-manure crop.

APPROXIMATE CARBON NITROGEN RATIOS OF COMMON ORGANIC MATERIALS

Material	C:N Ratio
Alfalfa	12:1
Sweet clover, young	12:1
Sweet clover, mature	24:1
Rotted manure	20:1
Oat straw	75:1
Corn stalks	80:1
Timothy	80:1
Sawdust	300:1

The particles of a soil are classified by size into sand, silt, and clay. The classification of soil-particle sizes is shown in the table.

Soil-Particle Size Classes (diameter, mm)

	2.0	0.02	0.002	0
Gravel	Sand	Silt	Clay	
Particles visible with the naked eye		Particles visible under microscope	Particles visible under electron microscope	

The percentage of sand, silt, and clay may be plotted on the diagram to determine the textural class of that soil.

Example: A soil containing 13% clay, 41% silt, and 46% sand would have a loam texture.

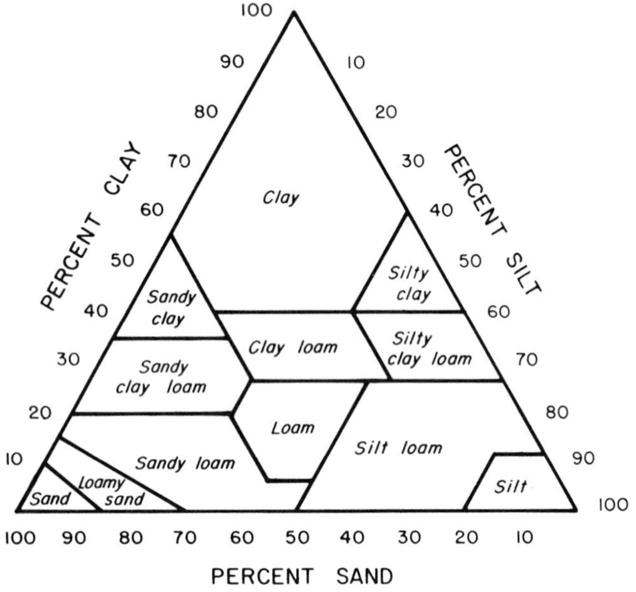

Soil textural triangle. From Soil Conservation Service, *Soil Survey Manual*, USDA Agricultural Handbook 18 (1951).

RELATIVE TOLERANCE OF VEGETABLE CROPS TO SOIL ACIDITY

Vegetables in the slightly tolerant group can be grown successfully on soils that are on the alkaline side of neutrality. They do well up to pH 7.6 if there is no deficiency of essential nutrients. Vegetables in the very tolerant group will grow satisfactory at a soil pH as low as 5.0. For the most part even the most tolerant crops grow better at pH 6.0–6.8 than in more acid soils. Calcium, phosphorus, magnesium, and molybdenum are the nutrients most likely to be deficient in acid soils.

Slightly Tolerant (pH 6.8–6.0)	Moderately Tolerant (pH 6.8–5.5)	Very Tolerant (pH 6.8–5.0)
Asparagus	Bean	Chicory
Beet	Bean, Lima	Dandelion
Broccoli	Brussels sprouts	Endive
Cabbage	Carrot	Fennel
Cauliflower	Collard	Potato
Celery	Corn	Rhubarb
Chard, Swiss	Cucumber	Shallot
Chinese cabbage	Eggplant	Sorrel
Cress	Garlic	Sweet potato
Leek	Gherkin	Watermelon
Lettuce	Horseradish	
Muskmelon	Kale	
New Zealand spinach	Kohlrabi	
Okra	Mustard	
Onion	Parsley	
Orach	Pea	
Parsnip	Pepper	
Salsify	Pumpkin	
Soybean	Radish	
Spinach	Rutabaga	
Watercress	Strawberry	
	Squash	
	Tomato	
	Turnip	

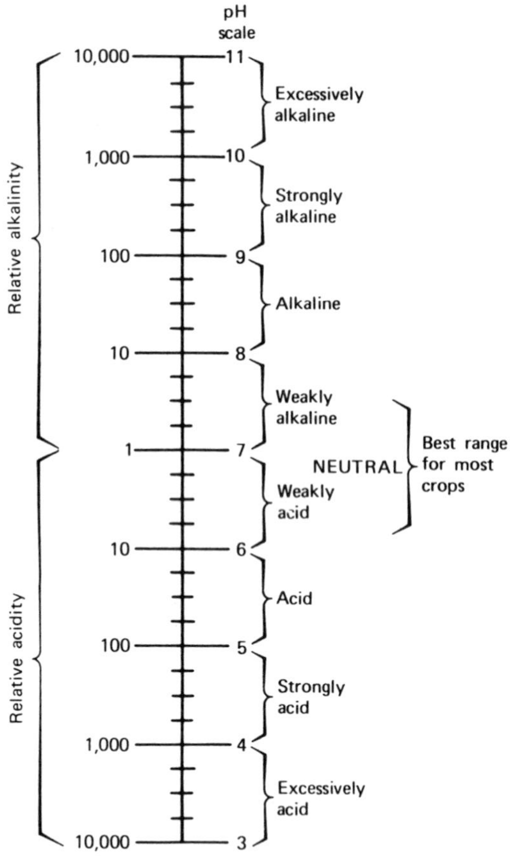

Relation Between pH, Alkalinity, Acidity, and Plant Growth.

EFFECT OF SOIL REACTION ON AVAILABILITY OF NUTRIENTS

Soil reaction affects plants by influencing the availability of nutrients. Changes in soil reaction caused by liming or by the use of sulfur and acid-forming fertilizers may increase or decrease the supply of the nutrients available to the plants.

The general relationship between soil reaction and availability of plant nutrients in organic soils differs from that in mineral soils. The diagrams depict nutrient availability for both mineral and organic soils. The width of the band indicates the availability of the nutrient. It does not indicate the actual amount present.

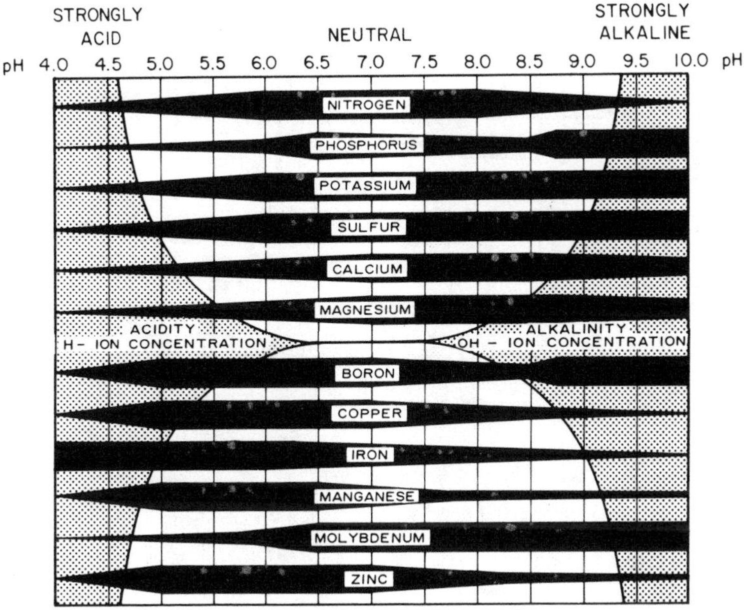

Influence of pH on the availability of plant nutrients in mineral soils; widest parts of the shaded areas indicate maximum availability of each element.

Adapted from L. B. Nelson (ed.), *Changing Patterns in Fertilizer Use*, Soil Science Society of America, Madison, WI (1968).

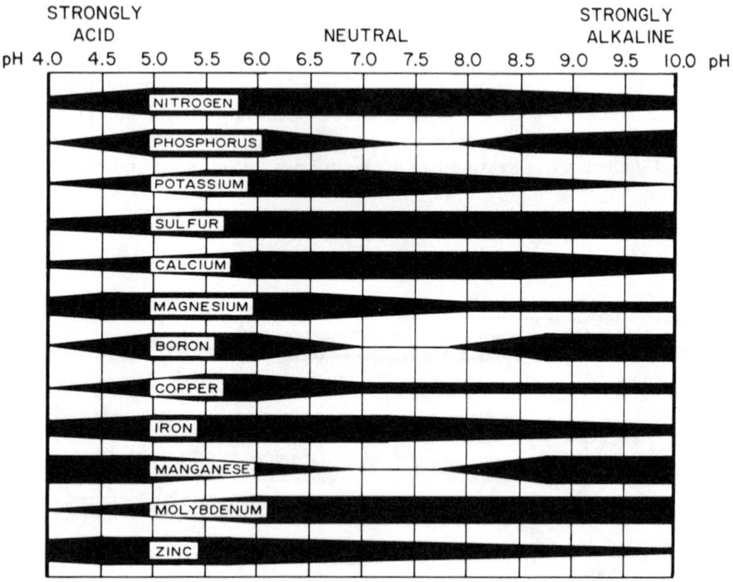

Influence of pH on the availability of plant nutrients in organic soils; widest parts of the shaded areas indicate maximum availability of each element.

Adapted from R. E. Lucas and J. F. Davis, Relationships between pH values of organic soils and availability of 12 plant nutrients, *Soil Science* 92:177–182 (1961).

CORRECTION OF SOIL ACIDITY

Soils differ greatly in their ability to resist a change in reaction caused by the addition of lime. The quantities given are a rough indication of the limestone needed to produce certain alterations in the reaction of mineral soils with an average organic-matter content of about 2%. In the far south somewhat smaller quantities can be used to obtain comparable changes. If a mineral soil is rich in organic matter, the rate of application should be increased by one-half or more.

LIMESTONE NEEDED TO CHANGE THE SOIL REACTION[1]

Change in pH Desired in Plow-Depth Layer	Limestone (lb/acre)					
	Sand	Sandy Loam	Loam	Silt Loam	Clay Loam	Muck
4.0–6.5	2600	5000	7000	8400	10,000	19,000
4.5–6.5	2200	4200	5800	7000	8,400	16,200
5.0–6.5	1800	3400	4600	5600	6,600	12,600
5.5–6.5	1200	2600	3400	4000	4,600	8,600
6.0–6.5	600	1400	1800	2200	2,400	4,400

[1] A high magnesium limestone is preferable wherever there is a possible lack of magnesium.

COMMON LIMING MATERIALS

Materials	Chemical Formula	Pure $CaCO_3$ Equivalent (%)	Liming Material (lb) Necessary to Equal 100 lb of Limestone
Burned lime	CaO	150	64
Hydrated lime	$Ca(OH)_2$	120	82
Dolomitic limestone	$CaCO_3$, $MgCO_3$	104	86
Limestone	$CaCO_3$	95	100
Marl	$CaCO_3$	95	100
Shell, oyster, etc.	$CaCO_3$	95	100

COMMON ACIDIFYING MATERIALS[1]

Material	Chemical Formula	Sulfur (%)	Acidifying Material (lb) Necessary to Equal 100 lb of Soil Sulfur
Soil sulfur	S	99.0	100
Sulfuric acid (98%)	H_2SO_4	32.0	306
Sulfur dioxide	SO_2	50.0	198
Lime–sulfur solution (32° Baumé)	CaS_x + water	24.0	417
Iron sulfate	$FeSO_4 \cdot 7H_2O$	11.5	896
Aluminum sulfate	$Al_2(SO_4)_3$	14.4	694

[1]Certain fertilizer materials also markedly increase soil acidity when used in large quantities (see page 113).

APPROXIMATE QUANTITY OF SOIL SULFUR NEEDED TO INCREASE SOIL ACIDICITY TO ABOUT pH 6.5

	Sulfur (lb/acre)		
Change in pH Desired	Sands	Loams	Clays
8.5–6.5	2000	2500	3000
8.0–6.5	1200	1500	2000
7.5–6.5	500	800	1000
7.0–6.5	100	150	300

EFFECT OF SOME FERTILIZER MATERIALS ON THE SOIL REACTION

Materials	N (%)	Pounds of Limestone ($CaCO_3$) Needed to Counteract the Acidity Produced: Per lb of N	Pounds of Limestone ($CaCO_3$) Needed to Counteract the Acidity Produced: Per 100 lb of the Fertilizer Material
Acidity-Forming			
Ammonium nitrate	33.5	1.80	60
Monoammonium phosphate	11	5.35	59
Ammonium phosphate sulfate	16	5.35	88
Ammonium sulfate	21	5.35	110
Anhydrous ammonia	82	1.80	148
Aqua ammonia	24	1.80	44
Aqua ammonia	30	1.80	54
Diammonium phosphate	16–18	1.80	70
Liquid phosphoric acid	52(P_2O_5)	—	110
Urea	46	1.80	84
Alkalinity-Forming			
Calcium cyanamide	22	2.85	63
Calcium nitrate	15.5	1.35	20
Potassium nitrate	13	1.80	23
Sodium nitrate	16	1.80	29

Neutral

Ammonium nitrate–lime	Potassium sulfate
Calcium sulfate (gypsum)	Superphosphate
Potassium chloride	

Based on the method of W. H. Pierre, Determination of equivalent acidity and basicity of fertilizers, *Industrial Engineering Chemical Analytical Edition*, 5:229–234 (1933).

RELATIVE SALT EFFECTS OF FERTILIZER MATERIALS ON THE SOIL SOLUTION

When fertilizer materials are placed close to seeds or plants they may increase the osmotic pressure of the soil solution and cause injury to the crop. The term "salt index" refers to the effect of a material in relation to that produced by sodium nitrate, which is given a rating of 100. The "partial index" shows the relationships per unit (20 lb) of the actual nutrient supplied. Any material with a high salt index must be used with great care.

Material	Salt Index	Partial Salt Index per Unit of Plant Food
Anhydrous ammonia	47.1	0.572
Ammonium nitrate	104.7	2.990
Ammonium nitrate–lime (Cal-Nitro)	61.1	2.982
Ammonium sulfate	69.0	3.253
Calcium carbonate (limestone)	4.7	0.083
Calcium nitrate	52.5	4.409
Calcium sulfate (gypsum)	8.1	0.247
Diammonium phosphate	29.9	1.614[1] 0.637[2]
Dolomite (calcium and magnesium carbonates)	0.8	0.042
Monoammonium phosphate	34.2	2.453[1] 0.485[2]
Monocalcium phosphate	15.4	0.274
Nitrogen solution, 37%	77.8	2.104
Potassium chloride, 50%	109.4	2.189
Potassium chloride, 60%	116.3	1.936
Potassium nitrate	73.6	5.336[1] 1.580[3]
Potassium sulfate	46.1	0.853
Sodium chloride	153.8	2.899
Sodium nitrate	100.0	6.060
Sulfate of potash–magnesia	43.2	1.971
Superphosphate, 20%	7.8	0.390
Superphosphate, 45%	10.1	0.224
Urea	75.4	1.618

Adapted from L. F. Rader, L. M. White, and C. W. Whittaker, The salt index—A measure of the effect of fertilizers on the concentration of the soil solution, *Soil Science* 55:201–218 (1943).

[1]N. [2]P_2O_5. [3]K_2O.

SOIL SALINITY

With an increase in soil salinity plant roots extract water less easily from the soil solution. This situation is more critical under hot and dry than under humid conditions. High soil salinity may result also in toxic concentrations of ions in plants. Soil salinity is determined by finding the electrical conductivity of the soil saturation extract (ECe). The electrical conductivity is measured in millimhos per centimeter (mmho/cm). One mmho/cm is equivalent to 1 decisiemens per meter (dS/m) and, on the average, to 640 ppm of salt.

CROP RESPONSE TO SALINITY

Salinity (expressed as ECe, mmho/cm, or as dS/m)	Crop Responses
0–2	Salinity effects mostly negligible
2–4	Yields of very sensitive crops may be restricted
4–8	Yields of many crops restricted
8–16	Only tolerant crops yield satisfactorily
Above 16	Only a few very tolerant crops yield satisfactorily

Adapted from Leon Bernstein, Salt tolerance of plants, USDA Agricultural Information Bulletin 283 (1970).

RELATIVE SALT TOLERANCE OF VEGETABLES

The indicated salt tolerances are based on growth rather than yield. With most crops there is little difference in salt tolerance among varieties. Boron tolerances may vary depending upon climate, soil condition, and crop varieties.

Vegetable	Maximum Soil Salinity Without Yield Loss (Threshold) (dS/m)	Decrease in Yield at Soil Salinities Above the Threshold (% per dS/m)
Sensitive crops		
Bean	1.0	19
Carrot	1.0	14
Strawberry	1.0	33
Onion	1.2	16
Moderately sensitive		
Turnip	0.9	9
Radish	1.2	13
Lettuce	1.3	13
Pepper	1.5	14
Sweet potato	1.5	11
Broad bean	1.6	10
Corn	1.7	12
Potato	1.7	12
Cabbage	1.8	10
Celery	1.8	6
Spinach	2.0	8
Cucumber	2.5	13
Tomato	2.5	10
Broccoli	2.8	9
Squash, scallop	3.2	16
Moderately tolerant		
Beet	4.0	9
Squash, zucchini	4.7	9

Adapted from E. V. Maas, Crop tolerance, *California Agriculture* (October, 1984).

1 decisiemens per meter (dS/m) = 1 mmho/cm
= approximately 640 mg/liter salt

FERTILIZER DEFINITIONS

Grade or *analysis* means the minimum guarantee of the percentage of total nitrogen, available phosphoric acid, and water-soluble potash in the fertilizer.

Example: 10–10–5 or 8–8–8.

Ratio is the grade reduced to its simplest terms.

Example: A 10–10–5 has a ratio of 2–2–1, as does an 8–8–4.

Formula shows the actual pound and percentage composition of the various ingredients or compounds that are mixed together to make up a ton of fertilizer. An *open-formula mix* carries the formula as well as the grade on the tag attached to each bag.
Carrier or *simple* is the material or compound in which a given plant nutrient is found or supplied.

Example: Ammonium nitrate and urea are simples or carriers that supply nitrogen.

Unit means 1% of 1 ton or 20 lb. On the basis of a ton, the units per ton are equal to the percentage composition or the pounds per 100 lb.

Example: Ammonium sulfate contains 21% nitrogen, or 21 lb of nitrogen/100 lb, or 21 units in a ton.

Primary nutrient refers to nitrogen, phosphorus, and potassium, which are used in considerable quantities by crops.

Secondary nutrient refers to calcium, magnesium, and sulfur, which are used in moderate quantities by crops and influence soil pH.

Micronutrient, trace, or *minor element* refers to the essential plant nutrients used in relatively small quantities.

APPROXIMATE COMPOSITION OF SOME CHEMICAL FERTILIZER MATERIALS[1]

Fertilizer Material	Total Nitrogen (% N)	Available Phosphorus (% P_2O_5)	Water-Soluble Potassium (% K_2O)
Nitrogen			
Ammonium nitrate	33.5	–	–
Ammonium nitrate–lime (A-N-L, Cal-Nitro)	20.5	–	–
Monoammonium phosphate	11.0	48.0	–
Ammonium phosphate–sulfate	16.0	20.0	–
Ammonium sulfate	21.0	–	–
Anhydrous ammonia	82.0	–	–
Aqua ammonia	20.0	–	–
Calcium cyanamide	21.0	–	–
Calcium nitrate	15.5	–	–
Calcium ammonium nitrate	17.0	–	–
Diammonium phosphate	16–18	46.0–48.0	–
Potassium nitrate	13.0	–	44.0
Sodium nitrate	16.0	–	–
Urea	46.0	–	–
Urea formaldehyde	38.0	–	–
Phosphorus			
Phosphoric acid solution	–	52.0–54.0	–
Normal superphosphate	–	18.0–20.0	–
Concentrated superphosphate	–	45.0–46.0	–
Potassium			
Potassium chloride	–	–	60.0–62.0
Potassium nitrate	13.0	–	44.0
Potassium sulfate	–	–	50.0–53.0
Sulfate of potash–magnesia	–	–	26.0

[1]See page 113 for effect of these materials on soil reaction.

SOLUBILITY OF FERTILIZER MATERIALS

Solubility of materials is an important factor in preparing starter solutions and foliar sprays. Hot water may be needed to get the chemicals dissolved.

Material	Solubility in Cold Water (lb/100 gal)
Primary Nutrients	
Ammonium nitrate	984
Ammonium sulfate	592
Calcium cyanamide	Decomposes
Calcium nitrate	851
Diammonium phosphate	358
Monoammonium phosphate	192
Potassium nitrate	108
Sodium nitrate	608
Superphosphate, single	17
Superphosphate, treble	33
Urea	651
Secondary Nutrients	
Ammonium molybdate	Decomposes
Borax	8
Calcium chloride	500
Copper oxide	Insoluble
Copper sulfate	183
Ferrous sulfate	242
Magnesium sulfate	592
Manganese sulfate	876
Sodium chloride	300
Sodium molybdate	467
Zinc sulfate	625

Multiply	By	To Obtain Equivalent Nutrient
Ammonia–NH_3	4.700	Ammonium nitrate–NH_4NO_3
Ammonia–NH_3	3.879	Ammonium sulfate–$(NH_4)_2SO_4$
Ammonia–NH_3	0.823	Nitrogen–N
Ammonium nitrate–NH_4NO_3	0.350	Nitrogen–N
Ammonium sulfate–$(NH_4)_2SO_4$	0.212	Nitrogen–N
Borax–$Na_2B_4O_7.10H_2O$	0.114	Boron–B
Boric acid–H_3BO_3	0.177	Boron–B
Boron–B	8.813	Borax–$Na_2B_4O_7.10H_2O$
Boron–B	5.716	Boric acid–H_3BO_3
Calcium–Ca	1.399	Calcium oxide–CaO
Calcium–Ca	2.498	Calcium carbonate–$CaCO_3$
Calcium–Ca	1.849	Calcium hydroxide–$Ca(OH)_2$
Calcium–Ca	4.296	Calcium sulfate–$CaSO_4.2H_2O$ (gypsum)
Calcium carbonate–$CaCO_3$	0.400	Calcium–Ca
Calcium carbonate–$CaCO_3$	0.741	Calcium hydroxide–$Ca(OH)_2$
Calcium carbonate–$CaCO_3$	0.560	Calcium oxide–CaO
Calcium carbonate–$CaCO_3$	0.403	Magnesia–MgO
Calcium carbonate–$CaCO_3$	0.842	Magnesium carbonate–$MgCO_3$
Calcium hydroxide–$Ca(OH)_2$	0.541	Calcium–Ca
Calcium hydroxide–$Ca(OH)_2$	1.351	Calcium carbonate–$CaCO_3$
Calcium hydroxide–$Ca(OH)_2$	0.756	Calcium oxide–CaO
Calcium oxide–CaO	0.715	Calcium–Ca
Calcium oxide–CaO	1.785	Calcium carbonate–$CaCO_3$
Calcium oxide–CaO	1.323	Calcium hydroxide–$Ca(OH)_2$
Calcium oxide–CaO	3.071	Calcium sulfate–$CaSO_4.2H_2O$ (gypsum)
Gypsum–$CaSO_4.2H_2O$	0.326	Calcium oxide–CaO
Gypsum–$CaSO_4.2H_2O$	0.186	Sulfur–S
Magnesia–MgO	2.480	Calcium carbonate–$CaCO_3$
Magnesia–MgO	0.603	Magnesium–Mg

Multiply	By	To Obtain Equivalent Nutrient
Magnesia—MgO	2.092	Magnesium carbonate—$MgCO_3$
Magnesia—MgO	2.986	Magnesium sulfate—$MgSO_4$
Magnesia—MgO	6.114	Magnesium sulfate—$MgSO_4.7H_2O$ (Epsom salts)
Magnesium—Mg	4.116	Calcium carbonate—$CaCO_3$
Magnesium—Mg	1.658	Magnesia—MgO
Magnesium—Mg	3.466	Magnesium carbonate—$MgCO_3$
Magnesium—Mg	4.951	Magnesium sulfate—$MgSO_4$
Magnesium—Mg	10.136	Magnesium sulfate—$MgSO_4.7H_2O$ (Epsom salts)
Magnesium carbonate—$MgCO_3$	1.187	Calcium carbonate—$CaCO_3$
Magnesium carbonate—$MgCO_3$	0.478	Magnesia—MgO
Magnesium carbonate—$MgCO_3$	0.289	Magnesium—Mg
Magnesium sulfate—$MgSO_4$	0.335	Magnesia—MgO
Magnesium sulfate—$MgSO_4$	0.202	Magnesium—Mg
Magnesium sulfate—$MgSO_4.7H_2O$ (Epsom salts)	0.164	Magnesia—MgO
Magnesium sulfate—$MgSO_4.7H_2O$ (Epsom salts)	0.099	Magnesium—Mg
Manganese—Mn	2.749	Manganese(ous) sulfate—$MnSO_4$
Manganese—Mn	4.060	Manganese(ous) sulfate—$MnSO_4.4H_2O$
Manganese(ous) sulfate—$MnSO_4$	0.364	Manganese—Mn
Manganese(ous) sulfate—$MnSO_4.4H_2O$	0.246	Manganese—Mn
Nitrate—NO_3	0.226	Nitrogen—N
Nitrogen—N	1.216	Ammonia—NH_3
Nitrogen—N	2.856	Ammonium nitrate—NH_4NO_3
Nitrogen—N	4.716	Ammonium sulfate—$(NH_4)_2SO_4$
Nitrogen—N	4.426	Nitrate—NO_3
Nitrogen—N	6.068	Sodium nitrate—$NaNO_3$
Nitrogen—N	6.250	Protein

Multiply	By	To Obtain Equivalent Nutrient
Phosphoric acid—P_2O_5	0.437	Phosphorus—P
Phosphorus—P	2.291	Phosphoric acid—P_2O_5
Potash—K_2O	1.583	Potassium chloride—KCl
Potash—K_2O	2.146	Potassium nitrate—KNO_3
Potash—K_2O	0.830	Potassium—K
Potash—K_2O	1.850	Potassium sulfate—K_2SO_4
Potassium—K	1.907	Potassium chloride—KCl
Potassium—K	1.205	Potash—K_2O
Potassium—K	2.229	Potassium sulfate—K_2SO_4
Potassium chloride—KCl	0.632	Potash—K_2O
Potassium chloride—KCl	0.524	Potassium—K
Potassium nitrate—KNO_3	0.466	Potash—K_2O
Potassium nitrate—KNO_3	0.387	Potassium—K
Potassium sulfate—K_2SO_4	0.540	Potash—K_2O
Potassium sulfate—K_2SO_4	0.449	Potassium—K
Sodium nitrate—$NaNO_3$	0.165	Nitrogen—N
Sulfur—S	5.368	Calcium sulfate—$CaSO_4.2H_2O$ (gypsum)
Sulfur—S	2.497	Sulfur trioxide—SO_3
Sulfur—S	3.059	Sulfuric acid—H_2SO_4
Sulfur trioxide—SO_3	0.401	Sulfur—S
Sulfuric acid—H_2SO_4	0.327	Sulfur—S

Examples: 80 lb of ammonia (NH_3) contains the same amount of N as 310 lb of ammonium sulfate [$(NH_4)_2SO_4$] $80\times 3.88 = 310$. 1000 lb of calcium carbonate multiplied by 0.400 equals 400 lb of calcium. A material contains 20% phosphoric acid. This percentage (20) multiplied by 0.437 equals 8.74% phosphorus.

AMOUNT OF CARRIERS NEEDED TO SUPPLY A CERTAIN AMOUNT OF NUTRIENT PER ACRE[1]

Nutrients (lb/acre):	20	40	60	80	100	120	160	200
% Nutrient in Carrier	Carriers Needed (lb)							
3	667	1333	2000					
4	500	1000	1500	2000				
5	400	800	1200	1600	2000			
6	333	667	1000	1333	1667	2000		
7	286	571	857	1142	1429	1714		
8	250	500	750	1000	1250	1500	2000	
9	222	444	667	889	1111	1333	1778	
10	200	400	600	800	1000	1200	1600	2000
11	182	364	545	727	909	1091	1455	1818
12	166	333	500	666	833	1000	1333	1666
13	154	308	462	615	769	923	1231	1538
15	133	267	400	533	667	800	1067	1333
16	125	250	375	500	625	750	1000	1250
18	111	222	333	444	555	666	888	1111
20	100	200	300	400	500	600	800	1000
21	95	190	286	381	476	571	762	952
25	80	160	240	320	400	480	640	800
30	67	133	200	267	333	400	533	667
34	59	118	177	235	294	353	471	588
42	48	95	143	190	238	286	381	476
45	44	89	133	178	222	267	356	444
48	42	83	125	167	208	250	333	417
50	40	80	120	160	200	240	320	400
60	33	67	100	133	167	200	267	333

[1]This table can be used in determining the acre rate for applying a material in order to supply a certain number of pounds of a nutrient.

Example: A carrier provides 34% of a nutrient. To get 200 lb of the nutrient, 588 lb of the material is needed; and for 60 lb of the nutrient, 177 lb of carrier is required.

APPROXIMATE RATES OF MATERIALS TO PROVIDE CERTAIN QUANTITIES OF NITROGEN PER ACRE

Fertilizer Material	% N	N (lb/acre): 15	30	45	60	75	100
		Material to Apply (lb/acre)					
Solids							
Ammonium nitrate	33	45	90	135	180	225	300
Ammonium phosphate (48% P_2O_5)	11	135	270	410	545	680	910
Ammonium phosphate–sulfate (20% P_2O_5)	16	95	190	280	375	470	625
Ammonium sulfate	21	70	140	215	285	355	475
Calcium nitrate	15.5	95	195	290	390	485	645
Potassium nitrate	13	115	230	345	460	575	770
Sodium nitrate	16	95	190	280	375	470	625
Urea	46	35	65	100	130	165	215
Liquids							
Anhydrous ammonia (approx. 5 lb/gal)[1]	82	20	35	55	75	90	120
Aqua ammonium phosphate (24% P_2O_5; approx. 10 lb/gal)	8	190	375	560	750	940	1250
Aqua ammonia (approx. 7½ lb/gal)[1]	20	75	150	225	300	375	500
Nitrogen solution (approx. 11 lb/gal)	32	50	100	150	200	250	330

[1]To avoid burning, especially on alkaline soils, these materials must be placed deeper and further away from the plant row than you would place dry fertilizers.

RATES OF APPLICATION FOR CERTAIN NITROGEN SOLUTIONS

Nitrogen (lb/acre)	Nitrogen Solution Needed (gal/acre)		
	21% Solution	32% Solution	41% Solution
20	8.9	5.6	5.1
25	11.1	7.1	6.4
30	13.3	8.5	7.7
35	15.6	9.9	9.0
40	17.8	11.3	10.3
45	20.0	12.7	11.5
50	22.2	14.1	12.8
55	24.4	15.5	14.1
60	26.7	16.5	15.4
65	28.9	18.4	16.7
70	31.1	19.8	17.9
75	33.3	21.2	19.2
80	35.6	22.6	20.5
85	37.8	24.0	21.8
90	40.0	25.4	23.1
95	42.2	26.8	24.4
100	44.4	28.2	25.6
110	48.9	31.1	28.2
120	53.3	33.9	30.8
130	57.8	36.7	33.3
140	62.2	39.6	35.9
150	66.7	42.4	38.5
200	88.9	56.5	51.3

Adapted from C. W. Gandt, W. C. Hulburt, and H. D. Brown, Hose pump for applying nitrogen solutions, USDA Farmer's Bulletin 2096 (1956).

DETERMINING THE KIND AND QUANTITY OF FERTILIZER TO USE

Many states issue suggested rates of application of fertilizers for specific vegetables. These recommendations are sometimes made according to the type of soil, that is, light or heavy, sands, loams, clays, peats, and mucks. Other factors often used in establishing these rates are whether manure or soil-improving crops are employed and whether an optimum moisture supply can be maintained. The nutrient requirements of the crop to be grown must be considered, as well as the past fertilizer and cropping history. The season of the year will affect nutrient availability. Broad recommendations are at best only a point from which to make variations to suit your conditions. Each field may require a different fertilizer program for the same vegetable.

Soil testing can give some idea of the levels of available phosphorus, potassium, lime, and magnesium in a soil. Soluble nitrogen leaches readily during the winter, so there may be little carry-over. Nitrification builds up the supply of nitrate in the soil as the season advances, particularly if organic matter is adequate.

The results of a soil test will depend on the solvent used to make the soil extract. With one extractant 10–25 lb of phosphorus per acre is considered a low level. When a different one is used, 25–50 lb would be a low level. Moreover, what would be an adequate level for one crop might be low for another. The soil test is one of the several pieces of information on which to base fertilizer practice.

Use the results of the soil test and the known general response by crops on that soil in the past as a guide to the rate and kind of fertilization. The quantity of nitrogen, phosphorus, and potassium that a crop will extract from the soil is given in the table on pages 128–129.

GENERAL CONSIDERATIONS REGARDING FERTILIZER USAGE

Drill deeply or plow down phosphorus and potassium. They will be available in the root zone where moisture can be maintained. They move but little from where they are placed.

Reduce the rate of phosphorus and potassium in relation to nitrogen if the land has been liberally fertilized in the past.

More fertilizer should be applied for closer rows and plant spacing.

Irrigation or rain can result in the leaching of the soluble nutrients, especially nitrogen, into the deeper areas of the soil out of the reach of shallow-rooted vegetables. You can compensate for this leaching by applying extra nitrogen during the growing season.

More fertilizer, especially phosphorus, must be supplied than the crop will utilize in plant growth. Most soils fix considerable quantities of phosphorus that becomes unavailable to the plants. Moreover, many vegetables have sparse root systems that are unable to explore the soil fully. They do not come in contact with all the fertilizer that has been placed there.

If a heavy rate of nitrogen fertilization is planned, apply one-half or two-thirds at the time of planting. Put the remainder on as a side dressing, either liquid or solid at the time of maximum growth rate.

Where the rows are 2 ft or more apart, put fertilizer in bands slightly below the level of the seeds or the roots of transplants and 3–4 in. to each side.

Do not put more than about 300 lb/acre of a high-analysis fertilizer in bands close to the rows or burning may result.

APPROXIMATE REMOVAL OF NUTRIENTS BY VEGETABLE CROPS

Some idea of the optimum fertility levels needed for vegetable production can be gained from the quantities of nutrients removed by crops. The removal will vary according to the natural soil content of nitrogen, phosphorus, and potassium. It is influenced by the quantities of these applied in fertilizers, and their availability as affected by soil moisture and temperature conditions. Plants absorb luxury amounts if the level of any nutrient is very high.

The data have been compiled from many sources. Where possible the nutrients removed by the plants are indicated as well as those in the harvested product. Those in the plant parts not taken from the field are eventually returned to the soil.

Experiments have shown that the greatest nutrient absorption takes place during the last third of the season in the case of lettuce, potato, pepper, and tomato. Yet you must put adequate quantities of fertilizer nutrients relatively close to the young plants. The meager root system can at that stage absorb what is needed for maximum growth.

APPROXIMATE ABSORPTION OF NUTRIENTS BY SOME VEGETABLE CROPS

Vegetable	Yield (cwt/acre)	Nutrient Absorption (lb/acre)		
		N	P	K
Broccoli	100 heads	20	2	45
	Other	145	8	165
		165	10	210
Brussels sprouts	160 sprouts	150	20	125
	Other	85	9	110
		235	29	235
Carrot	500 roots	80	20	200
	Tops	65	5	145
		145	25	345
Celery	1000 tops	170	35	380
	Roots	25	15	55
		195	50	435
Honeydew melon	290 fruits	70	8	65
	Vines	135	15	95
		205	23	160
Lettuce	350 plants	95	12	170
Muskmelon	225 fruits	95	17	120
	Vines	60	8	35
		155	25	155
Onion	400 bulbs	110	20	110
	Tops	35	5	45
		145	25	155
Pepper	225 fruits	45	6	50
	Plants	95	6	90
		140	12	140

APPROXIMATE ABSORPTION OF NUTRIENTS BY SOME VEGETABLE CROPS—Continued

Vegetable	Yield (cwt/acre)	Nutrient Absorption (lb/acre)		
		N	P	K
Pea, shelled	40 peas	100	10	30
	Vines	70	12	50
		170	22	80
Potato	400 tubers	150	19	200
	Vines	60	11	75
		210	30	275
Snap bean	100 beans	120	10	55
	Plants	50	6	45
		170	16	100
Spinach	200 plants	100	12	100
Sweet corn	130 ears	55	8	30
	Plants	100	12	75
		155	20	105
Sweet potato	300 roots	80	16	160
	Vines	60	4	40
		140	20	200
Tomato	600 fruits	100	10	180
	Vines	80	11	100
		180	21	280

PLANT ANALYSIS GUIDE FOR SAMPLING TIME, PLANT PART, AND NUTRIENT LEVELS OF VEGETABLE CROPS (DRY-WEIGHT BASIS)

Crop	Time of Sampling	Plant Part	Source	Nutrient[1]	Nutrient Level: Deficient	Nutrient Level: Sufficient
Asparagus	Midgrowth of fern	4-in. tip section of new fern branch	NO_3	N, ppm	100	500
			PO_4	P, ppm	800	1,600
				K, %	1	3
Bean, bush snap	Midgrowth	Petiole of 4th leaf from tip	NO_3	N, ppm	2,000	3,000
			PO_4	P, ppm	1,000	2,000
				K, %	3	5
	Early bloom	Petiole of 4th leaf from tip	NO_3	N, ppm	1,000	1,500
			PO_4	P, ppm	800	1,500
				K, %	2	4
Broccoli	Midgrowth	Midrib of young, mature leaf	NO_3	N, ppm	7,000	9,000
			PO_4	P, ppm	2,500	4,000
				K, %	3	5
	First buds	Midrib of young, mature leaf	NO_3	N, ppm	5,000	7,000
			PO_4	P, ppm	2,500	4,000
				K, %	2	4
Brussels sprouts	Midgrowth	Midrib of young, mature leaf	NO_3	N, ppm	5,000	7,000
			PO_4	P, ppm	2,000	3,500
				K, %	3	5

	Late growth	Midrib of young, mature leaf	NO_3	N, ppm	2,000	3,000
			PO_4	P, ppm	1,000	3,000
				K, %	2	4
Cabbage	At heading	Midrib of wrapper leaf	NO_3	N, ppm	5,000	7,000
			PO_4	P, ppm	2,500	3,500
				K, %	2	4
Chinese cabbage	At heading	Midrib of wrapper leaf	NO_3	N, ppm	8,000	10,000
			PO_4	P, ppm	2,000	3,000
				K, %	4	7
Carrot	Midgrowth	Petiole of young, mature leaf	NO_3	N, ppm	5,000	7,500
			PO_4	P, ppm	2,000	3,000
				K, %	4	6
Cauliflower	Buttoning	Midrib of young, mature leaf	NO_3	N, ppm	5,000	7,000
			PO_4	P, ppm	2,500	3,500
				K, %	2	4
Celery	Midgrowth	Petiole of newest fully elongated leaf	NO_3	N, ppm	5,000	7,000
			PO_4	P, ppm	2,500	3,000
				K, %	4	7
	Near maturity	Petiole of newest fully elongated leaf	NO_3	N, ppm	4,000	6,000
			PO_4	P, ppm	2,000	3,000
				K, %	3	5
Cucumber, pickling	Early fruit set	Petiole of 6th leaf from tip	NO_3	N, ppm	5,000	7,500
			PO_4	P, ppm	1,500	2,500
				K, %	3	5

PLANT ANALYSIS GUIDE FOR SAMPLING TIME, PLANT PART, AND NUTRIENT LEVELS OF VEGETABLE CROPS (DRY-WEIGHT BASIS)—Continued

Crop	Time of Sampling	Plant Part	Source	Nutrient[1]	Nutrient Level: Deficient	Nutrient Level: Sufficient
Cucumber, slicing	Early harvest period	Petiole of 6th leaf from growing tip	NO_3	N, ppm	5,000	7,500
			PO_4	P, ppm	1,500	2,500
				K, %	4	7
Eggplant	At first harvest	Petiole of young, mature leaf	NO_3	N, ppm	5,000	7,500
			PO_4	P, ppm	2,000	3,000
				K, %	4	7
Garlic	Early growth (prebulbing)	Newest fully elongated leaf	PO_4	P, ppm	2,000	3,000
				K, %	3	4
	Midseason (bulbing)	Newest fully elongated leaf	PO_4	P, ppm	2,000	3,000
				K, %	2	3
	Late season (postbulbing)	Newest fully elongated leaf	PO_4	P, ppm	2,000	3,000
				K, %	1	2
Lettuce	At heading	Midrib of wrapper leaf	NO_3	N, ppm	4,000	6,000
			PO_4	P, ppm	2,000	3,000
				K, %	2	4

	At harvest	Midrib of wrapper leaf	NO_3	N, ppm	3,000	5,000
			PO_4	P, ppm	1,500	2,500
				K, %	1.5	2.5
Muskmelon	Early growth (short runners)	Petiole of 6th leaf from growing tip	NO_3	N, ppm	8,000	12,000
			PO_4	P, ppm	2,000	3,000
				K, %	4	6
	Early fruit	Petiole of 6th leaf from growing tip	NO_3	N, ppm	5,000	8,000
			PO_4	P, ppm	1,500	2,500
				K, %	3	5
	First mature fruit	Petiole of 6th leaf from growing tip	NO_3	N, ppm	2,000	3,000
			PO_4	P, ppm	1,000	2,000
				K, %	2	4
	Early growth	Blade of 6th leaf from growing tip	NO_3	N, ppm	2,000	3,000
			PO_4	P, ppm	1,500	2,300
				K, %	1	2.5
	Early fruit	Blade of 6th leaf from growing tip	NO_3	N, ppm	1,000	1,500
			PO_4	P, ppm	1,300	1,700
				K, %	1	2.0
	First mature fruit	Blade of 6th leaf from growing tip	NO_3	N, ppm	500	800
			PO_4	P, ppm	1,000	1,500
				K, %	1	1.8
Onion	Early season	Tallest leaf	PO_4	P, ppm	1,000	2,000
				K, %	3	4.5
	Midseason	Tallest leaf	PO_4	P, ppm	1,000	2,000
				K, %	2	4
	Late season	Tallest leaf	PO_4	P, ppm	1,000	2,000
				K, %	2	3

PLANT ANALYSIS GUIDE FOR SAMPLING TIME, PLANT PART, AND NUTRIENT LEVELS OF VEGETABLE CROPS (DRY-WEIGHT BASIS)—Continued

Crop	Time of Sampling	Plant Part	Source	Nutrient[1]	Nutrient Level	
					Deficient	Sufficient
Pepper, chili	Early growth, first bloom	Petiole of young, mature leaf	NO_3	N, ppm	5,000	7,000
			PO_4	P, ppm	2,000	2,500
				K, %	3	5
	Early fruit set	Petiole of young, mature leaf	NO_3	N, ppm	1,000	1,500
			PO_4	P, ppm	1,500	2,000
				K, %	2	4
	Fruits, full size	Petiole of young, mature leaf	NO_3	N, ppm	750	1,000
			PO_4	P, ppm	1,500	2,000
				K, %	1.5	3
	Early growth, first bloom	Blade of young mature leaf	NO_3	N, ppm	1,500	2,000
			PO_4	P, ppm	1,500	2,000
				K, %	3	5
	Early fruit set	Blade of young mature leaf	NO_3	N, ppm	500	800
			PO_4	P, ppm	1,500	2,000
				K, %	2	4
Pepper, sweet	Early growth, first flower	Petiole of young, mature leaf	NO_3	N, ppm	8,000	10,000
			PO_4	P, ppm	2,000	3,000
				K, %	4	6

	Early fruit set, 1 in. diameter	Petiole of young, mature leaf	NO_3	N, ppm	3,000	5,000
			PO_4	P, ppm	1,500	2,500
				K, %	3	5
	Fruit ¾ size	Petiole of young, mature leaf	NO_3	N, ppm	2,000	3,000
			PO_4	P, ppm	1,200	2,000
				K, %	2	4
	Early growth, first flower	Blade of young, mature leaf	NO_3	N, ppm	2,000	3,000
			PO_4	P, ppm	1,800	2,500
				K, %	3	5
	Early fruit set, 1 in. diameter	Blade of young, mature leaf	NO_3	N, ppm	1,500	2,000
			PO_4	P, ppm	1,500	2,000
				K, %	2	4
Potato	Early season	Petiole of 4th leaf from growing tip	NO_3	N, ppm	8,000	12,000
			PO_4	P, ppm	1,200	2,000
				K, %	9	11
	Midseason	Petiole of 4th leaf from growing tip	NO_3	N, ppm	6,000	9,000
			PO_4	P, ppm	800	1,600
				K, %	7	9
	Late season	Petiole of 4th leaf from growing tip	NO_3	N, ppm	3,000	5,000
			PO_4	P, ppm	500	1,000
				K, %	4	6
Spinach	Midgrowth	Petiole of young, mature leaf	NO_3	N, ppm	4,000	6,000
			PO_4	P, ppm	2,000	3,000
				K, %	2	4
Summer squash (zucchini)	Early bloom	Petiole of young, mature leaf	NO_3	N, ppm	12,000	15,000
			PO_4	P, ppm	4,000	6,000
				K, %	6	10

PLANT ANALYSIS GUIDE FOR SAMPLING TIME, PLANT PART, AND NUTRIENT LEVELS OF VEGETABLE CROPS (DRY-WEIGHT BASIS)—Continued

Crop	Time of Sampling	Plant Part	Source	Nutrient[1]	Nutrient Level: Deficient	Nutrient Level: Sufficient
Sweet corn	Tasseling	Midrib of 1st leaf above primary ear	NO_3	N, ppm	500	1,000
			PO_4	P, ppm	500	1,000
				K, %	2	4
Sweet potato	Midgrowth	Petiole of 6th leaf from the growing tip	NO_3	N, ppm	1,500	2,500
			PO_4	P, ppm	1,000	2,000
				K, %	3	5
Tomato, cherry	Early fruit set	Petiole of 4th leaf from the growing tip	NO_3	N, ppm	8,000	10,000
			PO_4	P, ppm	2,000	3,000
				K, %	4	7
	Fruit ½ in. diameter	Petiole of 4th leaf from growing tip	NO_3	N, ppm	5,000	7,000
			PO_4	P, ppm	2,000	3,000
				K, %	3	5
	At first harvest	Petiole of 4th leaf from growing tip	NO_3	N, ppm	1,000	2,000
			PO_4	P, ppm	2,000	3,000
				K, %	2	4

Tomato, processing and determinate, fresh market	Early bloom	Petiole of 4th leaf from growing tip	NO_3	N, ppm	8,000	12,000
			PO_4	P, ppm	2,000	3,000
				K, %	3	6
	Fruit 1 in. diameter	Petiole of 4th leaf from growing tip	NO_3	N, ppm	4,000	6,000
			PO_4	P, ppm	1,500	2,500
				K, %	2	4
	First color	Petiole of 4th leaf from growing tip	NO_3	N, ppm	2,000	3,000
			PO_4	P, ppm	1,000	2,000
				K, %	1	3
Tomato, fresh market nondeterminate	Early bloom	Petiole of 4th leaf from growing tip	NO_3	N, ppm	10,000	14,000
			PO_4	P, ppm	2,500	3,000
				K, %	4	7
	Fruit 1 in. diameter	Petiole of 4th leaf from growing tip	NO_3	N, ppm	8,000	12,000
			PO_4	P, ppm	2,500	3,000
				K, %	3	5
	Full ripe fruit	Petiole of 4th leaf from growing tip	NO_3	N, ppm	4,000	6,000
			PO_4	P, ppm	2,000	2,500
				K, %	2	4
Watermelon	Early fruit set	Petiole of 6th leaf from growing tip	NO_3	N, ppm	5,000	7,500
			PO_4	P, ppm	1,500	2,500
				K, %	3	5

Adapted from H. M. Reisenauer (ed), Soil and plant tissue testing in California, University of California Division of Agricultural Science Bulletin 1879 (1983).

[1]Two percent acetic acid-soluble NO_3–N and PO_4–P and total K (dry-weight basis).

TOTAL NUTRIENT ANALYSES FOR DIAGNOSIS OF THE NUTRIENT LEVEL OF VEGETABLE CROPS

Crop	Time of Sampling	Plant Part	Nutrient	Nutrient Level (% dry weight) Deficient	Sufficient
Asparagus	Early fern growth (May–June)	4 in. tip section of new fern branch	N	4.00	5.00
			P	0.20	0.40
			K	2.00	4.00
	Mature fern (July–Sept.)	4 in. tip section of new fern branch	N	3.00	4.00
			P	0.20	0.40
			K	1.00	3.00
Bean, bush snap	Full bloom	Petiole: recent fully exposed trifoliate leaf	N	1.50	2.25
			P	0.15	0.30
			K	1.00	2.50
	Full bloom	Blade: recent fully exposed trifoliate leaf	N	1.25	2.25
			P	0.25	0.40
			K	0.75	1.50
Bean, Lima	Full bloom	Oldest trifoliate leaf	N	2.50	3.50
			P	0.20	0.30
			K	1.50	2.25
Celery	Midgrowth	Petiole	N	1.00	1.50
			P	0.25	0.55
			K	4.00	5.00

Garlic	Early season (prebulbing)	Newest fully elongated leaf	N	4.00	5.00
			P	0.20	0.30
			K	3.00	4.00
	Midseason (bulbing)	Newest fully elongated leaf	N	3.00	4.00
			P	0.20	0.30
			K	2.00	3.00
	Late season (postbulbing)	Newest fully elongated leaf	N	2.00	3.00
			P	0.20	0.30
			K	1.00	2.00
Lettuce	At heading	Leaves	N	1.50	3.00
			P	0.20	0.35
			K	2.50	5.00
	Nearly mature	Leaves	N	1.25	2.50
			P	0.15	0.30
			K	2.50	5.00
Muskmelon	Early growth	Petiole of 6th leaf from growing tip	N	2.50	3.50
			P	0.30	0.60
			K	4.00	6.00
	Early fruit	Petiole of 6th leaf from growing tip	N	2.00	3.00
			P	0.20	0.35
			K	3.00	5.00
	First mature fruit	Petiole of 6th leaf from growing tip	N	1.50	2.00
			P	0.15	0.30
			K	2.00	4.00
Onion	Early season	Tallest leaf	N	3.00	4.00
			P	0.10	0.20
			K	3.00	4.00

TOTAL NUTRIENT ANALYSES FOR DIAGNOSIS OF THE NUTRIENT LEVEL OF VEGETABLE CROPS

				Nutrient Level (% dry weight)	
Crop	Time of Sampling	Plant Part	Nutrient	Deficient	Sufficient
Onion	Midseason	Tallest leaf	N	2.50	3.00
			P	0.10	0.20
			K	2.50	4.00
	Late season	Tallest leaf	N	2.00	2.50
			P	0.10	0.20
			K	2.00	3.00
Pepper, sweet	Full bloom	Blade and petiole	N	2.00	3.50
			P	0.15	0.25
			K	1.50	2.50
	Full bloom, fruit ¾ size	Blade and petiole	N	1.50	2.50
			P	0.12	0.20
			K	1.00	2.00
Potato	Early, plants 12 in. tall	Petiole of 4th leaf from tip	N	2.50	3.50
			P	0.20	0.30
			K	9.00	11.00
	Midseason	Petiole of 4th leaf from tip	N	2.25	2.75
			P	0.10	0.20
			K	7.00	9.00

	Late, nearly mature	Petiole of 4th leaf from tip	N	1.50	2.25
			P	0.08	0.15
			K	4.00	6.00
	Early, plants 12 in. tall	Blade of 4th leaf from tip	N	4.00	6.00
			P	0.30	0.60
			K	3.50	5.00
	Midseason	Blade of 4th leaf from tip	N	3.00	5.00
			P	0.20	0.40
			K	2.50	3.50
	Late, nearly mature	Blade of 4th leaf from tip	N	2.00	4.00
			P	0.10	0.20
			K	1.50	2.50
Southern pea (cowpea)	Full bloom	Blade and petiole	N	2.00	3.50
			P	0.20	0.30
			K	1.00	2.00
Spinach	Midgrowth	Mature leaf blade and petiole	N	2.00	4.00
			P	0.20	0.40
			K	3.00	6.00
	At harvest	Mature leaf blade and petiole	N	1.50	3.00
			P	0.20	0.35
			K	2.00	5.00
Sweet corn	Tasseling	Sixth leaf from base of plant	N	2.75	3.50
			P	0.18	0.28
			K	1.75	2.25

TOTAL NUTRIENT ANALYSES FOR DIAGNOSIS OF THE NUTRIENT LEVEL OF VEGETABLE CROPS—Continued

Crop	Time of Sampling	Plant Part	Nutrient	Nutrient Level (% dry weight)	
				Deficient	Sufficient
Sweet corn (continued)	Silking	Leaf opposite first ear	N	1.50	2.00
			P	0.20	0.30
			K	1.00	2.00
Tomato (determinate)	Flowering	Leaf blade and petiole	N	2.00	3.00
			P	0.20	0.35
			K	2.50	4.00
	First ripe fruit	Leaf blade and petiole	N	1.50	2.50
			P	0.15	0.25
			K	1.50	3.00

Adapted from H. M. Reisenauer (ed.), Soil and plant tissue testing in California, University of California Division of Agricultural Science Bulletin 1879 (1983).

SOIL TESTING

Total analyses of nutrients in the soil are of limited value in predicting fertilizer needs. Consequently, various methods and extractants have been developed to measure the available soil nutrients and to serve as a basis for estimating fertilizer needs. Proper interpretation of the results of soil analysis is essential in recommending fertilizer need.

INTERPRETATION OF SOIL TEST RESULTS FOR PHOSPHORUS BY THE OLSON BICARBONATE EXTRACTION, FOR POTASSIUM AND MAGNESIUM BY AMMONIUM ACETATE EXTRACTION, AND FOR ZINC BY DPTA EXTRACTION

	Amount in Soil (ppm)			
Nutrient Need	Phosphorus[1] (PO_4-P)	Potassium[2] (K)	Magnesium[2] (Mg)	Zinc[3] (Zn)
Deficient levels for most vegetables	0–10	0–60	0–25	0–0.3
Deficient for susceptible vegetables	10–20	60–120	25–50	0.3–0.6
A few susceptible crops may respond	20–40	120–200	50–100	0.6–1.0
No crop response	Above 40	Above 200	Above 100	Above 1.0
Levels are excessive and could cause problems	Above 150	Above 2000	Above 1000	Above 3.0

Adapted from H. M. Reisenauer, (Ed.), Soil and plant tissue testing in California, University of California Division of Agricultural Science Bulletin 1879 (1976).

[1]Olson (0.5*M*, pH 8.5) sodium bicarbonate extractant.

[2]Exchangeable with *N* ammonium acetate extractant.

[3]DPTA extractable Zn.

INTERPRETATION OF SOIL TEST RESULTS OBTAINED BY THE DOUBLE-ACID ($0.05N$ HCl, $0.025N$ H_2SO_4) SOIL EXTRACTION METHOD

	Amount (lb/acre)			
Relative Level In Soil	Phosphorus (P)	Potassium (K)	Magnesium (Mg)	Calcium (Ca)
Very low	0–13	0–29	0–35	0–400
Low	14–27	30–70	36–70	401–800
Medium	28–45	71–134	71–125	801–1200
High	46–89	135–267	126–265	1201–1600
Very high	90+	268+	266+	1601+

Adapted from Commercial vegetable production recommendations, Maryland Cooperative Extension Service EB-236 rev. (1986).

INTERPRETATION OF SOIL TEST RESULTS FOR VEGETABLES, EXCEPT POTATOES, BY THE BRAY P_1 ($0.025N$ HCl, $0.03N$ NH_4F) SOIL EXTRACTION METHOD

	Amount (lb/acre)	
Relative Level In Soil	Phosphorus (P)	Potassium (K)
Very low	0–30	0–120
Low	31–60	121–180
Medium	61–90	181–300
High	91–150	301–450
Very High	151–200	>600
Excessively high	>200	

Adapted from K. A. Kelling et al., Soil test recommendations for field, vegetable and fruit crops, University of Wisconsin Extension Circular A2809 (1981).

GUIDE FOR DIAGNOSING NUTRIENT STATUS OF CALIFORNIA SOILS FOR VEGETABLE CROPS[1]

Vegetable	Nutrient[1]	Vegetable Yield Response to Fertilizer Application: Likely (soil ppm less than)	Vegetable Yield Response to Fertilizer Application: Not Likely (soil ppm more than)
Lettuce	P	15	25
	K	50	80
	Zn	0.5	1.0
Muskmelon	P	8	12
	K	80	100
	Zn	0.4	0.6
Onion	P	8	12
	K	80	100
	Zn	0.5	1.0
Potato (mineral soils)	P	12	25
	K	100	150
	Zn	0.3	0.7
Tomato	P	6	12
	K	50	80
	Zn	0.3	0.7
Warm-season vegetables	P	5	9
	K	50	70
	Zn	0.2	0.5
Cool-season vegetables	P	10	20
	K	50	80
	Zn	0.5	1.0

Adapted from Soil and plant testing in California, University of California Division Agricultural Science Bulletin 1879 (1983).

[1]Soil extracts:

PO_4-P: 0.5*M* pH 8.5 sodium bicarbonate ($NaHCO_3$).

K: 1.0*M* ammonium acetate (NH_4OAc).

Zn: 0.005*M* diethylenetriaminepentaacetic acid (DTPA).

INTERPRETATION OF MICRONUTRIENT SOIL TESTS

Element	Method	Range in Critical Level (ppm)[1]
Boron (B)	Hot H_2O	0.1–0.7
Copper (Cu)	$NH_4C_2H_3O_2$ (pH4.8)	0.2
	0.5*M* EDTA	0.75
	0.43*N* HNO_3	3–4
	Biological assay	2–3
Iron (Fe)	$NH_4C_2H_3O_2$ (pH 4.8)	2
	DTPA + $CaCl_2$ (pH 7.3)	2.5–4.5
Manganese (Mn)	0.05*N* HCl + 0.025*N* H_2SO_4	5–9
	0.1*N* H_3PO_4 and 3*N* $NH_4H_2PO_4$	15–20
	Hydroquinone + $NH_4C_2H_3O_2$	25–65
	H_2O	2
Molybdenum (Mo)	$(NH_4)_2C_2O_4$ (pH 3.3)	0.04–0.2
Zinc (Zn)	0.1*N* HCl	1.0–7.5
	Dithizone + $NH_4C_2H_3O_2$	0.3–2.3
	EDTA + $(NH_4)_2CO_3$	1.4–3.0
	DTPA + $CaCl_2$ (pH 7.3)	0.5–1.0

Reprinted with permission from S. S. Mortvedt, P. M. Giordano, and W. L. Lindsay (eds.), *Micronutrients in Agriculture*, Soil Science Society of America, Madison, WI (1972).

[1]Deficiencies are likely to occur when concentrations are below the critical level.

MANGANESE FERTILIZER NEEDS AS INDICATED BY SOIL TESTS FOR RESPONSIVE CROPS[1]

	Mineral Soils		Organic Soils	
Soil Test (ppm Mn)	pH 6.0–6.5	Above pH 6.5	pH 5.8–6.4	Above pH 6.4
	Mn (lb/acre)			
Below 5	6	8	12	16
5–10	4	6	8	12
11–20	0	4	4	8
21–40	0	0	0	4
Above 40	0	0	0	0

Adapted from D. D. Warncke, D. R. Christenson, and R. E. Lucas, Fertilizer recommendations for vegetable and field crops, Michigan Extension Bulletin E-550 (1976).

[1]0.1*N* HCl extraction.

ZINC FERTILIZER NEEDS AS INDICATED BY SOIL TESTS FOR RESPONSIVE CROPS IN MINERAL SOILS[1]

Soil Test (ppm Zn)	Below pH 6.7	pH 6.7–7.4	Above pH 7.4
	Zn (lb/acre)		
Below 2	2	3	5
3–5	0	3	3
5–10	0	2	3
11–15	0	0	2
Above 15	0	0	0

Adapted from D. D. Warncke, D. R. Christenson, and R. E. Lucas, Fertilizer recommendations for vegetable and field crops, Michigan Extension Bulletin E-550 (1976).

[1]0.1*N* HCl extraction.

RELATIVE RESPONSE OF VEGETABLES TO MICRONUTRIENTS[1]

Vegetable	Response to Micronutrient					
	Manganese	Boron	Copper	Zinc	Molybdenum	Iron
Asparagus	Low	Low	Low	Low	Low	Medium
Bean	High	Low	Low	High	Medium	High
Beet	High	High	High	Medium	High	High
Broccoli	Medium	Medium	Medium	—	High	High
Cabbage	Medium	Medium	Medium	—	Medium	Medium
Carrot	Medium	Medium	Medium	Low	Low	—
Cauliflower	Medium	High	Medium	—	High	High
Celery	Medium	High	Medium	—	Low	—
Cucumber	Medium	Low	Medium	—	—	—
Lettuce	High	Medium	High	—	High	—
Onion	High	Low	High	High	High	—
Pea	High	Low	Low	Low	Medium	—
Potato	High	Low	Low	Medium	Low	—
Radish	High	Medium	Medium	—	Medium	—
Spinach	High	Medium	High	—	High	High
Sweet corn	Medium	Low	Medium	High	Low	Medium
Tomato	Medium	Medium	Medium	Medium	Medium	High
Turnip	Medium	High	Medium	—	Medium	—

Adapted from M. L. Vitosh, D. D. Warncke, and R. E. Lucas, Secondary and micronutrients for vegetables and field crops, Michigan Extension Bulletin E-486 (1973).

[1]The crops listed will respond as indicated to applications of the respective micronutrient when that micronutrient concentration in the soil is low.

BORON REQUIREMENTS OF VEGETABLES ARRANGED IN APPROXIMATE ORDER OF DECREASING REQUIREMENTS

High Requirement (more than 0.5 ppm in soil)	Medium Requirement (0.1–0.5 ppm in soil)	Low Requirement (less than 0.1 ppm in soil)
Beet	Tomato	Corn
Turnip	Lettuce	Pea
Cabbage	Sweet potato	Bean
Broccoli	Carrot	Lima bean
Cauliflower	Onion	Potato
Asparagus		
Radish		
Brussels sprouts		
Celery		
Rutabaga		

Adapted from K. C. Berger, Boron in soils and crops, *Advances in Agronomy*, Vol. 1, Academic Press, New York (1949), pp. 321–351.

RELATIVE TOLERANCE OF VEGETABLES TO BORON, ARRANGED IN ORDER OF INCREASING SENSITIVITY TO BORON

Tolerant	Semitolerant	Sensitive
Asparagus	Celery	Jerusalem artichoke
Artichoke	Potato	Bean
Beet	Tomato	
Muskmelon	Radish	
Broad bean	Corn	
Onion	Pumpkin	
Turnip	Bell pepper	
Cabbage	Sweet potato	
Lettuce	Lima bean	
Carrot		

Adapted from L. V. Wilcox, Determining the quality of irrigation water, USDA Agricultural Information Bulletin 197 (1958).

SUGGESTED RATES OF FERTILIZERS FOR VEGETABLES

The table gives some suggested fertilizer rates for trial under unknown conditions; for individual cases, however, these rates must be adjusted.

Vegetable	Amount (lb/acre)		
	N	P_2O_5	K_2O
Potato	200	200	200
Leafy vegetables: lettuce, cabbage, spinach	150	100	150
Fruit crops: tomato, muskmelon, pepper	100	100	150
Root crops: sweet potato, carrot, beet	150	100	250
Legumes: bean, pea	50	75	50

Reprinted with permission from M. H. McVicar, G. L. Bridges, and L. B. Nelson (eds.), *Changing Patterns in Fertilizer Use*, Soil Science Society of America, Madison, WI (1968).

SUGGESTED CORRECTIVE FERTILIZER RATES FOR WISCONSIN VEGETABLE CROPS GROWING ON SANDS, SILTS, AND ORGANIC SOILS OF VARYING PHOSPHORUS AND POTASSIUM LEVELS[1]

Phosphorus (lb/acre)		Potassium (lb/acre)	
Soil P	Recommended P_2O_5	Soil K	Recommended K_2O
0–25	120	0–120	240
26–50	60	121–180	180
51–75	30	181–240	120
76–150	0	241–300	60
Over 150	0	301–500	0
		Over 500	0

Adapted from L. M. Walsh, E. E. Schulte, J. J. Genson, and E. A. Liegel, Soil test recommendations for field and vegetable crops, University of Wisconsin Extension Service A2809 (1976).

[1]As determined by Bray P_1 soil extractant (0.025*N* HCl, 0.03*N* NH_4F).

RATES OF FERTILIZERS RECOMMENDED FOR VEGETABLE CROPS IN MID-ATLANTIC STATES BASED ON SOIL ANALYSES[1]

Vegetable	Amount N (lb/acre)	Amount P_2O_5 (lb/acre)		Amount K_2O (lb/acre)	
		Low Soil P	High Soil P	Low Soil K	High Soil K
Asparagus	50	200	50	200	50
Bean	40–80	80	40	80	40
Beet	75–100	150	50	150	50
Broccoli	150–200	200	50	200	50
Cabbage	100–150	200	50	200	50
Carrot	50–80	150	50	150	50
Cauliflower	100–150	200	50	200	50
Celery	125–150	250	100	250	100
Cucumber	100–125	150	50	200	100
Eggplant	125–150	250	100	250	100
Lettuce	60–80	200	100	200	100
Leek	100–125	200	100	200	100
Muskmelon	85–100	150	50	200	100
Onion	75–100	200	50	200	50
Pea	40–60	120	40	120	40
Pepper	100–130	200	100	200	100
Potato	125–150	200	100	300	100
Pumpkin	50–75	150	50	200	100
Spinach	100–125	200	100	200	100
Squash (summer)	75–100	150	50	200	100
Strawberry	150–200	150	50	150	50
Sweet corn	125–150	160	80	160	80
Sweet potato	50–75	200	50	300	100
Tomato	80	200	100	300	100
Watermelon	125–150	150	50	200	100

Adapted from Commercial vegetable production recommendations, Maryland Cooperative Extension Service EB-236 rev. (1986).

[1]A common recommendation is to broadcast and work deeply into the soil one-third to one-half of the fertilizer at planting and to apply the balance as a side-dressing in one or two applications after the crop is fully established.

FERTILITY RECOMMENDATIONS FOR FLORIDA VEGETABLES GROWN ON IRRIGATED MINERAL SOILS TESTING VERY LOW IN PHOSPHORUS AND POTASSIUM

Vegetable	Amount (lb/acre)[1]		
	N	P_2O_5	K_2O
Bean	60	80	80
Bean, Lima	90	120	120
Beet	90	120	120
Broccoli	110	150	150
Cabbage	120	160	160
Carrot	110	150	150
Cauliflower (mulched)	150	200	200
Celery	150	150	200
Chinese cabbage	110	150	150
Collard	110	150	150
Cucumber	90	120	120
Eggplant	120	160	160
Lettuce	110	150	150
Muskmelon	120	160	160
Mustard	110	150	150
Okra	120	150	150
Onion	120	160	160
Pea	90	120	120
Pepper	160	160	160
Potato	150	115	135
Spinach	120	160	160
Sweet corn	90	120	120
Sweet potato	60	120	120
Strawberry (mulched)	120	160	160
Tomato (mulched)	220	160	300
Turnip	110	150	150
Watermelon	120	160	160

Adapted from G. J. Hochmuth, Florida vegetable fertilizer guide, *Florida Grower and Rancher* 78(8):176–20, 25–28 (1985).

[1]Approximately one-third to one-half of the N and K_2O is applied as the basic application and the balance in one to three supplemental applications. All of the P_2O_5 is applied as the basic application.

FERTILIZER RATES RECOMMENDED FOR VEGETABLE CROPS IN INDIANA

	Amount (lb/acre)[1]		
Vegetable	N	P_2O_5	K_2O
Asparagus	100	50	100
Bean	72	108	120
Broccoli	160	60	180
Beet	100	100	200
Cabbage	160	60	180
Carrot	100	100	200
Cauliflower	160	60	180
Cucumber	90	60	120
Eggplant	60	60	120
Endive	120	120	120
Lettuce	120	120	120
Muskmelon	90	60	120
Onion	60–160[2]	240	240
Parsnip	100	100	200
Pea	72	108	120
Pepper	100	100	200
Potato	70–120[2]	96	240
Radish	25	100	100
Rhubarb	125	75	75
Spinach	120	120	120
Squash	100	100	150
Sweet corn	132	48	120
Sweet potato	40	60	180
Tomato	50–120	100	240
Turnip	25	100	100
Watermelon	60	60	120

Adapted from R. X. Latin, J. E. Simon, and D. L. Matthew (eds.), Indiana vegetable production guide for commercial growers, Indiana Cooperative Extension ID-56 (1986).

[1]Total amounts are listed; application may be broadcast and plow down, band, side-dress, or topdress.
[2]Lower N rate suggested for organic soil.

SUGGESTED FERTILIZER RATES FOR NEW ENGLAND VEGETABLE CROPS GROWN ON SOILS OF AVERAGE SOIL FERTILITY[1]

	Amount (lb/acre)		
Vegetable	N	P_2O_5	K_2O
Asparagus[2]	50–80	100–150	150–225
Bean	20–40	70–100	70–100
Beet	100–160	50–150	50–150
Broccoli	150	100	100
Cabbage	150	100	100
Carrot	80–125	50–150	50–200
Cauliflower	100	100	100
Celery	120–150	150–200	150–200
Cucumber	105–130	100–150	100–150
Eggplant	130	100	100
Endive	90–120	120–180	120–180
Lettuce	90–120	120–180	120–180
Muskmelon	105–130	100–150	100–150
Onion	110–130	100–150	100–150
Parsnip	80–125	50–150	50–200
Pea	75	75	75
Pepper	105–145	100–150	100–150
Potato	150–180	180–200	180–200
Radish	40–75	40–100	50–200
Spinach	80–120	50–75	75–150
Squash and pumpkin	50	150	150
Sweet corn	90–170	170–220	150–220
Tomato	130–170	120–150	120–150
Turnip and rutabaga	70–135	40–100	50–200

Adapted from E. L. Bouton and C. W. Nicklow (eds.), New England vegetable production recommendations, Cooperative Services of the New England States (1986).

[1]Rates are for soils at recommended pH. Application of these amounts is by a combination of broadcast, band, and side-dress.

[2]For established plantings.

FERTILIZER RATES RECOMMENDED FOR VEGETABLE CROPS IN NEW YORK

	Amount (lb/acre)[1]		
Vegetable	N	P_2O_5	K_2O
Asparagus	130	160	160
Bean	50–75	20–80	20–40
Beet	150–175	50–150	50–300
Broccoli	80–180	50–160	50–160
Brussels sprouts	80–180	50–160	50–160
Cabbage	80–180	50–160	50–160
Carrot	80–135	50–150	50–200
Cauliflower	80–180	50–160	50–200
Celery	140–270	80–200	50–200
Cucumber	80–165	50–150	50–150
Eggplant	80–150	50–150	50–150
Endive	80–160	50–100	50–150
Lettuce	80–160	50–100	50–100
Muskmelon	80–165	50–150	50–150
Onion	80–125	40–150	40–150
Parsnip	80–180	50–150	50–200
Pea	40–50	50–100	50–150
Pepper	80–210	50–150	50–150
Potato	75–175	50–300	50–300
Pumpkin	80–135	50–100	50–150
Radish	40–75	40–100	50–200
Rhubarb	130	160	160
Rutabaga	70–135	40–100	50–200
Spinach	105–160	75–100	40–200
Squash, summer	80–135	50–100	50–150
Squash, winter	80–135	50–100	50–150
Sweet corn	110–200	40–80	40–100
Tomato	100–180	50–160	50–160
Turnip	70–135	40–100	50–200
Watermelon	80–165	50–150	50–150

Adapted from Cornell recommendation for commercial vegetable production, New York Cooperative Extension Service (1986).

[1]Total amounts are listed; application may be broadcast and plow down, broadcast and disk in, band, or side-dress. Actual rate of fertilization depends on soil type, previous cropping history, and soil test results.

AVERAGE RATES OF FERTILIZER APPLIED TO VEGETABLE CROPS IN CALIFORNIA[1]

	Amount (lb/acre)		
Vegetable	N	P_2O_5	K_2O
Asparagus	142	52	22
Bean	77	61	33
Beet	110	54	28
Broccoli	182	80	49
Cabbage	131	84	41
Carrot	120	95	40
Cauliflower	183	93	63
Celery	287	123	101
Cucumber	121	60	54
Garlic	180	116	44
Lettuce	159	93	48
Muskmelon	95	56	20
Onion	146	83	34
Pepper	162	90	60
Potato	189	86	98
Tomato	121	80	55

Adapted from R. S. Rauschkolb and D. S. Mikkelsen, Survey of fertilizer use in California, University of California Division of Agricultural Science Bulletin 1887 (1978).

[1]The rates represent statewide average of fertilizer applied. The rates for P_2O_5 and K_2O are lower than recommended for use on deficient soils, because some soils do not require application of either phosphorus or potassium.

SOIL AND FOLIAR APPLICATION OF SECONDARY AND TRACE NUTRIENTS

Vegetables differ in their requirements for these secondary nutrients. Availability in the soil is influenced by soil reaction and soil type. Use higher rates on muck and peat soils than on mineral soils and lower rates for band application than for broadcast. Foliar application is one means of correcting an evident deficiency that appears while the crop is growing.

Nutrient	Nutrient Application Rate (per acre basis)	Nutrient Source	Composition
Boron	0.5–3.5 lb (soil)	Borax ($Na_2B_4O_7 \cdot 10H_2O$)	11% B
		Boric acid (H_3BO_3)	17% B
		Sodium pentaborate ($Na_2B_{10}O_{16} \cdot 10H_2O$)	18% B
		Sodium tetraborate ($Na_2B_4O_7$)	21% B
Calcium	2–5 lb (foliar)	Calcium chloride ($CaCl_2$)	36% Ca
		Calcium nitrate ($CaNO_3 \cdot 2H_2O$)	20% Ca
		Liming materials and gypsum supply calcium when used as soil amendments	
Copper	2–6 lb (soil)	Cupric chloride ($CuCl_2$)	47% Cu
		Copper sulfate ($CuSO_4 \cdot H_2O$)	35% Cu
		Copper sulfate ($CuSO_4 \cdot 5H_2O$)	25% Cu
		Cupric oxide (CuO)	80% Cu
		Cuprous oxide (Cu_2O)	89% Cu
		Copper chelates	8–13% Cu

SOIL AND FOLIAR APPLICATION OF SECONDARY AND TRACE NUTRIENTS—Continued

Vegetables differ in their requirements for these secondary nutrients. Availability in the soil is influenced by soil reaction and soil type. Use higher rates on muck and peat soils than on mineral soils and lower rates for band application than for broadcast. Foliar application is one means of correcting an evident deficiency that appears while the crop is growing.

Nutrient	Nutrient Application Rate (per acre basis)	Nutrient Source	Composition
Iron	2–4 lb (soil)	Ferrous sulfate ($FeSO_4 \cdot 7H_2O$)	20% Fe
	0.5–1 lb (foliar)	Ferric sulfate [$Fe_2(SO_4)_3 \cdot 9H_2O$]	20% Fe
		Ferrous carbonate ($FeCO_3 \cdot H_2O$)	42% Fe
		Iron chelates	5–12% Fe
Magnesium	25–30 lb (soil)	Magnesium sulfate ($MgSO_4 \cdot 7HO$)	10% Mg
	2–4 lb (foliar)	Magnesium oxide (MgO)	55% Mg
		Dolomitic limestone	11% Mg
		Magnesium chelates	2–4% Mg
Manganese	20–100 lb (soil)	Manganese sulfate ($MnSO_4 \cdot 3H_2O$)	27% Mn
	2–5 lb (foliar)	Manganous oxide (MnO)	41–68% Mn
		Manganese chelates (Mn EDTA)	12% Mn

Molybdenum	25–400 g (soil)	Ammonium molybdate [$(NH_4)_6Mo_7O_{24} \cdot 4H_2O$]	54% Mo
	25 g (foliar)	Sodium molybdate ($Na_2MoO_4 \cdot 2H_2O$)	39% Mo
Sulfur	20–50 lb (soil)	Sulfur (S)	100% S
		Ammonium sulfate [$(NH_4)_2SO_4$]	24% S
		Potassium sulfate (K_2SO_4)	18% S
		Calcium sulfate ($CaSO_4$)	16–18% S
		Ferric sulfate [$Fe_2(SO_4)_3$]	18–19% S
Zinc	2–10 lb (soil)	Zinc oxide (ZnO)	80% Zn
	0.25 lb (foliar)	Zinc sulfate ($ZnSO_4 \cdot 7H_2O$)	23% Zn
		Zinc chelates (Na_2Zn EDTA)	14% Zn

BORON RECOMMENDATIONS BASED ON SOIL TESTS FOR VEGETABLE CROPS

Interpretation of Boron Soil Tests				
ppm	lb/acre	Relative Level	Crops That Often Need Additional Boron	Boron Recommendations (lb/acre)
0.0–0.35	0.0–0.70	Low	Broccoli, cauliflower, celery	3
			Asparagus, beet, cabbage, carrot, eggplant, horseradish, rutabaga, squash, sweet corn, tomato, turnip	2
			Pepper, sweet potato	1
0.36–0.70	0.71–1.40	Medium	Broccoli, cauliflower, celery	1 ½
			Asparagus, beet, cabbage, carrot, eggplant, horseradish, rutabaga, squash, sweet corn, tomato, turnip	1
>0.70	>1.40	High	All crops	0

Adapted from Commercial vegetable production recommendations, Maryland Cooperative Extension Service EB-236 rev. (1986).

TOLERANCE OF VEGETABLES TO A DEFICIENCY OF MAGNESIUM IN THE SOIL

Tolerant	Not Tolerant
Bean	Cabbage
Beet	Corn
Chard	Cucumber
Lettuce	Eggplant
Pea	Muskmelon
Radish	Pepper
Sweet potato	Potato
	Pumpkin
	Rutabaga
	Tomato
	Watermelon

Adapted from W. S. Ritchie and E. B. Holland, Minerals in nutrition, Massachusetts Agricultural Experiment Station Bulletin 374 (1940).

A KEY TO NUTRIENT-DEFICIENCY SYMPTOMS

Nutrient	Plant Symptoms	Occurrence
Primary		
Nitrogen	Stems are thin, erect, and hard. Leaves are smaller than normal, pale green or yellow; lower leaves are affected first, but all leaves may be deficient in severe cases. Plants grow slowly	Excessive leaching on light soils
Phosphorus	Stems are thin and shortened. Leaves develop purple coloration, first on undersides and later throughout. Plants grow slowly, and maturity is delayed	On acid soils. Temporary deficiencies on cold, wet soils
Potassium	Older leaves develop gray or tan areas near the margins. Eventually a scorch around the entire leaf margin may occur. Chlorotic areas may develop throughout leaf	Excessive leaching on light soils
Secondary and Micronutrients		
Boron	Growing points die; stems are shortened and hard; leaves are distorted. Specific deficiencies include browning of cauliflower, cracked stem of celery, blackheart of beet, and internal browning of turnip	On soils with a pH above 6.8 or on crops with a high boron requirement
Calcium	Stem elongation restricted by death of the growing point. Root tips die and root growth is restricted. Specific deficiencies include blossom-end rot of tomato, brownheart of escarole, celery blackheart, and carrot cavity spot	On acid soils, following leaching rains, on soils with very high potassium levels, or on very dry soils

A KEY TO NUTRIENT-DEFICIENCY SYMPTOMS—Continued

Nutrient	Plant Symptoms	Occurrence
Secondary and Micronutrients		
Copper	Yellowing of leaves. Leaves may become elongated. Onion bulbs are soft, with thin, pale-yellow scales	Most cases of copper deficiency occur on muck or peat soils
Iron	Distinct yellow or white areas appear between the veins on the youngest leaves	On soils with a pH above 6.8
Magnesium	Initially, older leaves show yellowing between the veins; continued deficiency causes younger leaves to become affected. Older leaves may fall with prolonged deficiency	On acid soils, on soils with very high potassium levels, or on very light soils subject to leaching
Manganese	Yellow mottled areas, not as intense as with iron deficiency, appear on the youngest leaves. This finally results in an overall pale appearance. In beet, foliage becomes densely red. Onion and corn show narrow stripping of yellow	On soils with a pH above 6.7
Molybdenum	Pale, distorted, very narrow leaves with some interveinal yellowing on older leaves. Whiptail of cauliflower; small, open, loose curds	On very acid soils
Zinc	Small reddish-brown spots on cotyledon leaves of bean. Green and yellow broad stripping at base of leaves of corn. Interveinal yellowing with marginal burning on beet	On wet soils in early spring; often related to heavy phosphorus fertilization

Each time a distributer is used it is wise to check it to ensure that the proper quantity of fertilizer is being supplied. Fertilizers vary greatly in the way they flow through the equipment. Movement is influenced by the humidity of the atmosphere as well as the degree of granulation of the material.

Adjustment of Row Crop Distributor

1. Disconnect from one hopper, the downspout or tube to the furrow opener for a row.
2. Attach a can just below the fertilizer hopper.
3. Fill the hopper under which the can is placed.
4. Engage the fertilizer attachment and drive the tractor the suggested distance, according to the number of inches between rows.

Distance Between Rows (in.)	Distance to Pull the Distributor (ft)
20	261
24	218
30	174
36	145
38	138
40	131
42	124

5. Weigh the fertilizer in the can. Each pound in it equals 100 lb/acre. Each tenth of a pound equals 10 lb/acre.
6. Adjust the distributor for the rate of application desired, and then adjust the other distributor or distributors to the same setting.

Adjustment of Grain-Drill-Type Distributor

1. Remove four downspouts or tubes.
2. Attach a paper bag to each of the four outlets.
3. Fill the part of the drill over the bagged outlets.
4. Engage the distributor and drive the tractor the suggested distance, according to the inches between the drill rows.

ADJUSTMENT OF FERTILIZER DISTRIBUTORS—Continued

Adjustment of Grain-Drill-Type Distributor

Distance Between Drill Rows (in.)	Distance to Pull the Drill (ft)
7	187
8	164
10	131
12	109
14	94

5. Weigh total fertilizer in the four bags. Each pound equals 100 lb/acre. Each tenth of a pound equals 10 lb/acre.

CALIBRATION OF FERTILIZER DRILLS

Set drill at opening estimated to give the desired rate of application. Mark level of the fertilizer in the hopper. Operate the drill for 100 ft. Weigh a pail full of fertilizer. Refill hopper to marked level and again weigh pail. The difference is the pounds of fertilizer used in 100 ft. Consult the column under the row spacing you are using. The left-hand column opposite the amount you used will then show the rate in pounds per acre at which the fertilizer has been applied. Adjust setting of the drill if necessary and re-check.

Distance Between Rows (in.):	18	24	20	36	48
Rate (lb/acre)	Approximate Amount of Fertilizer (lb/100 ft of row)				
250	0.9	1.1	1.4	1.7	2.3
500	1.7	2.3	2.9	3.5	4.6
750	2.6	3.4	4.3	5.2	6.9
1000	3.5	4.6	5.8	6.9	9.2
1500	5.2	6.8	8.6	10.4	13.8
2000	6.8	9.2	11.6	13.0	18.4
3000	10.5	14.0	17.5	21.0	28.0

PART 5
WATER AND IRRIGATION

ROOTING OF VEGETABLES

SOIL MOISTURE

SURFACE IRRIGATION

OVERHEAD IRRIGATION

DRIP OR TRICKLE IRRIGATION

WATER QUALITY

WATER AND SOIL SOLUTION CONVERSION FACTORS

POWER AND ENERGY CONVERSION FACTORS

SUGGESTIONS ON SUPPLYING WATER TO VEGETABLES

Plants in hot, dry areas lose more moisture into the air than those in cooler, more humid areas. Vegetables utilize and evaporate more water in the later stages of growth when size and leaf area are greater. The root system becomes deeper and more widespread as the plant ages.

Some vegetables, especially lettuce and sweet corn, have sparse root systems that do not come into contact with all the soil moisture in their root-depth zone. Cool-season vegetables normally root to a shallower depth than do warm-season vegetables and perennials.

When applying water, use enough to bring the soil-moisture content of the effective rooting zone of the crop up to field capacity. This is the quantity of water that the soil will hold against the pull of gravity.

The frequency of irrigation will depend on the total supply of available moisture reached by the roots and the rate of water use. The first is affected by soil type, depth of wetted soil, and the depth and dispersion of roots. The latter is influenced by weather conditions and the age of the crops. Add water when the moisture in the root zone has been used to about the half-way point in the range of available moisture. Do not wait until vegetables show signs of wilting or develop color or texture changes that indicate they are not growing rapidly.

A general rule is that vegetables will need about 1 in. of water per week from rain or supplemental irrigation in order to grow vigorously. In arid regions about 2 in./week is required.

ROOTING DEPTH OF VEGETABLES

The depth of rooting of vegetables is influenced by the soil profile. If there is a clay pan, hard pan, compacted layer, or other dense formation, the normal depth of rooting is not possible.

CHARACTERISTIC ROOTING DEPTHS OF VARIOUS VEGETABLES

Shallow (18–24 in.)	Moderately Deep (36–48 in.)	Deep (More than 48 in.)
Broccoli	Bean, bush	Artichoke
Brussels sprouts	Bean, pole	Asparagus
Cabbage	Beet	Bean, Lima
Cauliflower	Carrot	Parsnip
Celery	Chard	Pumpkin
Chinese cabbage	Cucumber	Squash, winter
Corn	Eggplant	Sweet potato
Endive	Muskmelon	Tomato
Garlic	Mustard	Watermelon
Leek	Pea	
Lettuce	Pepper	
Onion	Rutabaga	
Parsley	Squash, summer	
Potato	Turnip	
Radish		
Spinach		
Strawberry		

DETERMINING MOISTURE IN SOIL BY APPEARANCE OR FEEL

A shovel will serve to obtain a soil sample from a shallow soil or when a shallow-rooted crop is being grown. A soil auger or soil tube is necessary to draw samples from great depths in the root zone.

Squeeze the soil sample in the hand and compare its behavior with those of the soils listed in the Practical Soil-Moisture Interpretation Chart to get a rough idea of its moisture content.

PRACTICAL SOIL-MOISTURE INTERPRETATION CHART

Amount of Readily Available Moisture Remaining for the Plant	Sand (gritty when moist, almost like beach sand)	Sandy Loam (gritty when moist; dirties fingers; contains some silt and clay)	Clay Loam (sticky and plastic when moist)	Clay (very sticky when moist; behaves like modeling clay)
Close to 0%. Little or no moisture available	Dry, loose, single-grained; flows through fingers	Dry, loose, flows through fingers	Dry clods that break down into powdery condition	Hard, baked, cracked surface. Hard clods difficult to break, sometimes has loose crumbs on surface
50% or less. Approaching time to irrigate	Still appears to be dry; will not form a ball with pressure	Still appears to be dry; will not form a ball	Somewhat crumbly, but will hold together with pressure	Somewhat pliable; will ball under pressure

50%–75%. Enough available moisture	Same as sand under 50%	Tends to ball under pressure but seldom will hold together	Forms a ball, somewhat plastic; will sometimes stick slightly with pressure	Forms a ball; will ribbon out between thumb and forefinger
75% to field capacity. Plenty of available moisture	Tends to stick together slightly, sometimes forms a very weak ball under pressure	Forms weak ball, breaks easily, will not become slick	Forms a ball and is very pliable; becomes slick readily if high in clay	Easily ribbons out between fingers; feels slick
At field capacity. Soil will not hold any more water (after draining)	Upon squeezing, no free water appears; but moisture is left on hand	Same as sand	Same as sand	Same as sand
Above field capacity. Unless water drains out, soil will be water-logged	Free water appears when soil is bounced in hand	Free water will be released with kneading	Can squeeze out free water	Puddles and free water form on surface

Adapted from R. W. Harris, and R. H. Coppock (eds.), Saving water in landscape irrigation, University of California Division of Agricultural Science Leaflet 2976 (1978).

APPROXIMATE SOIL-WATER CHARACTERISTICS FOR TYPICAL SOIL CLASSES

Characteristic	Sandy Soil	Loamy Soil	Clayey Soil
Dry weight 1 cu ft	90 lb	80 lb	75 lb
Field capacity—% of dry weight	10%	20%	35%
Permanent wilting percentage	5%	10%	19%
Percent available water	5%	10%	16%
Water available to plants			
lb/cu ft	4 lb	8 lb	12 lb
in./ft depth	¾ in.	1½ in.	2¼ in.
gal/cu ft	½ gal	1 gal	1½ gal
Approximate depth of soil that will be wetted by each 1 in. of water applied if half the available water has been used	24 in.	16 in.	11 in.
Suggested lengths of irrigation runs	330 ft	660 ft	1320 ft

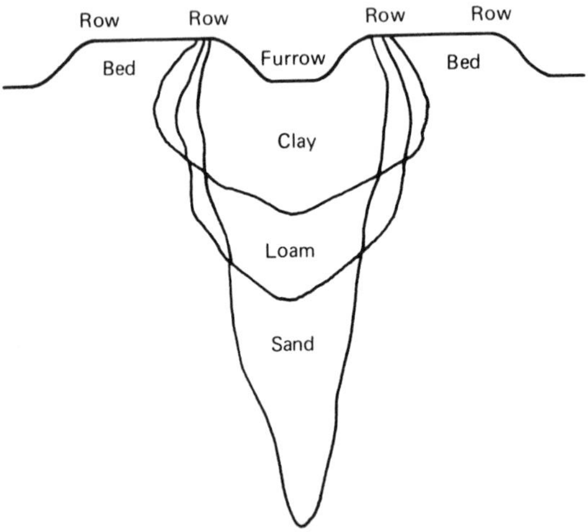

Arrangement of beds for furrow irrigation. Beds intended for two rows are usually on 36-, 40-, or 42-in. centers, with the surface 4–6 in. above the bottom of the furrow. The depth of penetration of an equal quantity of water varies with the class of soil as indicated.

RATES OF WATER APPLICATION FOR VARIOUS IRRIGATION METHODS

The infiltration rate has an important bearing on the rapidity with which water should be applied by any method of irrigation.

Normally, sandy soils have a high infiltration rate and clay soils have a low one. The rate is affected by soil texture, structure, dispersion, and the depth of the water table. The longer the water is allowed to run, the more the infiltration rate decreases.

With furrows, use a flow of water initially two to three times that indicated to fill the run as quickly as possible. Then cut back the flow to the indicated amount. This prevents excessive penetration at the head and equalizes the application of water throughout the whole furrow.

APPROXIMATE FLOW OF WATER PER FURROW AFTER IT HAS REACHED END OF THE FURROW

	Slope of Land (%):	0–0.2	0.2–0.5	0.5–1
Infiltration Rate of Soil (in./hr)	Length of Furrow (ft)	Flow of Water per Furrow (gal/min)		
High (1.5 or more)	330	9	4	3
	660	20	9	7
	1320	45	20	15
Medium (0.5–1.5)	330	4	3	1.5
	660	10	7	3.5
	1320	25	15	7.5
Low (0.1–0.5)	330	2	1.5	1
	660	4	3.5	2
	1320	9	7.5	4

SUGGESTED MAXIMUM WATER INFILTRATION RATES FOR VARIOUS SOIL TYPES

Soil Type	Infiltration Rate[1] (in./hr)
Sand	2.0
Loamy sand	1.8
Sandy loam	1.5
Loam	1.0
Silt and clay loam	0.5
Clay	0.2

[1]Assumes a full crop cover. For bare soil reduce the rate by one-half.

PERCENT OF AVAILABLE WATER DEPLETED FROM SOILS AT VARIOUS TENSIONS

Tension — less than— (bars)[1]	Loamy Sand	Sandy Loam	Loam	Clay
0.3	55	35	15	7
0.5	70	55	30	13
0.8	77	63	45	20
1.0	82	68	55	27
2.0	90	78	72	45
5.0	95	88	80	75
15.0	100	100	100	100

Adapted from Cooperative Extension, University of California Soil and Water Newsletter No. 26 (1975).

[1]1 bar = 100 kilopascals

SPRINKLER IRRIGATION: APPROXIMATE APPLICATION OF WATER

Infiltration Rate of Soil (in./hr)	Slope of Land (%): 0–5	5–12
	Approximate Application (in./hr)	
High (1.5 or more)	1.0	0.75
Medium (0.5–1.5)	0.5	0.40
Low (0.1–0.5)	0.2	0.15

BASIN IRRIGATION: APPROXIMATE AREA

Infiltration Rate of Soil (in./hr)	Quantity of Water to be Supplied: 450 gal/min or 1 cu ft/sec	900 gal/min or 2 cu ft/sec
	Approximate Area (acre/basin)	
High (1.5 or more)	0.1	0.2
Medium (0.5–1.5)	0.2	0.4
Low (0.1–0.5)	0.5	1.0

VOLUME OF WATER APPLIED FOR VARIOUS FLOW RATES AND TIME PERIODS

	Volume (acre-in.) Applied			
Flow Rate (gpm)	1 hr	8 hr	12 hr	1 Day
25	0.06	0.44	0.66	1.33
50	0.11	0.88	1.33	2.65
100	0.22	1.77	2.65	5.30
200	0.44	3.54	5.30	10.60
300	0.66	5.30	7.96	15.90
400	0.88	7.07	10.60	2.12
500	1.10	8.84	13.30	26.50
1000	2.21	17.70	26.50	53.00
1500	3.32	26.50	39.80	79.60
2000	4.42	35.40	53.00	106.00

Adapted from A. Smajstila and D. S. Harrison, Florida Cooperative Extension, Agricultural Engineering Fact Sheet AE18 (1982).

APPROXIMATE TIME REQUIRED TO APPLY VARIOUS DEPTHS OF WATER PER ACRE WITH DIFFERENT FLOWS[1]

Flow of Water			Approximate Time Required per Acre for a Depth of:							
			1 in.		2 in.		3 in.		4 in.	
gpm	sec-ft	Approximate acre-in./hr	hr	min	hr	min	hr	min	hr	min
50	0.11	1/8	9	03	18	06	27	09	36	12
100	0.22	1/4	4	32	9	03	13	35	18	06
150	0.33	5/16	3	01	6	02	9	03	12	04
200	0.45	7/16	2	16	4	32	6	47	9	03
250	0.56	9/16	1	49	3	37	5	26	7	14
300	0.67	11/16	1	31	3	01	4	32	6	02
350	0.78	3/4	1	18	2	35	3	53	5	10
400	0.89	7/8	1	08	2	16	3	24	4	32
450	1.00	1	1	00	2	01	3	01	4	01
500	1.11	1 1/8		54	1	49	2	43	3	37
550	1.23	1 3/16		49	1	39	2	28	3	18
600	1.34	1 5/16		45	1	31	2	16	3	01
650	1.45	1 7/16		42	1	24	2	05	2	48

APPROXIMATE TIME REQUIRED TO APPLY VARIOUS DEPTHS OF WATER PER ACRE WITH DIFFERENT FLOWS[1]—Continued

Flow of Water			Approximate Time Required per Acre for a Depth of:							
			1 in.		2 in.		3 in.		4 in.	
gpm	sec-ft	Approximate acre-in./hr	hr	min	hr	min	hr	min	hr	min
700	1.56	$1\frac{9}{16}$		39	1	18	1	56	2	35
750	1.67	$1\frac{21}{32}$		36	1	12	1	49	2	24
800	1.78	$1\frac{3}{4}$		34	1	08	1	42	2	16
850	1.89	$1\frac{7}{8}$		32	1	04	1	36	2	08
900	2.01	2		30	1	00	1	31	2	01
950	2.12	$2\frac{3}{32}$		29		57	1	26	1	54
1000	2.23	$2\frac{3}{16}$		27		54	1	21	1	49
1050	2.34	$2\frac{5}{16}$		26		52	1	18	1	44
1100	2.45	$2\frac{7}{16}$		25		49	1	14	1	38
1150	2.56	$2\frac{1}{2}$		24		47	1	11	1	34
1200	2.67	$2\frac{5}{8}$		23		45	1	08	1	31
1300	2.90	$2\frac{7}{8}$		21		42	1	03	1	24
1400	3.12	$3\frac{1}{16}$		20		39		58	1	18
1500	3.34	$3\frac{5}{16}$		18		36		54	1	12

[1]If a sprinkler system is used the time required should be increased by 2–10% to compensate for the water that will evaporate before reaching the soil.

TO DETERMINE THE WATER NEEDED TO WET VARIOUS DEPTHS OF SOIL

Example: You wish to wet a loam soil to a 12-in. depth when half the available water in that zone is gone. Move across the chart from the left on the 12-in. line. Stop when you reach the diagonal line marked "loams." Move upward from that point to the scale at the top of the chart. You will see that about ¾ in. of water is needed.

Depth of water required, inches, based on depletion of about half the available water in the effective root zone.

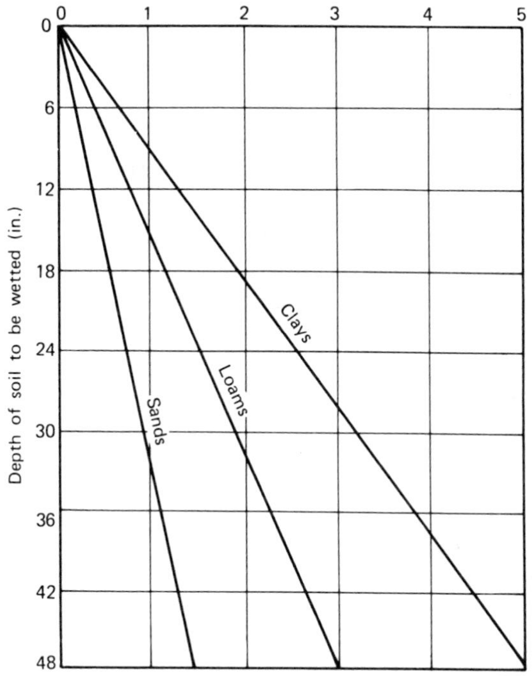

Chart for determining the amount of water needed to wet various depths of soil.

Siphons of metal, plastic, or rubber can be used to carry water from a ditch to the area or furrow to be irrigated.

The inside diameter of the pipe and the head—the vertical distance from the surface of the water in the ditch to the surface of the water on the outlet side—determine the rate of flow.

When the outlet is not submerged, the head is measured to the center of the siphon outlet. You can determine how many gallons per minute are flowing through each siphon from the chart below.

Example: You have a head of 4 in. and are using 2-in. siphons. Follow the 4-in. line across the chart until you reach the curve for 2-in. siphons. Move straight down to the scale at the bottom. You will find that you are putting on about 28 gal/minute.

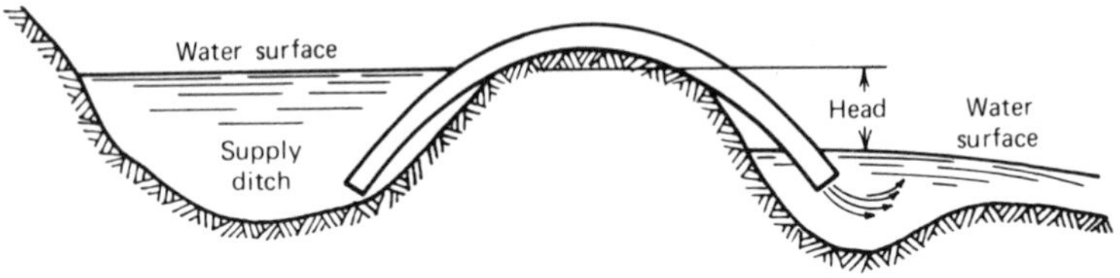

Method of measuring the head for water carried from a supply ditch to a furrow by means of a siphon. Adapted from University of California Division of Agricultural Science Leaflet 2956 (1977).

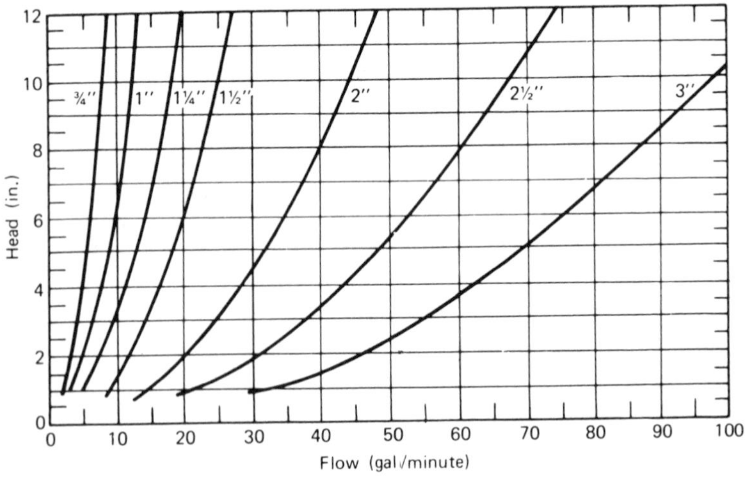

Chart for determining the flow of water through small siphons. Adapted from University of California Division of Agricultural Science Leaflet 2956 (1977).

APPLICATION OF FERTILIZER IN WATER FOR FURROW IRRIGATION

There are certain limitations to the method of applying fertilizer solutions or soluble fertilizers in water supplied by furrow irrigation. You do not get uniform distribution of the fertilizer over the whole irrigated area. More of the dissolved material may enter the soil near the head than at the end of the furrow. You must know how long it will be necessary to run water in order to irrigate a certain area so as to meter out the fertilizer solution properly. Soils vary considerably in their ability to absorb water.

Fertilizer solutions can be dripped from containers into the water. Devices are available that meter dry fertilizer materials into the irrigation water where they dissolve.

The rate of flow of dry soluble fertilizer or of fertilizer solutions into an irrigation head ditch can be calculated as follows:

$$\frac{\text{Area to be irrigated (acres/hr)} \times \text{amount of nutrient wanted (lb/acre)}}{\text{nutrients in solution (lb/gal)}} = \text{flow rate of fertilizer solution (gal/hr)}$$

$$\frac{\text{Area to be irrigated (acres)} \times \text{amount of soluble fertilizer (lb/acre or gal/acre)}}{\text{time of irrigation (hr)}} = \text{flow rate of fertilizer solution (lb/hr or gal/hr)}$$

Knowing the gallons of solution per hour that are to be added to the irrigation water, you can adjust the flow from the tank as directed by the following table.

RATE OF FLOW OF FERTILIZER SOLUTIONS

Amount of Solution Desired (gal/hr)	Approximate Time (sec) to Fill a 4-oz Jar	Approximate Time (sec) to Fill an 8-oz Jar
½	225	450
1	112	224
2	56	112
3	38	76
4	28	56
5	22	44
6	18	36
7	16	32
8	14	28
9	12	24
10	11	22
12	9	18
14	8	16
16	7	14
18	6	12
20	5.5	11

LAYOUT OF A SPRINKLER SYSTEM

Each irrigation system presents a separate engineering problem. The advice of a competent engineer is essential. Many factors must be taken into consideration in developing a plan for the equipment:

Water supply available at period of greatest use.

Distance from source of water to field to be irrigated.

Height of field above water source and topography of the land.

Type of soil (rate at which it will absorb water and its water-holding capacity).

Area to be irrigated.

Desired frequency of irrigation.

Quantity of water to be applied.

Time in which application is to be made.

Type of power available.

Normal wind velocity and direction.

Possible future expansion of the installation.

Specific details of the plan must then include the following:

Size of power unit and pump to do the particular job.

Pipe sizes and lengths for mains and laterals.

Operating pressures of sprinklers.

Size and spacing of sprinklers.

Friction losses in the system.

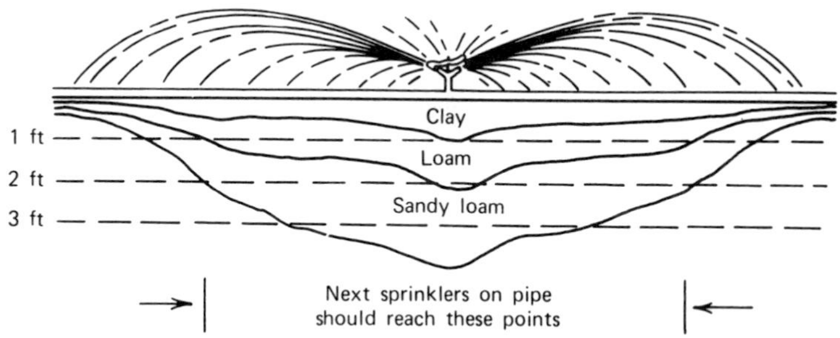

To avoid uneven water distribution, there should be enough distance between sprinklers to allow a 40% overlap in diameter of the area they are to cover. The diagram shows the approximate depth of penetration of available water from a 3-in. irrigation on various classes of soil.

ACREAGE COVERED BY MOVES OF PIPE OF VARIOUS LENGTHS

Lateral Move of Pipe (ft)	Length of Sprinkler Pipe (ft)	Area Covered per Move (acres)
20	2640	1.21
20	1320	0.61
20	660	0.30
20	330	0.15
30	2640	1.82
30	1320	0.91
30	660	0.46
30	330	0.23
40	2640	2.42
40	1320	1.21
40	660	0.61
40	330	0.30
50	2640	3.03
50	1320	1.52
50	660	0.76
50	330	0.38
60	2640	3.64
60	1320	1.82
60	660	0.91
60	330	0.46
80	2640	4.85
80	1320	2.42
80	660	1.21
80	330	0.61
100	2640	6.06
100	1320	3.03
100	660	1.52
100	330	0.76

CALCULATION OF RATES OF SPRINKLER APPLICATIONS

To determine the output per sprinkler you need to put on your desired rate of application:

$$\frac{\text{Distance between sprinklers (ft)} \times \text{distance between line settings (ft)} \times \text{precipitation rate (in./hr)}}{96.3}$$

$= \text{sprinkler rate (gal/minute)}$

Example: $\dfrac{30 \times 50 \times 0.4}{96.3} = 6.23$ gal/minute per sprinkler

To determine the rate at which you are applying water:

$$\frac{\text{Sprinkler rate (gal/minute)} \times 96.3}{\text{Distance between sprinklers (ft)} \times \text{distance between line settings (ft)}} = \text{precipitation rate (in./hr)}$$

Manufacturer's specifications give the gallons per minute for each type of sprinkler at various pressures.

Example: $\dfrac{10 \times 96.3}{40 \times 50} = 0.481$ in./hr

PRECIPITATION RATES FOR VARIOUS NOZZLE SIZES, PRESSURE, AND SPACINGS

Nozzle Size (in.)	Pressure (psi)	Discharge[1] (gpm)	Diameter of Spray[2] (ft)	Precipitation Rate at Spacings (in./hr)[1]		
				30 × 40 ft	30 × 45 ft	40 × 40 ft
1/16	45	0.76	60–72	0.061		
1/16	50	0.80	61–73	0.064		
1/16	55	0.85	62–74	0.068		
1/16	60	0.88	63–75	0.071		
1/16	65	0.93	64–76	0.075		
5/64	45	1.19	59–73	0.095	0.085	
5/64	50	1.25	62–72	0.100	0.089	
5/64	55	1.30	64–74	0.104	0.094	0.079
5/64	60	1.36	67–76	0.110	0.097	0.082
5/64	65	1.45	68–77	0.116	0.103	0.087

3/32	45	1.72	68–76	0.138	0.123	0.103
3/32	50	1.80	69–77	0.145	0.128	0.108
3/32	55	1.88	70–78	0.151	0.134	0.113
3/32	60	1.98	71–79	0.159	0.141	0.119
3/32	65	2.08	72–80	0.167	0.148	0.125
7/64	45	2.32	71–78	0.186	0.165	0.140
7/64	50	2.44	72–80	0.196	0.174	0.147
7/64	55	2.56	74–81	0.205	0.182	0.154
7/64	60	2.69	76–82	0.216	0.192	0.161
7/64	65	2.79	77–83	0.224	0.199	0.168
1/8	45	3.04	76–82	0.244	0.217	0.183
1/8	50	3.22	78–82		0.230	0.193
1/8	55	3.39	79–83		0.242	0.204
1/8	60	3.55	80–84		0.253	0.213
1/8	65	3.70	81–85			0.222

Adapted from A. W. Marsh et al., Solid set sprinklers for starting vegetable crops, University of California Division of Agricultural Science Leaflet 2265 (1977).

[1]Three-digit numbers are shown here only to indicate the progression as nozzle size and pressure increase.

[2]Range of diameters of spray for different makes and models of sprinklers.

GUIDE FOR SELECTING SIZE OF ALUMINUM PIPE FOR SPRINKLER LATERAL LINES

Sprinkler Discharge (gpm)	Maximum Number of Sprinklers to Use on Single Lateral Line: 30-ft Sprinkler Spacing for Pipe Diameter (in.): 2	3	4	40-ft Sprinkler Spacing for Pipe Diameter (in.): 2	3	4
0.75	47	95	200	43	85	180
1.00	40	80	150	36	72	125
1.25	34	69	118	31	62	104
1.50	30	62	100	28	56	92
1.75	27	56	92	25	50	83
2.00	25	51	84	23	46	76
2.25	23	47	78	21	43	71
2.50	21	44	73	19	40	66
2.75	20	42	68	18	38	62
3.00	19	40	65	17	36	58
3.25	18	38	62	16	34	56
3.50	17	36	59	15	32	53
3.75	16	34	56	14	31	51
4.00	16	33	54	14	30	48

Adapted from A. W. Marsh et al., Solid set sprinklers for starting vegetable crops, University of California Division of Agricultural Science Leaflet 2265 (1977).

GUIDE TO MAIN-LINE PIPE SIZES[1]

Distance (ft)	Water Flow (gpm) for Pipe Diameter (in.): 200	400	600	800	1000	1200	1400	1600	1800
200	3	4	5	5	6	6	6	7	7
400	4	5	5	6	6	7	7	8	8
600	4	5	6	7	7	7	8	8	8
800	4	5	6	7	7	8	8	8	10
1000	5	6	6	7	8	8	8	10	10
1200	5	6	7	7	8	8	10	10	10

Adapted from A. W. Marsh et al., Solid set sprinklers for starting vegetable crops, University of California Division of Agricultural Science Leaflet 2265 (1977).

[1] Using aluminum pipe (C = 120) with pressure losses ranging from 5 to 15 psi, average about 10.

CONTINUOUS POWER OUTPUT REQUIRED AT TRACTOR POWER TAKEOFF TO PUMP WATER

Pressure[1] (psi)	Head[1] (ft)	Flow (gpm) 100	200	300	400	500	600	700	800	1000
		Horsepower Required[2]								
50	116	3.9	7.8	11.7	16	20	23	27	31	39
55	128	4.3	8.7	13	17	22	26	30	35	43
60	140	4.7	9.5	14	19	24	28	33	38	47
65	151	5.1	10	15	20	25	30	36	41	51
70	162	5.5	11	16	22	27	33	38	44	55
75	173	5.8	12	17	23	29	35	41	47	58
80	185	6.2	12	19	25	31	37	44	50	62

Adapted from A. W. Marsh et al., Solid set sprinklers for starting vegetable crops, University of California Division of Agricultural Science Leaflet 2265 (1977).

[1] Including nozzle pressure, friction loss, and elevation lift.
[2] Pump assumed to operate at 75% efficiency.

FLOW OF WATER REQUIRED TO OPERATE SOLID SET SPRINKLER SYSTEMS

	Area Irrigated per Set (acres)									
Irrigation rate (in./hr)	4		8		12		16		20	
	gpm[1]	cfs[2]	gpm	cfs	gpm	cfs	gpm	cfs	gpm	cfs
0.06	108	0.5	217	0.5	326	1.0	435	1.0	543	1.5
0.08	145	0.5	290	1.0	435	1.0	580	1.5	725	2.0
0.10	181	0.5	362	1.0	543	1.5	724	2.0	905	2.5
0.12	217	0.5	435	1.0	652	1.5	870	2.0	1086	2.5
0.15	271	1.0	543	1.5	815	2.0	1086	2.5	1360	3.5
0.20	362	1.0	724	2.0	1086	2.5	1448	2.5	1810	4.5

Adapted from A. W. Marsh et al., Solid set sprinklers for starting vegetable crops, University of California Division of Agricultural Science Leaflet 2265 (1977).

[1] Gallons per minute pumped into the sprinkler system to provide an average precipitation rate as shown. Pump must have this much or slightly greater capacity.

[2] Cubic feet per second—the flow of water to the next larger 1/2 cfs that must be ordered from the water district, assuming that the district accepts orders only in increments of 1/2 cfs. Actually, 1/2 cfs = 225 gpm.

APPLYING FERTILIZER THROUGH A SPRINKLER SYSTEM

Anhydrous ammonia, aqua ammonia, and nitrogen solutions containing free ammonia should not be applied by sprinkler irrigation because of the excessive loss of the volatile ammonia. Ammonium nitrate, ammonium sulfate, calcium nitrate, sodium nitrate, and urea are all suitable materials for use through a sprinkler system. The water containing the ammonia salts should not have a reaction that is on the alkaline side of neutrality or the loss of ammonia will be considerable.

It is best to put phosphorus fertilizers directly in the soil by a band application. Potash fertilizers can be used in sprinkler lines. However, a soil application ahead of or at planting time will usually prove adequate and can be made efficiently at that time.

Manganese, boron, or copper can be applied through the sprinkler system. See page 147 for possible rates of application.

The fertilizing material is dissolved in a tank of water. Calcium nitrate, ammonium sulfate, and ammonium nitrate will dissolve completely. The solution can then be introduced into the water line, either by suction or by pressure from a pump. See page 119 for relative solubility of fertilizer materials.

Introduce the fertilizer into the line slowly, taking 10–20 min to complete the operation.

After enough of the fertilizer solution has passed into the pipe lines, shut the valve if suction by pump has been used. This prevents unpriming the pump. Then run the system for 10–15 min to wash the fertilizer off the leaves. This will also flush out the lines, valves, and pump if one has been used to force or suck the solution into the main line.

AMOUNT OF FERTILIZER TO USE FOR EACH SETTING OF THE SPRINKLER LINE

Length of Line (ft)	Lateral Move of Line (ft)	Nutrient per Setting of Sprinkler Line (lb): 10	20	30	40	50	60	70	80	90	100
		Nutrient Application Desired (lb/acre)									
330	40	3	6	9	12	15	18	21	24	27	30
	60	4	9	12	18	22	27	31	36	40	45
	80	6	12	18	24	30	36	42	48	54	60
660	40	6	12	18	24	30	36	42	48	54	60
	60	9	18	24	36	45	54	63	72	81	90
	80	12	24	36	48	60	72	84	96	108	120
990	40	9	18	24	36	45	54	63	72	81	90
	60	13	27	40	54	67	81	94	108	121	135
	80	18	36	54	72	90	108	126	144	162	180
1320	40	12	24	36	48	60	72	84	96	108	120
	60	18	36	54	72	90	108	126	144	162	180
	80	24	48	72	96	120	144	168	192	216	240

It is necessary to calculate the actual pounds of a fertilizing material that must be dissolved in the mixing tank in order to supply a certain number of pounds of the nutrient to the acre at each setting of the sprinkler line. This is done as follows. To apply 40 lb of nitrogen to the acre when the sprinkler line is 660 ft long and will be moved 80 ft, if sodium nitrate is used, divide 48 (as shown in the table) by 0.16 (the percentage of nitrogen in sodium nitrate). This equals 300 lb, which must be dissolved in the tank and applied at each setting of the pipe. Do the same with ammonium nitrate: divide 48 by 0.33, which equals about 145 lbs.

METHODS OF INJECTING FERTILIZER AND OTHER CHEMICAL SOLUTIONS INTO IRRIGATION PIPELINE

There are three principal methods used to inject fertilizers and other solutions into drip-irrigation systems: (1) pressure differential; (2) the venturi (vacuum); and (3) metering pumps. It is essential that drip-irrigation systems equipped with a chemical injection system have a vacuum breaker (anti-siphon device) and a backflow preventer (check valve) installed upstream from the injection point. The vacuum-breaking valve and backflow preventer will prevent chemical contamination of the water source in case of a water pressure loss or power failure.

METHODS FOR INJECTION OF FERTILIZERS AND OTHER SOLUTIONS INTO DRIP IRRIGATION SYSTEMS

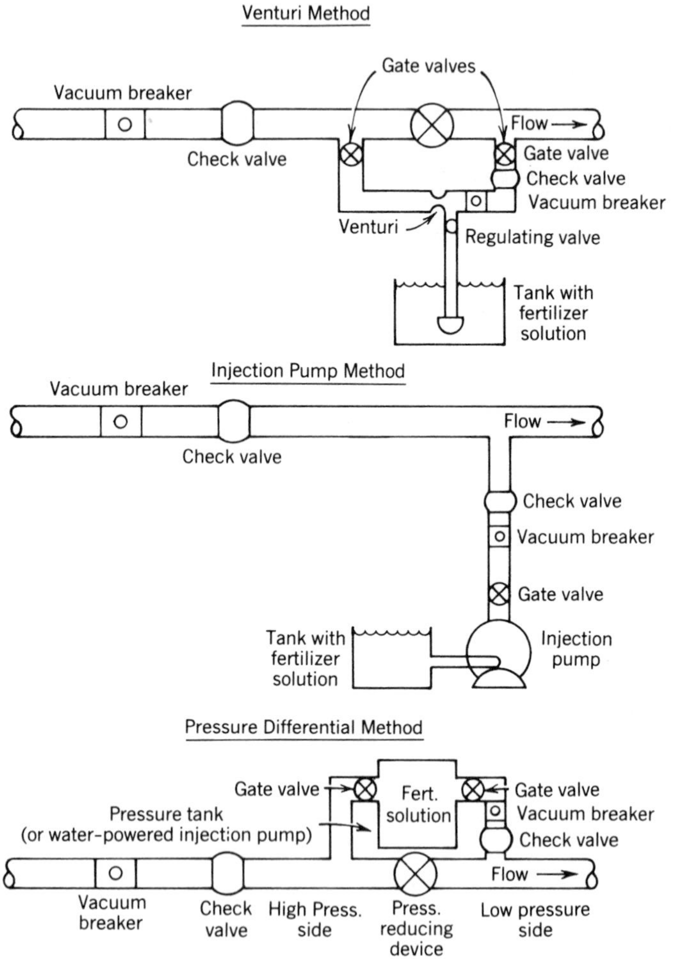

Adapted from S. P. Kovach, Injection of fertilizers into drip irrigation systems for vegetables, Florida Cooperative Extension Service Circular 606 (1984).

SPRINKLER IRRIGATION FOR COLD PROTECTION

Sprinklers are often used to protect vegetables from freezing. Sprinkling provides cold protection because the latent heat of fusion is released when water changes from liquid to ice. When water is freezing, its temperature is near 32°F. The heat liberated as the water freezes maintains the temperature of the vegetable near 32°F even though the surroundings may be colder. As long as there is a mixture of both water and ice present, the temperature remains near 32°F. For all of the plant to be protected, it must be covered or encased in the freezing ice–water mixture. Enough water must be applied so that the latent heat released will compensate for the heat losses.

APPLICATION RATE RECOMMENDED FOR COLD PROTECTION UNDER DIFFERENT WIND AND TEMPERATURE CONDITIONS

Minimum Temperature Expected (°F)	Wind Speed (mph)		
	0–1	2–4	5–8
27	0.10	0.10	0.10
26	0.10	0.10	0.14
24	0.10	0.16	0.30
22	0.12	0.24	0.50
20	0.16	0.30	0.60

Adapted from D. S. Harrison, J. F. Gerber, and R. E. Choate, Sprinkler irrigation for cold protection, Florida Cooperative Extension Circular 348 (1974).

Drip or trickle irrigation refers to the frequent slow application of water directly to the base of the plants. Vegetables are usually irrigated by double-wall or by thin-wall tubing to supply a uniform rate along the entire row.

Pressure in the drip lines varies from 1 to 3 psi and about 12 psi in the submains. Length of the drip lines may be as long as 600 ft but 200–250 ft is more common. Rate of water application is about 1/4 gpm/100 ft of row. One acre of plants in rows 100 ft long and 4 ft apart will use about 30 gpm of water. Unless clear sediment-free water is available, it is necessary to install a filter in the main line in order to prevent clogging of the small pores in the drip lines.

Drip irrigation allows for considerable saving in water application, particularly during early plant growth. Because water is applied only next to plants in the row, the aisles between rows remain dry.

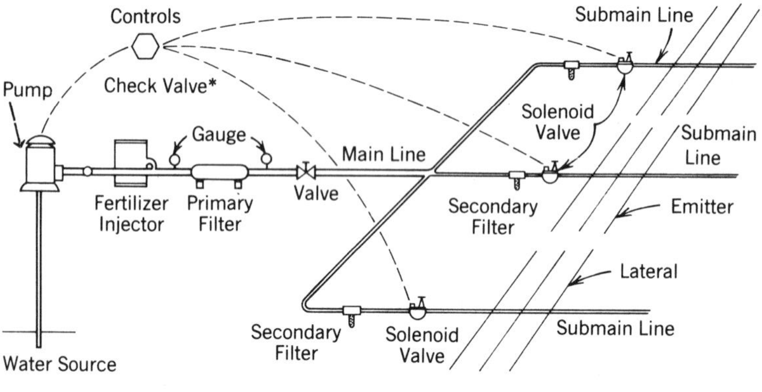

*A backflow preventer or vacuum breaker is required in some areas.

Drip or trickle irrigation system components.

WATER QUALITY GUIDELINES FOR IRRIGATION[1]

Type of Problem	Degree of Problem		
	None	Increasing	Severe
Salinity			
EC (dS/m) or	Less than 0.75	0.75–3.0	More than 3.0
TDS (mg/liter)	Less than 480	480–1920	More than 1920
Permeability			
Low EC (dS/m) or	More than 0.5	0.5–0	—
Low TDS (mg/liter)	More than 320	320–0	—
SAR	Less than 6.0	6.0–9.0	More than 9.0
Toxicity of Specific Ions to Sensitive Crops			
ROOT ABSORPTION			
Sodium (evaluated by SAR)	SAR less than 3	3–9	More than 9

WATER QUALITY GUIDELINES FOR IRRIGATION[1]—Continued

Type of Problem	Degree of Problem		
	None	Increasing	Severe
Toxicity of Specific Ions to Sensitive Crops			
Chloride			
meq/liter	Less than 2	2–10	More than 10
mg/liter	Less than 70	70–345	More than 345
Boron (mg/liter)	1.0	1.0–2.0	2.0–10.0
RELATED TO FOLIAR ADSORPTION (SPRINKLER IRRIGATED)			
Sodium			
meq/liter	Less than 3.0	More than 3	—
mg/liter	Less than 70	70	—
Chloride			
meq/liter	Less than 3.0	More than 3	—
mg/liter	Less than 100	100	—
MISCELLANEOUS			
NH_4 and NO_3-N (mg/liter)	Less than 5	5–30	More than 30
HCO_3			
meq/liter	Less than 1.0	1.5–8.5	More than 8.5
mg/liter	Less than 40	40–520	More than 520
pH	Normal range: 6.5–8.3	More than 8.3	—

Adapted from D. S. Farnham, R. F. Hasek, and J. L. Paul, Water quality, University of California Division of Agricultural Science Leaflet 2995 (1985).

[1] Interpretation is related to type of problem and its severity, but is modified by circumstances of soil, crop, and locality.

MAXIMUM CONCENTRATIONS OF TRACE ELEMENTS IN IRRIGATION WATERS

Element	For Waters Used Continuously on All Soils (mg/liter)	For Use up to 20 Years on Fine-Textured Soils of pH 6.0–8.5 (mg/liter)
Aluminum	5.0	20.0
Arsenic	0.10	2.0
Beryllium	0.10	0.50
Boron	0.75	2.0–10.0
Cadmium	0.01	0.05
Chromium	0.10	1.0
Cobalt	0.05	5.0
Copper	0.20	5.0
Fluoride	1.0	15.0
Iron	5.0	20.0
Lead	5.0	10.0
Lithium	2.5	2.5
Manganese	0.20	10.0
Molybdenum	0.01	0.05[1]
Nickel	0.20	2.0
Selenium	0.02	0.02
Vanadium	0.10	1.0
Zinc	2.00	10.0

Adapted from D. S. Farnham, R. F. Hasek, and J. L. Paul, Water quality, University of California Division of Agricultural Science Leaflet 2995 (1985).

[1] Only for acid, fine-textured soils or acid soils with relatively high iron oxide contents.

YIELD LOSS EXPECTED OWING TO SALINITY OF IRRIGATION WATER

Crop	Electrical Conductivity of Water (mmho/cm or dS/m) for Following % Yield Loss:			
	0	10	25	50
Bean	0.7	1.0	1.5	2.4
Carrot	0.7	1.1	1.9	3.1
Strawberry	0.7	0.9	1.2	1.7
Onion	0.8	1.2	1.8	2.9
Radish	0.8	1.3	2.1	3.4
Lettuce	0.9	1.4	2.1	3.4
Pepper	1.0	1.5	2.2	3.4
Sweet potato	1.0	1.6	2.5	4.0
Sweet corn	1.1	1.7	2.5	3.9
Potato	1.1	1.7	2.5	3.9
Cabbage	1.2	1.9	2.9	4.6
Spinach	1.3	2.2	3.5	5.7
Muskmelon	1.5	2.4	3.8	6.1
Cucumber	1.7	2.2	2.9	4.2
Tomato	1.7	2.3	3.4	5.0
Broccoli	1.9	2.6	3.7	5.5
Beet	2.7	3.4	4.5	6.4

Adapted from R. S. Ayers, *Journal of the Irrigation and Drainage Division* 103:135–154 (1977).

RELATIVE TOLERANCE OF VEGETABLE CROPS TO BORON IN IRRIGATION WATERS[1]

10–15 ppm Boron	4–6 ppm Boron	2–4 ppm Boron	1–2 ppm Boron	0.5–1 ppm Boron
Asparagus	Beet	Artichoke	Broccoli	Bean
	Parsley	Cabbage	Carrot	Garlic
	Tomato	Cauliflower	Cucumber	Lima bean
		Celery	Pea	Onion
		Corn	Pepper	
		Lettuce	Potato	
		Muskmelon	Radish	
		Turnip		

Adapted from E. V. Mass, Salt tolerance of plants, *Applied Agricultural Research* 1(1):12–26 (1986).

[1]Maximum concentrations of boron in soil water without yield reduction.

Concentration

1 decisiemens per meter (dS/m) = 1 millimho per centimeter (mmho/cm)

1 decisiemens per meter (dS/m) = approximately 640 milligrams per liter salt

1 part per million (ppm) = 1/1,000,000

1 percent = 0.01 or 1/100

1 ppm × 10,000 = 1 percent

ppm × 0.00136 = tons per acre-foot of water

ppm = milligrams per liter

ppm = 17.12 × grains per gallon

grains per gallon = 0.0584 × ppm

ppm = 0.64 × micromohos per centimeter (in range of 100–5000 micromhos per centimeter)

ppm = 640 × millimhos per centimeter (in range of 0.1–5.0 millimhos per centimeter)

ppm = grams per cubic meter

mho = reciprocal ohm

millimho = 1000 micromhos

millimho = approximately 10 milliequivalents per liter (meq/liter)

milliequivalents per liter = equivalents per million

millimhos per centimeter = EC × 10^3 (EC × 1000) at 25°C (EC = electrical conductivity)

micromhos per centimeter = EC × 10^6 (EC × 1,000,000) at 25°C

millimhos per centimeter = 0.1 siemens per meter

millimhos per centimeter = (EC × 10^3) = decisiemens per meter (dS/m)

1000 micromhos per centimeter = approximately 700 ppm

1000 micromhos per centimeter = approximately 10 milliequivalents per liter

1000 micromhos per centimeter = 1 ton of salt per acre-foot of water

milliequivalents per liter = 0.01 × (EC × 10^6) (in range of 100–5000 micromhos per centimeter)

milliequivalents per liter = 10 × (EC × 10^3) (in range of 0.1–5.0 millimhos per centimeter)

Pressure and Head

1 atmosphere at sea level = 14.7 pounds per square inch

1 atmosphere at sea level = 29.9 inches of mercury

Pressure and Head—Continued

1 atmosphere at sea level = 33.9 feet of water
1 atmosphere = 0.101 megapascal (MPa)
1 bar = 0.10 megapascal (MPa)
1 foot of water = 0.8826 inch of mercury
1 foot of water = 0.4335 pound per square inch
1 inch of mercury = 1.133 feet of water
1 inch of mercury = 0.4912 pound per square inch
1 inch of water = 0.07355 inch of mercury
1 inch of water = 0.03613 pound per square inch
1 pound per square inch = 2.307 feet of water
1 pound per square inch = 2.036 inches of mercury
1 pound per square foot = 47.9 pascals

Weight and Volume (U.S. Measurements)

1 acre-foot of soil = about 4,000,000 pounds
1 acre-foot of water = 43,560 cubic feet
1 acre-foot of water = 12 acre-inches
1 acre-foot of water = about 2,722,500 pounds
1 acre-foot of water = 325,851 gallons
1 cubic foot of water = 7.4805 gallons
1 cubic foot of water at 59°F = 62.37 pounds
1 acre-inch of water = 27,154 gallons
1 gallon of water at 59°F = 8.337 pounds
1 gallon of water = 0.1337 cubic foot or 231 cubic inches

Flow (U.S. Measurements)

1 cubic foot per second = 448.8 gallons per minute
1 cubic foot per second = about 1 acre-inch per hour
1 cubic foot per second = 23.80 acre-inches per hour
1 cubic foot per second = 3600 cubic feet per hour
1 cubic foot per second = 3600 cubic feet per hour
1 cubic foot per second = about 7½ gallons per second
1 gallon per minute = 0.00223 cubic feet per second
1 gallon per minute = 0.053 acre-inch per 24 hours

Flow (U.S. Measurements)–Continued

1 gallon per minute = 1 acre-inch in 4½ hours
1000 gallons per minute = 1 acre-inch in 27 minutes
1 acre-inch per 24 hours = 18.86 gallons per minute
1 acre-foot per 24 hours = 226.3 gallons per minute
1 acre-foot per 24 hours = 0.3259 million gallons per 24 hours

U.S.–Metric Equivalents

1 cubic meter = 35.314 cubic feet
1 cubic meter = 1.308 cubic yards
1 cubic meter = 1000 liters
1 liter = 0.0353 cubic feet
1 liter = 0.2642 U.S. gallon
1 liter = 0.2201 British or Imperial gallon
1 cubic centimeter = 0.061 cubic inch
1 cubic foot = 0.0283 cubic meter
1 cubic foot = 28.32 liters
1 cubic foot = 7.48 U.S. gallons
1 cubic foot = 6.23 British gallons
1 cubic inch = 16.39 cubic centimeters
1 cubic yard = 0.7645 cubic meter
1 U.S. gallon = 3.7854 liters
1 U.S. gallon = 0.833 British gallon
1 British gallon = 1.201 U.S. gallons
1 British gallon = 4.5436 liters
1 acre-foot = 43,560 cubic feet
1 acre-foot = 1,233.5 cubic meters
1 acre-inch = 3,630 cubic feet
1 acre-inch = 102.8 cubic meters
1 cubic meter per second = 35.314 cubic feet per second
1 cubic meter per hour = 0.278 liter per second
1 cubic meter per hour = 4.403 U.S. gallons per minute
1 cubic meter per hour = 3.668 British gallons per minute
1 liter per second = 0.0353 cubic feet per second
1 liter per second = 15.852 U.S. gallons per minute

U.S.–Metric Equivalents—Continued

1 liter per second = 13.206 British gallons per minute
1 liter per second = 3.6 cubic meters per hour
1 cubic foot per second = 0.0283 cubic meter per second
1 cubic foot per second = 28.32 liters per second
1 cubic foot per second = 448.8 U.S. gallons per minute
1 cubic foot per second = 373.8 British gallons per minute
1 cubic foot per second = 1 acre-inch per hour (approximately)
1 cubic foot per second = 2 acre-feet per day (approximately)
1 U.S. gallon per minute = 0.06309 liter per second
1 British gallon per minute = 0.07573 liter per second

Power and Energy

1 horsepower = 550 foot-pounds per second
1 horsepower = 33,000 foot-pounds per minute
1 horsepower = 0.7457 kilowatts
1 horsepower = 745.7 watts
1 horsepower-hour = 0.7457 kilowatt-hour
1 kilowatt = 1.341 horsepower
1 kilowatt-hour = 1.341 horsepower-hours
1 acre-foot of water lifted 1 foot = 1.372 horsepower-hours of work
1 acre-foot of water lifted 1 foot = 1.025 kilowatt-hours of work

PART 6
VEGETABLE PESTS AND PROBLEMS

AIR POLLUTION

INTEGRATED PEST MANAGEMENT

PESTICIDE-USE PRECAUTIONS

EQUIPMENT AND APPLICATION

NEMATODES

DISEASES

INSECTS

Plant damage by pollutants depends on meteorological factors leading to air stagnation, the presence of a pollution source, and the susceptibility of the plants.

Among the pollutants that affect vegetable crops are sulfur dioxide (SO_2), ozone (O_3), peroxyacetyl nitrate (PAN), chlorine (Cl), and ammonia (NH_3).

Sulfur Dioxide: SO_2 causes acute and chronic plant injury. Acute injury is characterized by dead tissue between the veins or on leaf margins. The dead tissue may be bleached, ivory, tan, orange, red, reddish-brown, or brown, depending on the plant species, time of year, and weather. Chronic injury is marked by brownish-red, turgid, or bleached white areas on the leaf blade. Young leaves rarely display damage, whereas fully expanded leaves are very sensitive.

Ozone: Common symptoms of O_3 injury are very small irregularly shaped spots that are dark brown to black (stipplelike) or light tan to white (flecklike) on the upper leaf surface. Very young and old leaves are normally resistant to ozone. Recently matured leaves are most susceptible. Injury is usually more pronounced at the leaf tip and along the margins. With severe damage, symptoms may extend to the lower leaf surface.

Peroxyacetyl Nitrate: Typically, PAN affects the underleaf surface of newly matured leaves and causes bronzing, glazing, or silvering on the lower surface of sensitive leaf areas.

The leaf apex of broad-leaved plants becomes sensitive to PAN approximately 5 days after leaf emergence. About four leaves on a shoot are sensitive at any one time. PAN toxicity is specific for tissue in a particular stage of development. Only with successive exposure to PAN will the entire leaf develop injury. Injury may consist of bronzing or glazing with little or no tissue collapse on the upper leaf surface. Pale green to white stipplelike areas may appear on upper and lower leaf surfaces. Complete tissue collapse in a diffuse band across the leaf is helpful in identifying PAN injury.

Chlorine: Injury from chlorine is usually of an acute type and is similar in pattern to sulfur dioxide injury. Foliar necrosis and bleaching are common. Necrosis is marginal in some species but scattered in others either between or along veins. Lettuce plants exhibit necrotic injury on the margins of outer leaves, which often extends in solid areas toward the center and base of the leaf. Inner leaves remain unmarked.

Ammonia: Field injury from NH_3 has been primarily due to accidental spillage.

Slight amounts of the gas produce color changes in the pigments of vegetable skin. The dry outer scales of red onion may become greenish or black, whereas scales of yellow or brown onion may turn dark brown.

Hydrochloric Acid Gas: HCl causes an acid-type burn. The usual acute response is a bleaching of tissue. Leaves of lettuce, endive, and escarole exhibit a tipburn that progresses toward the center of the leaf and soon dries out. Tomato plants develop interveinal bronzing.

Adapted from Commercial vegetable production recommendations, Maryland Agricultural Extension Service EB-236 (1986).

REACTION OF VEGETABLE CROPS TO AIR POLLUTANTS

Vegetable crops may be injured following exposure to high concentrations of various atmospheric pollutants. Prolonged exposure to lower concentrations may also result in plant damage.

Injury appears progressively as leaf chlorosis (yellowing), necrosis (death), and perhaps restricted growth and yields. On occasion plants may be killed, but usually not until they have suffered persistent injury.

Symptoms of air pollution damage vary with the individual crops and plant age, specific pollutant, concentration, duration of exposure, and environmental conditions.

RELATIVE SENSITIVITY OF VEGETABLE CROPS TO AIR POLLUTANTS

Pollutant	Sensitive	Intermediate	Tolerant
Ozone	Bean Broccoli Onion Potato Radish Spinach Sweet corn Tomato	Carrot Endive Parsley Parsnip Turnip	Beet Cucumber Lettuce
Sulfur dioxide	Bean Beet Broccoli Brussels sprouts Carrot Endive Lettuce Okra Pepper Pumpkin Radish Rhubarb Spinach Squash Sweet potato Swiss chard Turnip	Cabbage Pea Tomato	Cucumber Onion Sweet corn
Fluoride	Sweet corn		Asparagus Squash Tomato
Nitrogen dioxide	Lettuce		Asparagus Bean
PAN	Bean Beet Celery Endive Lettuce	Carrot	Broccoli Cabbage Cauliflower Cucumber Onion

RELATIVE SENSITIVITY OF VEGETABLE CROPS TO AIR POLLUTANTS—Continued

Pollutant	Sensitive	Intermediate	Tolerant
PAN (Continued)	Mustard Pepper Spinach Sweet corn Swiss chard Tomato		Radish Squash
Ethylene	Bean Cucumber Pea Southern pea Sweet potato Tomato	Carrot Squash	Beet Cabbage Endive Onion Radish
2,4-D	Tomato	Potato	Bean Cabbage Eggplant Rhubarb
Chlorine	Mustard Onion Radish Sweet corn	Bean Cucumber Southern pea Squash Tomato	Eggplant Pepper
Ammonia	Mustard	Tomato	
Mercury vapor	Bean	Tomato	
Hydrogen sulfide	Cucumber Radish Tomato	Pepper	Mustard

Adapted from J. S. Jacobson and A. C. Hill (eds.), *Recognition of Air Pollution Injury to Vegetation*, Air Pollution Control Association, Pittsburgh, PA (1970); M. Treshow, *Environment and Plant Response*, McGraw-Hill, New York (1970); and R. G. Pearson et al., Air pollution and horticultural crops, Ontario Ministry of Agriculture and Food AGDEX 200/691 (1973).

Integrated Pest Management (IPM) attempts to make the most efficient use of the strategies available to control pest populations by taking action to prevent problems, suppress damage levels and use chemical pesticides only where needed. Rather than seeking to eradicate all pests entirely, IPM strives to prevent their development or to suppress their population numbers below levels that would be economically damaging.

Integrated means that a broad, interdisciplinary approach is taken using scientific principles of crop protection in order to fuse into a single system a variety of methods and tactics.

Pest includes insects, mites, nematodes, plant pathogens, weeds, and vertebrates that adversely affect crop quality and yield.

Management refers to the attempt to control pest populations in a planned, systematic way by keeping their numbers or damage within acceptable levels.

Effective IPM consists of four basic principles:

Exclusion seeks to prevent pests from entering the field in the first place.

Suppression refers to the attempt to suppress pests below the level at which they would be economically damaging.

Eradication strives to eliminate entirely certain pests.

Plant resistance stresses the effort to develop healthy, vigorous strains that will be resistant to certain pests.

In order to carry out these four basic principles, the following steps are often taken:

1. *The identification of key pests and beneficial organisms* is a necessary first step.
2. *Preventive cultural practices* are selected to minimize pest population development.
3. *Pest populations must be monitored* by trained "scouts" who routinely sample fields.
4. *A prediction of loss and risks* involved is made by setting an economic threshold. Pests are controlled only when the pest population threatens acceptable levels of quality and yield. The level at which the pest population or its damage endangers quality and yield is often called the economic threshold. The economic threshold is set by predicting potential loss and risks at a given population density.
5. *An action decision must be made.* In some cases pesticide application will be necessary to reduce the crop threat, whereas in other cases, a decision will be made to wait and rely on closer monitoring.

6. *Evaluation and follow-up* must occur throughout all stages in order to make corrections, assess levels of success, and project future possibilities for improvement.

To be effective, IPM must make use of the following tools:

1. *Pesticides.* Some pesticides are applied preventively, for example, herbicides, fungicides, and nematicides. In an effective IPM program pesticides are applied on a prescription basis tailored to the particular pest, and chosen so as to have minimum impact on people and the environment. They are applied only when a pest population has been diagnosed as large enough to threaten acceptable levels of yield and quality.
2. *Resistant crop varieties* are bred and selected when available in order to protect against key pests.
3. *Natural enemies* are used to regulate the pest population whenever possible.
4. *Pheromone (sex lure) traps* are used to lure and destroy male insects, thus helping monitoring procedures.
5. *Preventive measures* such as soil fumigation for nematodes and assurance of good soil fertility help to provide a healthy, vigorous plant.
6. *Avoidance* of peak pest populations can be brought about by a change in planting times or pest-controlling crop rotation.
7. *Improved application* is achieved by keeping equipment up-to-date and in excellent shape.
8. *Other assorted cultural practices* such as flooding, row spacing, and plot spacing can influence pest populations.

Adapted from K. Hoeller (ed.), IPM, An integrated pest management primer, Florida Cooperative Extension Service IPM-1 (1978).

Soil solarization is a nonchemical control method that is particularly effective in areas having high temperatures and long days for the required 4–6 weeks. In the northern hemisphere, this generally means that solarization is done during the summer months in preparation for a fall crop or for a crop in the following spring.

Soil solarization captures radiant heat energy from the sun, thereby causing physical, chemical, and biological changes in the soil. Transparent polyethylene plastic placed on moist soil during the hot summer months increases soil temperatures to levels lethal to many soil-borne plant pathogens, weed seeds, and seedlings (including parasitic seed plants), nematodes, and some soil-residing mites. Soil solarization also improves plant nutrition by increasing the availability of nitrogen and other essential nutrients.

Time of Year

Highest soil temperatures are obtained when the days are long, air temperatures are high, the sky is clear, and there is no wind.

Plastic Color

Clear polyethylene should be used, not black plastic. Transparent plastic results in greater transmission of solar energy to the soil.

Plastic Thickness

Polyethylene 1 mil thick is the most efficient and economical for soil heating. However, it is easier to rip or puncture and is less able to withstand high winds than thicker plastic. Users in windy areas may prefer to use plastic 1½–2 mils thick. Thick transparent plastic (4–6 mils) reflects more solar energy than does thinner plastic (1–2 mils) and results in slightly lower temperatures.

Preparation of the Soil

It is important that the area to be treated is level and free of weeds, plants, debris, and large clods that would raise the plastic off the ground. Maximum soil heating occurs when the plastic is close to the soil; therefore, air pockets caused by large clods or deep furrows should be avoided.

Partial vs. Complete Soil Coverage

Polyethylene tarps may be applied in strips (a minimum of 2–3 ft wide) over the planting bed or as continuous sheeting glued, heat-fused, or held in place by soil. In some cases strip coverage may be more practical and economical than full soil coverage, because less plastic is needed and plastic connection costs are avoided.

Soil Moisture

Soil must be moist for maximum effect because moisture not only makes organisms more sensitive to heat, but it also conducts heat faster and deeper into the soil.

Duration of Soil Coverage

Killing of pathogens and pests is related to time and temperature exposure. The longer the soil is heated, the deeper the control. Although some pest organisms are killed within days, 4–6 weeks of treatment in full sun during the summer is usually best.

Adapted from G. S. Pullman, J. E. DeVay, C. L. Elmore, and W. H. Hart, Soil solarization, California Cooperative Extension Leaflet 21377 (1984).

PRECAUTIONS IN THE USE OF PESTICIDES

All chemicals are potentially hazardous and should be used carefully. Follow exactly the directions, precautions and limitations given on the container label. Store all chemicals in a safe place where children, pets, and livestock cannot reach them. Do not reuse pesticide containers. Avoid inhaling fumes and dust from pesticides. Avoid spilling chemicals; if they are accidently spilled, remove contaminated clothing and thoroughly wash the skin with soap and water immediately.

Observe the following rules:

1. Avoid drift from the application area to adjacent areas occupied by humans or livestock or to bodies of water.
2. Wear goggles, an approved respirator, and neoprene gloves when loading or mixing pesticides. Aerial applicators should be loaded by a ground crew.
3. Pour chemicals at a level well below the face to avoid splashing or spilling onto the face or eyes.
4. Have plenty of soap and water on hand to wash contaminated skin in the event of spilling.
5. Change clothing and bathe after the job is completed.
6. Know the insecticide, the symptoms of overexposure to it, and a physician who can be called quickly. In case symptoms appear (contracted pupils, blurred vision, nausea, severe headache, dizziness), stop operations at once and contact a physician.

TOXICITY OF PESTICIDES

Hazard	Unit	Category: I Danger and Poison	II Warning	III Caution	IV Caution
Oral LD_{50}	mg/kg	50 or less	50–500	500–5,000	More than 5,000
Inhalation LD_{50}	mg/liter	0.2 or less	0.2–2.0	2.0–20	More than 20
Dermal LD_{50}	mg/kg	200 or less	200–2,000	2,000–20,000	More than 20,000
Eye effects		Irreversible corneal opacity at 7 days	Corneal opacity reversible within 7 days or irritation persisting for 7 days	No corneal opacity irritation reversible within 7 days	No irritation
Skin irritation		Corrosive	Severe irritation at 72 hr	Moderate irritation at 72 hr	Mild or slight irritation at 72 hr

Adapted from *Farm Chemicals Handbook*, Meister Publishing Co., Willoughby, OH (1987).

LD_{50} (median lethal dose) is a measure of the toxicity of a chemical. It indicates the amount of toxicant necessary to effect a 50% kill of the animals being tested. The lower the number, the more toxic the chemical.

FARM WORKER PROTECTION STANDARDS

These standards provide for the safety of farm workers who enter fields that have been treated with pesticides.

1. Appropriate and timely warnings of pesticide applications are to be given to farm workers orally, by posting, or both. If a worker does not read or does not speak English, every effort must be made to ensure that the warnings are understood.
2. Pesticide applications are not permitted if unprotected workers or other persons not involved in the spraying are within the area to be treated.
3. Unprotected workers may not enter any field treated with a pesticide until the sprays have dried or the dusts have settled. Protective clothing must include at least a hat or other suitable head covering, a long-sleeved shirt and long-legged trousers or a coverall-type garment, shoes, and socks.
4. Specific reentry times have been established in regard to chemicals that are highly toxic to workers. Reentering workers must wear protective clothing during these periods.

24 hr	48 hr
azinphos-methyl	demeton
disulfoton	methidathion
endosulfan	methyl parathion
ethion	monocrotophos
phosalone	oxydemeton-methyl
	parathion
	phorate

5. These general regulations do not replace label restrictions on individual pesticide products. If the label directions specify more stringent precautions, follow the label directions.

Honeybees and other bees are necessary for pollination of vegetables in the gourd family—cucumber, muskmelon and other melons, pumpkin, squash, and watermelon. Bees and other pollinating insects are necessary for all of the cross-pollinated vegetables grown for seed production. Some pesticides are extremely toxic to bees and other pollinating insects, so certain precautions are necessary to avoid injury to them.

Recommendations for Vegetable Growers and Pesticide Applicators:

1. Participate actively in areawide integrated crop management programs.
2. Follow pesticide label directions and recommendations.
3. Apply hazardous chemicals in late afternoon, night, or early morning (generally 6 p.m. to 7 a.m.) when honeybees are not actively foraging. Evening applications are generally somewhat safer than morning applications.
4. Use pesticides that are relatively nonhazardous to bees whenever this is consistent with other pest-management strategies. Choose the least hazardous pesticide formulations or tank mixes.
5. Become familiar with bee foraging behavior and types of pesticide applications that are hazardous to bees.
6. Know the location of all apiaries in the vicinity of fields to be sprayed.
7. Avoid drift, overspray, and dumping of toxic materials in noncultivated areas.
8. Survey pest populations and be aware of current treatment thresholds in order to avoid unnecessary pesticide use.
9. Determine if bees are foraging in target area so protective measures can be taken.

RELATIVE TOXICITY OF PESTICIDES TO HONEYBEES[1]

Group I. Highly Toxic: *Severe losses may be expected if these pesticides are used when bees are present at treatment or within a day thereafter.*

Insecticides and Acaracides

Afugan (pyrazophos)	Guthion (azinphosmethyl)	PayOff (flucythrinate)
Ambush (permethrin)	Imidan (phosmet)	Penncap-M (microencapsulated methyl parathion)
Azodrin (monocrotophos)	Lannate (methomyl)	Phosdrin (mevinphos)
Baygon (propoxur)	lindane	Pounce (permethrin)
Baytex (fenthion)	Lorsban (chlorpyrifos)	Pydrin (fenvalerate)
Cygon (dimethoate)[2]	malathion	resmethrin
Cythion (malathion)	Metacil	Sevin (carbaryl)
Dasanit (fensulfothion)	Mesurol (methiocarb)	Spectracide (diazinon)
DDVP (dichlorvos)	methyl parathion	Supracide (methadathion)
De-Fend (dimethoate)[2]	Monitor (methamidophos)	Tamoron (methamidophos)
Dibrom (naled)	Nemacur P (phenamiphos)	Temik (aldicarb)[2]
Dimecron (phosphamidon)[2]	Nudrin (methomyl)	Vapona (dichlorvos)
Dursban (chlorpyrifos)	Orthene (acephate)	Zectran (mexacarbate)
Furadan (carbofuran)	parathion	
Gardona (tetrachlorvinphos)		

Herbicides, Defoliants, and Desiccants

2,4,5-T	Gramoxone (paraquat)	Silvex (2,4,5-TP)

Fungicides

Captan	Dithane M-22	Maneb

RELATIVE TOXICITY OF PESTICIDES TO HONEYBEES[1]—Continued

Group II. Moderately Toxic: *These can be used around bees if dosage, timing, and method of application are correct, but should not be applied directly on bees in the field or at the colonies.*

Abate (temophos)
Agritox (trichloronate)
Banol (carbanolate)
Broot (trimethacarb) (G)[3]
Carzol (formetanate hydrochloride)
Ciodrin (crotoxyphos)
Counter (terbufos) (G)

diazinon (G)[3]
Di-Syston (disulfoton) (G)[2]
Dyfonate (fonofos) (G)
Furadan (carbofuran) (G)
Lorsban (chlorpyrifos) (G)
Meta-Systox-R (oxydemetonmethyl)[2]
Mocap (ethoprop) (G)

Pyramat
Systox (demeton)[2]
Thimet (phorate) (G)[2]
Thiodan (endosulfan)
Trithion (carbophenothion)
Vydate (oxamyl)
Zolone (phosalone)

Group III. Relatively Nontoxic: *These can be used around bees and cause a minimum of injury.*

Insecticides and Acaracides

Acaraben (chlorobenzilate)
allethrin
Altosid (methoprene)
Bacillus thuringiensis (Accoate, Biotrol, Dipel, Thuricide)
Birlane (chlorvinphos)
Delnav (dioxathion)
Dessin (dinobuton)
Dimilin (diflubenzuron)

Dylox (trichlorfon)
Eradex (chinothionat)
Fundal (chlordimeform)
Galecron (chlordimeform)
Heliothis polyhedrosis virus
methoxychlor
Morestan (oxythioquinox)
Morocide (binapacryl)
Murvesco (fenson)
Nemagon (dibromochlorpropane)

Neotran (oxythane)
Pentac (dienochlor)
Plictran (cyhexatin)
pyrethrum (natural)
rotenone
ryania
Tedion (tetradifon)
Torak (dialifor)

Herbicides, Defoliants, and Desiccants

AAtrex	Eptam (EPTC)	Ramrod (propachlor)
Amiben (chloramben)	Hyvar (bromacil)	Randox (CDAA)
Ammate (AMS)	Karmex (diuron)	Sancap (diproptryn)
Balan (benefin)	Kerb (proamide)	Sencor (metribuzin)
Banvel (dicamba)	Lasso (alachlor)	Sinbar (terbacil)
Bladex (cyanazine)	Lorox (linuron)	Surflan (oryzalin)
cacodylic acid	MCPA	Sutan (butylate)
Casoron (dichlobenil)	Modown (bifenox)	Telvar (monuron)
2,4-D	Paarlan (isopropalin)	Tordon (picloram)
dalapon	Pramitol (prometone)	Treflan (trifluralin)
2,4-DB	Preforan (fluorodifen)	
DNBP (dinitrobutylphenyl)	Princep (simazine)	
2,4-DP (dichlorprop)		

Fungicides

Arasan (thiram)	Dithane M-45 (mancozeb)	Mylone (dazomet, tiazon)
Benlate (benomyl)	Dithane Z-78 (zineb)	Phaltan (folpet)
Bordeaux mixture	DU-Ter (fentin hydroxide)	Polyram (metiram)
Bravo (chlorothalonil)	Dyrene (anilazine)	Sulfur
copper oxychloride sulfate	Glyoxide (glyodin)	Vitavax (carboxin)
Cyprex (dodine)	Karathane (dinocap)	
Difolatan (captafol)	Kocide (cupric hydroxide)	

Adapted from J. L. Wedberg and E. H. Erickson, Protecting honeybees in Wisconsin from pesticides and other toxic chemicals, Wisconsin Cooperative Extension Service A3086 (1986).

[1]On vegetables, use only those pesticides that are labeled. Others are listed because they may be used on other crops in adjoining fields.
[2]Systemic insecticide.
[3]Granular.

To calculate approximately the acreage of a crop in the field, multiply the length of the field by the number of rows or beds. Divide by the factor for spacing of beds.

Examples: Field 726 ft long with 75 rows 48 in. apart.

$$\frac{726 \times 75}{10890} = 5 \text{ acres}$$

Field 500 ft long with 150 beds on 40-in. centers.

$$\frac{500 \times 150}{13068} = 5.74 \text{ acres}$$

Row or Bed Spacing (in.)	Factor
12	43,560
18	29,040
24	21,780
30	17,424
36	14,520
40	13,068
42	12,445
48	10,890
60	8,712
72	7,260
84	6,223

DISTANCE TRAVELED AT VARIOUS TRACTOR SPEEDS

mph	ft/min	mph	ft/min
1.0	88	3.1	273
1.1	97	3.2	282
1.2	106	3.3	291
1.3	114	3.4	299
1.4	123	3.5	308
1.5	132	3.6	317
1.6	141	3.7	325
1.7	150	3.8	334
1.8	158	3.9	343
1.9	167	4.0	352
2.0	176	4.1	361
2.1	185	4.2	370
2.2	194	4.3	378
2.3	202	4.4	387
2.4	211	4.5	396
2.5	220	4.6	405
2.6	229	4.7	414
2.7	237	4.8	422
2.8	246	4.9	431
2.9	255	5.0	440
3.0	264		

CALCULATIONS OF SPEED OF EQUIPMENT AND AREA WORKED

To review the actual performance of a tractor determine the number of seconds required to travel a certain distance. Then use the formula

$$\text{Speed (mph)} = \frac{\text{distance traveled (ft)} \times 0.682}{\text{time to cover distance (secs)}}$$

or the formula

$$\text{Speed (mph)} = \frac{\text{distance traveled (ft)}}{\text{time to cover distance (secs)} \times 1.47}$$

Another method is to walk beside the machine counting the number of normal paces (2.93 ft) covered in 20 secs. Point off one place. Result equals tractor speed (mph).

CALCULATIONS OF SPEED OF EQUIPMENT AND AREA WORKED—Continued

Example: 15 paces/20 secs = 1.5 mph.

The working width of an implement multiplied by mph equals the number of acres covered in 10 hr. This includes an allowance of 17.5% for turning at the ends of the field. By moving the decimal point one place, which is equivalent to dividing by 10, the result is the acreage covered in 1 hr.

Example: A sprayer with a 20-ft boom is operating at 3.5 mph. So $20 \times 3.5 = 70$ acres/10 hr or 7 acres/hr.

APPROXIMATE TIME REQUIRED TO WORK AN ACRE[1]

Rate (mph):	1	2	3	4	5	10
Rate (ft/min):	88	176	264	352	440	880
Effective Working Width of Equipment (in.)	Approximate Time Required (min/acre)					
18	440	220	147	110	88	44
24	330	165	110	83	66	33
36	220	110	73	55	44	22
40	198	99	66	50	40	20
42	189	95	63	47	38	19
48	165	83	55	41	33	17
60	132	66	44	33	26	13
72	110	55	37	28	22	11
80	99	50	33	25	20	10
84	94	47	31	24	19	9
96	83	42	28	21	17	8
108	73	37	24	19	15	7
120	66	33	22	17	13	6
240	33	17	11	8	7	3
360	22	11	7	6	4	2

[1]These figures have been calculated on the basis of 75% field efficiency to allow for turning and other lost time.

Ground Application

Boom-Type Sprayers: High-pressure, high-volume sprayers have been used for row-crop pest control for many years. Now a trend exists toward the use of sprayers that utilize lower volumes and pressures.

Airblast-Type Sprayers: Airblast sprayers are used in the vegetable industry to control insects and diseases. Correct operation of an airblast sprayer is more critical than for a boom-type sprayer.

Do not operate an airblast sprayer under high wind conditions. Wind speed below 5 mph is preferable unless it becomes necessary to apply the pesticide for timely control measures, but drift and nearby crops must be considered.

Do not overextend the coverage of the machine. Considerable visible mist from the machine moves into the atmosphere and does not deposit on the plant. If in doubt, use black plastic indicator sheets in the rows to determine deposit and coverage before a pest problem appears as evidence.

Use correct gallonage and pressures to obtain proper droplet size to ensure uniform coverage across the effective swath width.

Adjust the vanes and nozzles on the sprayer unit to give best coverage. Vane adjustment must occur in the field, depending on terrain, wind, and crop.

Cross drives in the field allow the material to be blown down the rows instead of across them and help to give better coverage in some crops, such as tomato.

Aerial Application

Spraying should occur when wind is not excessive—less than 6 mph. A slight crosswind during spraying is advantageous in equalizing the distribution of the spray within the swath and between swaths.

Proper nozzle angle and arrangements along the boom are critical and necessary to obtain proper distribution at ground level. Use black plastic indicator sheets in the rows to determine deposit and coverage patterns. Cover a swath no wider than is reasonable for the aircraft and boom being used.

Fields of irregular shape or topography and ones bounded by woods, power lines, or other flight hazards should not be sprayed by aircraft.

Adapted from Ohio vegetable production guide, Ohio Cooperative Extension Service Bulletin 672 (1986).

Width of Boom: The boom coverage is equal to the number of nozzles multiplied by the space between two nozzles.

Ground Speed (mph): Careful control of ground speed is very important for accurate spray application. Select a gear and throttle setting to maintain constant speed. A speed of 2–3 mph is desirable. From a "running start," mark off the beginning and ending of a 30-sec run. The distance traveled in this 30-sec period divided by 44 will equal the speed in miles per hour (see page 223).

Sprayer Discharge (gpm): Run the sprayer at a certain pressure, and catch the discharge from each nozzle for a known length of time. Collect all the discharge and measure the total volume. Divide this volume by the time in minutes to determine discharge in gallons per minute.

Before Calibrating:

1. Thoroughly clean all nozzles, screens, etc., to ensure proper operation.
2. Check to be sure that all nozzles are the same.
3. Check the spray patterns of all nozzles for uniformity. Check the volume of delivery by placing similar containers under each nozzle. Replace nozzles that do not have uniform patterns or do not fill containers at the same rate.
4. Select an operating speed. Note the tachometer reading or mark the throttle setting. When spraying, be sure to use the same speed as used for calibrating.
5. Select an operating pressure. Adjust to desired pressure (psi) while pump is operating at normal speed and water is actually flowing through the nozzles. This pressure should be the same during calibration and field spraying.

Calibration (Jar Method): Either a special calibration jar or a homemade one can be used. If you buy one, carefully follow the manufacturer's instructions.

Make accurate speed and pressure readings and jar measurements. Make several checks.

Any 1-qt or larger container, such as a jar or measuring cup, if calibrated in fluid ounces, can easily be used in the following manner:

1. Measure a course on the same type of surface (sod, plowed, etc.) and same type of terrain (hilly, level, etc.) as that to be sprayed, according to nozzle spacing as follows:

Nozzle spacing (in.)	16	20	24	28	32	36	40
Course length (ft)	255	204	170	146	127	113	102

2. Time the seconds it takes the sprayer to cover the measured distance at the desired speed.
3. With the sprayer standing still, operate at selected pressure and pump speed. Catch the water from several nozzles for the number of seconds measured in Step 2.
4. Determine the average output per nozzle in ounces. The ounces per nozzle equal the gallons per acre applied for one nozzle per spacing.

Calibration (Boom or Airblast Sprayer):

1. Fill sprayer with water.
2. Spray a measured area (width of area covered × distance traveled) at constant speed and pressure selected from manufacturer's information.
3. Measure amount of water necessary to refill tank (gallons used).
4. Multiply gallons used by 43,560 and divide by the number of square feet in area sprayed. This gives gallons per acre.

$$\text{Gal/acre} = \frac{\text{gal used} \times 43{,}560}{\text{area sprayed (sq ft)}}$$

5. Add correct amount of spray material to tank to give the recommended rate per acre.

EXAMPLE

Assume: 10 gal of water used to spray an area 660 ft long and 20 ft wide
Tank size: 100 gal
Spray material: 2 lb (actual)/acre

Calculation:

$$\frac{\text{Gal used} \times 43{,}560}{\text{area sprayed (sq ft)}} = \frac{10 \times 43{,}560}{660 \times 20} = 33 \text{ gal/acre}$$

$$\frac{\text{Tank capacity}}{\text{gal/acre}} = \frac{100 \text{ (tank size)}}{33} = 3.03 \text{ acres sprayed per tank}$$

$$3.03 \times 2 \text{ (lb/acre)} = 6.06 \text{ lb material per tank}$$

If 80% material is used:

$$\frac{6.06}{0.8} = 7.57 \text{ lb material needed per tank to give 2 lb/acre rate}$$

Adapted from Commercial vegetable production recommendations, Maryland Agricultural Extension Service EB-236 (1986).

CALIBRATION OF GRANULAR APPLICATORS

Sales of granular fertilizer, herbicides, insecticides, etc., for application through granular application equipment have been on the increase.

Application rates of granular application equipment are affected by several factors: gate openings or settings, ground speed of the applicator, shape and size of granular material, and roughness of the ground.

Broadcast Application:

1. From the label, determine the application rate.
2. From the operator's manual, set dial or feed gate to apply desired rate.
3. On a level surface, fill hopper to a given level and mark this level.
4. Measure test area—length of run will depend on size of equipment. It need not be one long run but can be multiple runs at shorter distances.
5. Apply material to measured area, operating at the speed applicator will travel during application.
6. Weigh amount of material required to refill hopper to the marked level.
7. Determine application rate:

$$\text{Area covered} = \frac{\text{number of runs} \times \text{length of run} \times \text{width of application}}{43{,}560}$$

$$\text{Application rate} = \frac{\text{amount applied (pounds to refill hopper)}}{\text{area covered}}$$

Note. Width of application is width of the spreader for drop or gravity spreaders. For spinner applicators, it is the working width (distance between runs). Check operator's manual for recommendations, generally one-half to three-fourths of overall width spread.

EXAMPLE

Assume: 50 lb/acre rate
Test run: 200 ft
Four runs made
Application width: 12 ft
11.5 lb to refill hopper

Calculation:

$$\text{Area covered} = \frac{4 \times 200 \times 12}{43{,}560} = 0.22 \text{ acre}$$

$$\text{Application rate} = \frac{11.5}{0.22} = 52.27 \text{ lb}$$

8. If application rate is not correct, adjust feed gate opening and recheck.

Band Application:

1. From the label, determine application rate.
2. From the operator's manual, determine applicator setting and adjust accordingly.
3. Fill hopper half full.
4. Operate applicator until all units are feeding.
5. Stop applicator; remove feed tubes at hopper.
6. Attach paper or plastic bag over hopper openings.
7. Operate applicator over measured distance at the speed equipment will be operated.
8. Weigh and record amount delivered from each hopper. (Compare to check that all hoppers deliver the same amount.)

9. Calculate application rate:

$$\text{Area covered in bands} = \frac{\text{length of run} \times \text{band width} \times \text{number of bands}}{43{,}560}$$

Application rate:

$$\text{Amount applied in bands} = \frac{\text{total amount collected}}{\text{area covered in bands}}$$

Changing from broadcast to band application:

$$\frac{\text{Band width in inches}}{\text{row spacing in inches}} \times \text{broadcast rate per acre} = \text{amount needed per acre}$$

Adapted from Commercial vegetable production recommendations, Maryland Agricultural Extension Service EB-236 (1986).

CALIBRATION OF AERIAL SPRAY EQUIPMENT

Calculation:

$$\text{Acres covered} = \frac{\text{length of swath (miles)} \times \text{width (ft)}}{8.25}$$

$$\text{Acres/min} = \frac{2 \times \text{swath width} \times \text{mph}}{1000}$$

$$\text{GPM} = \frac{2 \times \text{swath width} \times \text{mph} \times \text{gal/acre}}{1000}$$

Adapted from O. C. Turnquist et al., Weed, insect, and disease control guide for commercial vegetable growers, Minnesota Agricultural Extension Service Special Report 5 (1978).

CALIBRATION OF DUSTERS

Select a convenient distance that multiplied by the width covered by the duster, both expressed in feet, equals a convenient fraction of an acre. With the hopper filled to a marked level, operate the duster at this distance. Take a known weight of dust in a bag or other container and refill hopper to the marked level. Weigh the dust remaining in the container. The difference is the quantity of dust applied to the fraction of an acre covered.

Example:
Distance duster is operated × width covered by duster = area dusted

$$= 108.9 \text{ ft} \times 10 \text{ ft} = 1089 \text{ sq ft} \; \frac{1089 \text{ sq ft}}{43560} = \frac{1}{40} \text{ acre}$$

If it takes 1 lb of dust to refill the hopper, the rate of application is 40 lb/acre.

Pesticide containers give directions usually in terms of pounds or gallons of material in 100 gal of water. The following tables make easy the conversion for smaller quantities of spray solution.

Solid Equivalent Table

100 gal	25 gal	5 gal	1 gal
4 oz	1 oz	3/16 oz	1/2 tsp
8 oz	2 oz	3/8 oz	1 tsp
1 lb	4 oz	7/8 oz	2 tsp
2 lb	8 oz	1 3/4 oz	4 tsp
3 lb	12 oz	2 3/8 oz	2 tbsp
4 lb	1 lb	3 1/4 oz	2 tbsp + 2 tsp

Liquid Equivalent Table

100 gal	25 gal	5 gal	1 gal
1 gal	1 qt	6 1/2 oz	1 1/4 oz
2 qt	1 pt	3 1/4 oz	5/8 oz
1 qt	1/2 pt	1 9/16 oz	5/16 oz
1 1/2 pt	6 oz	1 1/4 oz	1/4 oz
1 pt	4 oz	7/8 oz	3/16 oz
8 oz	2 oz	7/16 oz	1/2 tsp
4 oz	1 oz	1/4 oz	1/4 tsp

Dilution of Liquid Pesticides to Various Concentrations

Dilution	1 gal	3 gal	5 gal
1:100	2 tbsp + 2 tsp	1/2 cup	3/4 cup + 5 tsp
1:200	4 tsp	1/4 cup	6 1/2 tbsp
1:800	1 tsp	1 tbsp	1 tbsp + 2 tsp
1:1000	3/4 tsp	2 1/2 tsp	1 tbsp + 1 tsp

Adapted from Cornell recommendations for commercial vegetable production, New York Cooperative Extension Service (1986).

PESTICIDE DILUTION CHART

Amounts of a commercial product (formulation) needed to provide various amounts of actual insecticide (chemical) per 100 gal or per acre.

Commercial Products (lb of insecticide/gal of formulated material)[1]	Pounds of Actual Insecticide Wanted per 100 gal			
	½ lb	1 lb	3 lb	5 lb
1.5 EC (1½ lb/gal)	1⅓ qt	2⅔ qt	2 gal	3⅓ gal
2 EC (2 lb/gal)	1 qt	2 qt	1½ gal	2½ gal
4 EC (4 lb/gal)	1 pt	1 qt	3 qt	5 qt
6 EC (6 lb/gal)	⅔ pt	1⅓ pt	2 qt	3⅓ qt
8 EC (8 lb/gal)	½ pt	1 pt	1½ qt	2½ qt
15 WP	3⅓ lb	6⅔ lb	20 lb	33⅓ lb
25 WP	2 lb	4 lb	12 lb	20 lb
40 WP	1¼ lb	2½ lb	7½ lb	12½ lb
1% dust or granules	50 lb	100 lb	300 lb	500 lb
1½% dust or granules	33 lb	67 lb	200 lb	333 lb
2½% dust or granules	20 lb	40 lb	120 lb	200 lb
5% dust or granules	10 lb	20 lb	60 lb	100 lb

Adapted from E. L. Bouton and C. W. Nicklow (eds.), New England vegetable production recommendations, Cooperative Extension Service of the New England States (1986).

[1] WP = wettable powder; EC = emulsifiable concentrate (liquid).

PESTICIDE APPLICATION RATES FOR SMALL PLANTINGS

Distance Between Rows (ft)	Amount (gal/ acre)	Amount (per 100 ft of row)	Length of Row Covered (ft/gal)
1	75	22 oz	581
	100	30 oz	435
	125	1 qt, 5 oz	348
	150	1 qt, 12 oz	290
	175	1 qt, 20 oz	249
	200	1 qt, 27 oz	218
2	75	1 qt, 12 oz	290
	100	1 qt, 27 oz	218
	125	2 qt, 10 oz	174
	150	2 qt, 24 oz	145
	175	3 qt, 7 oz	124
	200	3 qt, 21 oz	109
3	75	2 qt, 2 oz	194
	100	2 qt, 24 oz	145
	125	3 qt, 14 oz	116
	150	4 qt, 4 oz	97
	175	4 qt, 26 oz	83
	200	5 qt, 16 oz	73

GUIDELINES FOR EFFECTIVE PEST CONTROL

Often failure to control a pest is blamed on the pesticide when frequently the cause lies elsewhere. Some common reasons for failure follow:

1. Delaying applications until pests are already well established.
2. Making applications with insufficient gallonage or clogged or poorly arranged nozzles.
3. Selecting the wrong pesticide.

The following points are suggested for more effective pest control:

1. *Inspect field regularly.* Frequent examinations (at least twice per week) help determine the proper timing of the next pesticide application.

2. *Control insects and mites according to economic thresholds or schedule.* Economic thresholds assist in determining whether pesticide applications or other management actions are needed to avoid economic loss from pest damage. Thresholds for insect pests are generally expressed as a numerical count of a given life stage or as a damage level based on certain sampling techniques. They are intended to reflect the population size that will cause economic damage and thus would warrant the cost of treatment. Guidelines for other pests are usually based on the field history, crop development, variety, weather conditions, and other factors.

   Rather than using economic thresholds, many pest problems can be predicted to occur at approximately the same time year after year. One application before buildup often eliminates the need for several applications later in the season. Often less toxic and safer-to-handle chemicals are effective when pests are small in size and population.

   Weather conditions. Spray only when wind velocity is less than 10 mph. Dust only when it is perfectly calm. Do not spray when sensitive plants are wilted during the heat of the day. If possible, make applications when ideal weather conditions prevail.

   Biological insecticides are ineffective in cool weather. Some pyrethroid insecticides (fenvalerate, permethrin) do not perform well when field temperatures reach 85°F and above. Best control results with these insecticides are achieved when the temperature is in the 70s or low 80s (evening or early morning).

   Sprinkler irrigation washes pesticide deposits from foliage. Wait at least 48 hr after pesticide application before sprinkler irrigating. More frequent pesticide applications may be needed during and after periods of heavy rainfall.

3. *Strive for adequate coverage of plants.* The principal reason aphids, mites, cabbage loopers, and diseases are serious pests is that they occur beneath leaves, where they are protected from spray deposit or dust particles. Improved control can be achieved by adding and arranging nozzles so that the application is directed toward the plants from the sides as well as from the tops. In some cases, nozzles should be arranged so that the application is directed beneath the leaves. As the season progresses, plant size increases, as does the need for increased spray gallonage to ensure adequate coverage. Applying sprays with sufficient spray volume and pressure is important. Sprays from high-volume, high-pressure rigs (airblast) should be applied at 40–100 gal/acre at approximately 400 psi pressure. Sprays from low-volume, low-pressure rigs (boom type) should be applied at 50–100 gal/acre at approximately 100–300 psi pressure.

4. *Select the proper pesticide.* Know the pests to be controlled and choose the recommended pesticide and rate of application.

   For certain pests that are extremely difficult to control or are resistant, it may be important to alternate labeled insecticides, especially with different classes of insecticides; for example, alternate a pyrethroid insecticide with either a carbamate or an organophosphate insecticide.

5. *Pesticide compatibility.* To determine if two pesticides are compatible, using the following "jar test" before you tank mix pesticides or pesticides and fluid fertilizers:
   a. Add 1 pint of water or fertilizer solution to a clean quart jar. Then add the pesticide to the water or fertilizer solution in the same proportion as used in the field.
   b. To a second clean quart jar, add 1 pint of water or fertilizer solution. Then add ½ teaspoon of an adjuvant to keep the mixture emulsified. Finally, add the pesticide to the water–adjuvant or fertilizer–adjuvant in the same proportion as to be used in the field.
   c. Close both jars tightly and mix thoroughly by inverting 10 times. Inspect the mixtures immediately and again after standing for 30 min. If the mix in either jar remains uniform for 30 min, the combination can be used. If either mixture separates but readily remixes, constant agitation is required. If nondispersible oil, sludge, or clumps of solids form, do not use the mixture.

6. *Calibrate application equipment.* Periodic calibration of sprayers, dusters, and granule distributors is necessary to ensure accurate delivery rates of pesticides per acre. See pages 225–231.

7. *Select correct sprayer tips.* The selection of proper sprayer tips for use with various pesticides is very important. Flat fan-spray tips are designed for preemergence and postemergence application of herbicides. They can also be used with insecticides, fertilizers, and other pesticides. Flat fan-spray tips produce a tapered-edge spray pattern for uniform coverage where patterns overlap. Some flat fan-spray tips (SP) are designed to operate at low pressure (15–40 psi) and are usually used for preemergence herbicide applications. These lower pressures result in larger spray particles than those from standard flat tips operating at higher pressures (30–60 psi). Spray nozzles with even flat-spray tips (often designated E) are designed for band spraying where uniform distribution is desired over a zone 8–14 in. wide; they are generally used for herbicides. See page 305 for nozzle information.

   Flood-type nozzle tips are generally used for complete fertilizer, liquid nitrogen, and so on, and sometimes for spraying herbicides onto the soil surface prior to incorporation. They are less suited for spraying postemergence herbicides or for applying fungicides or insecticides to plant foliage. Coverage of the target is often less uniform and complete when flood-type nozzles are used, compared with the coverage obtained with other types of nozzles. Space flood-type nozzles a maximum of 20 in. apart, rather than the standard 40-in. spacing for better coverage. This will result in an overlapping spray pattern. Spray at the maximum pressure recommended for the nozzle.

Wide-spray angle tips with full or hollow cone patterns are usually used for fungicides and insecticides. They are used at higher water volume and spray pressures than are commonly recommended for herbicide application with flat fan or flood-type nozzle tips.

8. *pH and pesticides.* Unsatisfactory results with some pesticides may be related to the pH of the mixing water. Some materials carry a label cautioning the user against mixing the pesticide with alkaline materials because they undergo a chemical reaction known as "alkaline hydrolysis." This reaction occurs when the pesticide is mixed in water with a pH greater than 7.

   Many manufacturers provide information on the rate at which their product hydrolyzes. The rate is expressed as "half-life," meaning the time it takes for 50% hydrolysis or breakdown to occur.

   Check the pH of the water. If acidification is necessary, there are several commercial nutrient buffer materials available on the market.

Adapted from Commercial vegetable production recommendations, Maryland Agricultural Extension Service EB-236 (1986).

SPRAY ADJUVANTS OR ADDITIVES

Adjuvants are chemicals that, when added to a liquid spray, make it mix, wet, spread, stick, or penetrate better. Water is almost a universal diluent for pesticide sprays. However, water is not compatible with oily pesticides, and an *emulsifier* may be needed in order to obtain good mixing. Furthermore, water from sprays often remains as large droplets on leaf surfaces. A *wetting agent* lowers the interfacial tension between the spray droplet and the leaf surface and thus moistens the leaf. *Spreaders* are closely related to wetters and help to build a deposit on the leaf and improve weatherability. *Stickers* cause pesticides to adhere to the sprayed surface and are often called spray-stickers. They are oily and serve to increase the amounts of suspended solids held on the leaves or fruits by holding the particles in a resinlike film. *Extenders* form a sticky, elastic film that holds the pesticide on the leaves and thus reduces the rate of loss caused by sunlight and rainfall.

There are a number of adjuvants on the market. Read the label not only for dosages, but also for crop uses and compatibilities, because some adjuvants must not be used with certain pesticides. Although many formulations of pesticides contain adequate adjuvants, some do require additions on certain crops, especially cabbage, cauliflower, onion, and pepper.

Spray adjuvants for use with herbicides often serve a function distinctly different from that of adjuvants used with insecticides and fungicides. For example, adjuvants such as oils used with atrazine greatly improve penetration of the chemical into crop and weed leaves, rather than just give more uniform coverage. Do not use any adjuvant with herbicides unless there are specific recommendations for its use. Plant damage or even crop residues can result from using an adjuvant that is not recommended.

Adapted from Cornell recommendations for commercial vegetable production, New York Cooperative Extension Service (1986).

VEGETABLE SEED TREATMENTS

Various vegetable seed treatments prevent early infection by seedborne diseases, protect the seed from infection by soil microorganisms, and guard against a poor crop stand or crop failure caused by attacks on seeds by soil insects. Commercial seed is often supplied with the appropriate treatment.

Two general categories of vegetable seed treatments are used. Eradication treatments kill disease-causing agents on or within the seed, whereas protective treatments are applied to the surface of the seed to protect against seed decay, damping-off, and soil insects. Hot-water treatment is the principal means of eradication, and chemical treatments usually serve as protectants. Follow time–temperature directions precisely for hot-water treatment and label directions for chemical treatment. When insecticides are used, seeds should also be treated with a fungicide.

Hot-Water Treatment

To treat seeds with hot water, fill cheesecloth bags half full, wet seed and bag with warm water, and treat at exact time and temperature while stirring to maintain a uniform temperature. Use an accurate thermometer.

HOT-WATER TREATMENT OF SEEDS

Seed	Temperature (°F)	Time (min)	Diseases Controlled
Broccoli, cauliflower, collard, kale, kohlrabi, turnip	122	20	Alternaria, blackleg, black rot
Brussels sprouts, cabbage	122	25	Alternaria, blackleg, black rot
Celery	118	30	Early blight, late blight
Eggplant	122	30	Phomopsis blight, anthracnose
Pepper	122	25	Bacterial spot, rhizoctonia
Tomato	122	25	Bacterial canker, bacterial spot, bacterial speck
	132	30	Anthracnose

Chemical Seed Treatments

The most frequently used fungicides for vegetable seeds are thiram and captan applied as a dust or slurry. Large-seeded vegetables may require treatment with a labeled insecticide as well as a fungicide. Always follow label directions when pesticides are used.

Certain bacterial diseases on the seed surface can be controlled by other chemical treatments:

1. *Tomato Bacterial Canker.* Soak seeds in 1.05% sodium hypochlorite solution for 20–40 min or 5% hydrochloric acid for 5–10 hr, rinse, and dry.
2. *Tomato Bacterial Spot.* Soak seeds in 1.3% sodium hypochlorite for 1 min, rinse, and dry.
3. *Pepper Bacterial Spot.* Soak seeds in 1.3% sodium hypochlorite for 1 min, rinse, and dry.

   DO NOT USE CHEMICALLY TREATED SEED FOR FOOD OR FEED.

Adapted from Indiana vegetable production guide for commercial growers, Cooperative Extension Service ID-56 (1985–86) and A. F. Sherf and A. A. MacNab, *Vegetable Diseases and Their Control*, Wiley, New York (1986).

PLANT PARASITIC NEMATODES

Nematodes are unsegmented round worms that range in size from microscopic to many inches long. Some nematodes, usually those that are microscopic or barely visible without magnification, attack vegetable crops and cause maladies, restrict yields, or in severe cases, lead to total crop failure.

A large number of various nematodes are known to infest the roots and aboveground plant parts of vegetable crops. Their common names are usually descriptive of the affected plant part and the resulting injury.

Common Name	Scientific Name
Awl nematode	*Dolichodorus* spp.
Bud and leaf nematode	*Aphelenchoides* spp.
Cyst nematode	*Heterodera* spp.
Dagger nematode	*Xiphinema* spp.
Lance nematode	*Hopolaimus* spp.
Root-lesion nematode	*Pratylenchus* spp.
Root-knot nematode	*Meloidogyne* spp.
Spiral nematode	*Helicotylenchus* spp. and *Scutellonema* spp.
Sting nematode	*Belonolaimus* spp.
Stubby-root nematode	*Trichodorus* spp.
Stunt nematode	*Tylenchorhynchus* spp.

Nematodes are the most troublesome in areas with mild winters where soils are not subject to freezing and thawing. Management practices and chemical control are both required to keep nematode numbers low enough to permit normal plant growth where populations are not kept in check naturally by severe winters.

The first and most obvious control for nematodes is avoiding their introduction into uninfected fields or areas. This may be done by quarantine over large geographical areas or by means of good sanitation in smaller areas.

Once nematodes have been introduced into a field, several management practices will help to control them: rotating with crops that a particular species of nematode does not attack, frequent disking during hot weather, and alternating flooding and drying cycles.

If soil management practices are not possible or are ineffective, chemicals may have to be used to control nematodes (nematicides). Some fumigants are effective against soil-borne disease, insects, and weed seeds—these are termed multipurpose soil fumigants. Growers should select a chemical for use against the primary problem to be controlled and use it according to label directions.

CHEMICALS FOR CONTROL OF NEMATODES AND OTHER SOIL PESTS[1]

Nematicide	Some Trade Names	Effectiveness[2] against				Comments
		Nematodes	Soil Insects	Soil Fungi	Weed Seeds	
aldicarb	Temik	+	+	–	–	Apply to moist soil before planting or at emergence
carbofuran	Furadan	+	+	–	–	Apply before planting
chloropicrin	Larvacide	+	+	+	+	Keep soil moist and covered with polyethylene for at least 2 days. Aerate for 2 weeks before planting
	Picfume	+	+	+	+	
	various mixtures					
1,3-D	D-D	+	–	–	–	Apply as preplant soil fumigants
	Telone	+	–	+	+	
	Terr-O-Cide	+	+	–	–	
	Vorlex	+	+	+	+	
ethoprop	Mocap	+	+	–	–	Mix thoroughly with soil
fensulfothion	Dasanit	+	+	–	–	Place and mix properly
metham	Vapam	+	+	+	+	Improve effectiveness with a water seal

methyl bromide	Brom-O-Gas Brozone Dowfume Terr-O-Gas	+	+	+	+	Apply preplanting as a soil fumigant
oxamyl	Vydate	+	+	–	–	Apply before, at, or after planting
phenamiphos	Nemacur	+	–	–	–	Apply before planting and incorporate
terbufos	Counter	+	+	–	–	Apply at planting

Adapted from *Guidelines for the Control of Plant Diseases and Nematodes*, USDA Agricultural Handbook 656 (1986) and Crop Protection Chemicals Reference, Wiley, New York (1986).

[1]Follow label directions for use and observe the precautions listed.

[2]+ denotes effective, – denotes not effective.

TOXICITY OF PESTICIDES: NEMATICIDES

	Acute LD_{50} Levels (mg/kg)		
Nematicide	Oral	Dermal	Vapor
aldicarb	1	5	—
carbofuran	11	10,200	—
chloropicrin	250	—	—
1,3-D	250–500	—	500
ethoprop	61	2.4	—
fensulfothion	2–10	3–30	—
metham	1,700–1,800	—	—
methyl bromide	—	—	200
oxamyl	5.4	2,960	—
phenamiphos	8–10	178–225	—
terbufos	4–9	1	—

Adapted from *Farm Chemicals Handbook*, Meister Publishing Co., Willoughby, OH (1985).
Refer to Toxicity of Pesticides (page 216) for definitions.

NEMATODE CONTROL FOR VEGETABLES

Chloropicrin, 1,3-D, and metham can be considered for use as nematicides for preplant treatments in soil in which vegetable crops are to be grown. General conditions of use of these nematicides are similar for all vegetables, and they do not require tolerances. However, rate restrictions may apply to specific crops as indicated in the tables beginning on page 247. Other chemicals, listed under specific vegetable crops, can also be considered for use as nematicides, but these require more specific conditions of use or tolerances, or both.

Vegetable Crops	Nematicide[1]	Rate (lb a.i./acre)	Application	General Comments
		General Vegetable Crop Uses		
All	chloropicrin	480–630	Preplant for seedbed soil. Preplant for bulk treatment of rooting soil	Exposure period 24–48 hr. After exposure period, aerate 7–14 days before planting
	1,3-D	84–250	Preplant overall for mineral soils	Wait 14–21 days before planting for mineral soils, 21 days or more for organic soils. These periods must be extended in case of heavy rains or temperatures below 60°F. A minimum of 300 lb/acre on mineral soils for control of cyst nematodes; for this
		220–600	Preplant overall for organic soils	
		42–100	Preplant in row for mineral soils	

NEMATODE CONTROL FOR VEGETABLES—Continued

Vegetable Crops	Nematicide[1]	Rate (lb a.i./acre)	Application	General Comments
		General Vegetable Crop Uses		
All (Continued)		84–200	Preplant in row for organic soils	treatment the waiting period before planting is 21–28 days
	metham	160–400 300–400	Preplant overall for fields Preplant overall for seedbeds	For soil injection or flood irrigation, plastic cover can be used; keep in place 24–48 hr. Wait at least 21 days before planting, 30 days at low temperature or at high rates of application

Vegetable Crop	Nematicide[1]	Rate (lb a.i./acre)	Application	Restrictions and Remarks
		Specific Vegetable Crop Uses		
Asparagus	1,3-D	14–33	Preplanting in row or overall	See general comments
Bean, Lima	1,3-D	14–33	Preplanting in row or overall	See general comments
	ethoprop	2.0–3.0	Preplanting. Incorporate in a 12- to 15-in. band on the row	Wait 0–3 days and seed
Bean, snap	ethoprop	2.0–3.0 6.0–8.0	Preplanting. Incorporate in a 12- to 15-in. band on the row	Wait 0–3 days and seed
Bean, dry	aldicarb	0.92–1.71	Preplanting. Incorporate in a 6- to 8-in. band or cover with 1 to 2 in. of soil	
Broccoli	1,3-D	14–33	Preplanting in row or overall	See general comments
	methyl bromide	150–235	Preplanting overall for seedbeds and plant beds	Expose to fumigation under plastic tarpaulin for at least 24 hr (up to 84 hr). Aerate for a minimum of 3 days before seeding or 5–14 days before setting transplants
Brussels sprouts (transplants)	phenamiphos	4.0–6.0 1.5–3.0	Preplanting overall Preplanting in 12- to 15-in. band on row	Plant after incorporating granules 2–6 in. in soil

NEMATODE CONTROL FOR VEGETABLES—Continued

Vegetable Crop	Nematicide[1]	Rate (lb a.i./acre)	Application	Restrictions and Remarks
			Specific Vegetable Crop Uses	
Cabbage (transplants and direct seeded)	phenamiphos	4.0–6.0	Preplanting overall	Plant after incorporating granules 2–6 in. in soil
		1.5–3.0	Preplanting in 12–15-in. band on row	
Carrot	1,3-D	14–33	Preplanting in row or overall	See general comments
	oxamyl	4–8 in 20 gal water	Preplanting broadcast, incorporate 4–6 in. deep	
		2–4 in 20 gal water	At planting seed furrow, incorporate 4–6 in. deep	
Cauliflower	1,3-D	14–33	Preplanting in row or overall	See general comments
	methyl bromide	150–235	Preplanting overall for seedbeds and plant beds	Expose to fumigation under plastic tarpaulin for at least 24 hr (up to 48 hr). Aerate for a minimum of 3 days before seeding or 5–14 days before setting transplants
Cucumber	carbofuran	2.0	For 60-in. rows, apply in 12- to 15-in. band and incorporate in the top 3 in. of soil	
	1,3-D	14–33	Preplanting in row or overall	See general comments

	ethoprop	3.9	Apply on 12- to 15-in. band of row, immediately mix 2–3 in. deep, and seed	
	oxamyl	2–4	Preplanting. Broadcast, incorporate 2–4 in. into the soil	
		0.6–1.34	For 40-in. rows, preplanting Incorporate 2–4 in. into the soil	
		0.5–1.0	Foliar spray—apply sufficient water for uniform coverage of foliage	First application 2–4 weeks after planting, repeat 14–21 days later. Do not treat within 7 days of harvest
Eggplant	1,3-D	14–33	Preplanting in row or overall	See general comments
	methyl bromide	150–235	Preplanting overall for seedbeds and plant beds	Expose to fumigation under plastic tarpaulin for at least 24 hr (up to 48 hr). Aerate for a minimum of 3 days before seeding or 5–14 days before setting transplants
Lettuce	1,3-D	14–33	Preplanting in row or overall	See general comments
Melons	carbofuran	2.0	For 60-in. rows, apply in 12- to 15-in. band and incorporate in the top 3 in. of soil	
	1,3-D	14–33	Preplanting in row or overall	See general comments
Honeydew melon	oxamyl	2–4	Preplanting. Broadcast, incorporate 2–4 in. into the soil	
		0.6–1.34	For 40-in. rows, preplanting. Incorporate 2–4 in. into the soil	

NEMATODE CONTROL FOR VEGETABLES—Continued

Vegetable Crop	Nematicide[1]	Rate (lb a.i./acre)	Application	Restrictions and Remarks
		Specific Vegetable Crop Uses		
Honeydew melon (Continued)		0.5–1.0	Foliar spray—apply sufficient water for uniform coverage of foliage	First application 2–4 weeks after planting, repeat 14–21 days later. Do not treat within 7 days of harvest
Muskmelon	Methyl bromide	150–235	Preplanting overall for seedbeds and plant beds	Expose to fumigation under plastic tarpaulin for at least 24 hr (up to 48 hr). Aerate for a minimum of 3 days before seeding or 5–14 days before setting transplants
	oxamyl	2–4	Preplanting. Broadcast, incorporate 2–4 in. into the soil	
		0.6–1.34	For 40-in. rows, preplanting. Incorporate 2–4 in. into the soil	
		0.5–1.0	Foliar spray—apply sufficient water for uniform coverage of foliage	First application 2–4 weeks after planting, repeat 14–21 days later. Do not treat within 7 days of harvest

Okra	1,3-D	14–33	Preplanting in row or overall	See general comments
Pepper	1,3-D	14–33	Preplanting in row or overall	See general comments
	methyl bromide	150–235	Preplanting overall for seedbeds and plant beds	Expose to fumigation under plastic tarpaulin for at least 24 hr (up to 48 hr). Aerate for a minimum of 3 days before seeding or 5–14 days before transplanting
Pepper (bell)	oxamyl	0.5	Apply in 200 gal of water during transplanting	Do not treat within 7 days of harvest
Potato (white)	aldicarb	3.0	Apply granules with seed pieces in planting furrow and cover with soil, or apply granules in an 8-in. band and work into the soil or cover with soil to a depth of 4 in. Plant seed pieces in treated zone	Do not make more than one application per crop. Do not allow livestock to graze in treated areas before harvest. Do not apply granular material to soil surface unless immediately incorporated into the soil with rototiller or other device. Apply at least 90 days before harvest for planting application, 50 days for postemergence application
	1,3-D	14–33	Preplanting in row or overall	See general comments
Pumpkin	carbofuran	2.0	For 60-in. rows, apply in 12- to 15-in. band and incorporate in the top 3 in. of soil	
Squash	carbofuran	2.0	For 60-in. rows, apply in 12- to 15-in. band and incorporate in the top 3 in. of soil	

NEMATODE CONTROL FOR VEGETBLES—Continued

Vegetable Crop	Nematicide[1]	Rate (lb a.i./acre)	Application	Restrictions and Remarks
		Specific Vegetable Crop Uses		
Squash (Continued)	oxamyl	2–4	Preplanting. Broadcast, incorporate 2–4 in. into the soil	
		0.6–1.34	For 40-in. rows, preplanting. Incorporate 2–4 in. into the soil	
		0.5–1.0	Foliar spray—apply sufficient water for uniform coverage of foliage	First application 2–4 weeks after planting, repeat 14–21 days later. Do not treat within 7 days of harvest
Strawberry	methyl bromide	180–240	Preplanting	Expose to fumigation under gasproof tarpaulin for 48 hr. Aerate soil for 2 weeks before planting
	oxamyl	0.5 to 1/100 gal water	Foliar spray	Do not use 365 days before harvest
		0.5 to 1/100 gal water	Dip bare root for 1–30 min	Do not use 365 days before harvest

Sweet corn	1,3-D	14–33	Preplanting in row or overall	See general comments
	ethoprop	6.0	Preplanting. Incorporate overall	Plant after incorporating granules in soil. Do not use as a seed furrow treatment
		1.5–2.0	Preplanting. Incorporate 2–4 in. deep in 12- to 15-in. band on 40-in. rows	
	fensulfothion	1.83	Apply 12-in. band on row and incorporate 3 in.	
	terbufos	8 oz formulation per 1000 feet of row	Place granules directly in the seed furrow behind planter shoe	
Sweet potato	ethoprop	6.0–8.0	Preplanting. Incorporate 4–8 in. deep, overall	Allow at least 14–21 days before planting. Limit is 4.0 lb active per 12,400 linear bed feet
	fensulfothion	3.0–6.9	Preplanting. Incorporate 6 in. deep, overall	Plant after incorporating granules in soil. No waiting period before planting
Swiss chard	aldicarb	3.0	Apply 12- to 15-in. band on row and incorporate 4–8 in. deep, plant	
	oxamyl	4–6	Apply in 20 gal water per acre. Thoroughly incorporate into soil 4–6 in. deep	
		2–6	Apply in 200 gal transplant water per acre	
Tomato	fensulfothion	10–20	Preplant. Incorporate 6 in. deep, overall	Plant after incorporating granules or liquid in soil

NEMATODE CONTROL FOR VEGETABLES—Continued

Vegetable Crop	Nematicide[1]	Rate (lb a.i./acre)	Application	Restrictions and Remarks
			Specific Vegetable Crop Uses	
Tomato (Continued)		3.2–6.3	Preplanting. Incorporate 6 in. deep in a 12-in. band on row	
	methyl bromide	180–350	Preplanting overall for seedbeds and plant beds	Expose to fumigation under gasproof tarpaulin for 48 hr. Aerate soil for 2 weeks before planting
Watermelon	oxamyl	2–4	Preplanting. Broadcast, incorporate 2–4 in. into the soil	
		0.6–1.34	For 40-in. rows, preplanting. Incorporate 2–4 in. into the soil	
		0.5–1.0	Foliar spray—apply sufficient water for uniform coverage of foliage	First application 2–4 weeks after planting, repeat 14–21 days later. Do not treat within 7 days of harvest

Adapted from *Guidelines for the Control of Plant Diseases and Nematodes*, USDA Agricultural Handbook 656 (1986).

[1]See page 242 for trade names.

VEGETABLE DISEASES

Diseases of vegetable crops are caused by fungi, bacteria, viruses, and mycoplasms. For a disease to occur, organisms must be transported to a susceptible host plant. This may be done by infected seeds or plant material, contaminated soil, wind, water, animals including humans, or insects. Suitable environmental conditions must be present for the organism to infect and thrive on the crop plant.

Effective disease control requires knowledge of the disease life cycle, time of likely infection, agent of distribution, plant part affected, and the symptoms produced by the disease. Control methods include:

1. *Use of resistant varieties.* Often this is the best and cheapest control measure.
2. *Use of noninfested soil.*
3. *Soil fumigation.* It reduces the population of soil organisms, allowing the crop to be grown. Fumigation will probably be necessary periodically to lower the population of organisms to an acceptable level.
4. *Use of clean seed.* The use of certified seed or seed grown in disease-free areas prevents the introduction of organisms to the crop.
5. *Seed treatment.* Disease organisms carried on or in the seed may be killed by chemicals or hot-water treatments, respectively.
6. *Control of weed hosts.* Many disease organisms persist in weeds during the off-season. Weed control around fields limits this potential source of infection.
7. *Insect control.* Some bacterial and virus diseases are spread by insects. Effective control of beetles, aphids, and leafhoppers can limit the introduction of these diseases.
8. *Proper use of fungicides.* This includes use of the correct material applied at the recommended dosage. The fungicide must be directed at the plant parts attacked, and must be applied at the right time.

TOXICITY OF PESTICIDES: FUNGICDES

Fungicide	Some Trade Names	Acute Oral LD_{50} (mg/kg)	Acute Dermal LD_{50} (mg/kg)
anilazine	Dyrene	5,000	9,400
benomyl	Benlate	10,000	10,000
	Tersan		
	Fungicide 1991		
captan	Orthocide	9,000	—
chlorothalonil	Bravo	10,000	10,000
	DAC 2787		
	Daconil		
	Termil		
copper compounds	COCS	—	—
	Citcop		
	Copper Count N		
	Fixed copper		
	Kocide		
	Oxycop		
DCNA	Botran	5,000	—
	Allisan		
iprodione	Rovral	10,000	5,000
mancozeb	Dithane M-45	8,000	—
	Manzate 200		
maneb	Dithane M-22	7,990	—
	Manzate		
	Tersan		
maneb-zinc	Dithane M-22 Special	7,990	—
	Manzate D		
metalaxyl	Ridomil 2E	669	3,100
PCNB	Terraclor	15,000	—
sulfur	several	—	—
thiophanate-methyl	Topsin M	7,500	—
thiram	Arasan	780	—
	Spotrete		
	Tersan		
	Thiramad		
	Thylate		
triadimefon	Bayleton	400–1,000	1,000
vinclozolin	Ronilan	10,000	—
zineb	Dithane Z-78	5,200	—
	Parzate		

Adapted from *Farm Chemical Handbook*, Meister Publishing Co., Willoughby, OH (1987).

Refer to Toxicity of Pesticides (page 216) for definitions.

DISEASE CONTROL FOR VEGETABLES

When using fungicides, read the label and carefully follow the instructions. Do not exceed maximum rates given, observe the interval between application and harvest, and apply only to those crops for which use has been approved. Make a record of the product used, trade name, concentration of the fungicide, dilution, rate applied per acre, and dates of application. Fungicides listed are for planning purposes. Follow local recommendations for efficacy and label for proper use.

Crop	Disease	Description	Control
Asparagus	Fusarium root rot	Damping-off of seedlings. Yellowing, stunting, or wilting of the growing stalks; vascular bundle discoloration. Crown death gives fields a spotty appearance	Use diseasefree crowns. Select fields where asparagus has not grown for 8 years. Preplanting crown dip; Benomyl
	Rust	Reddish or black pustules on stems and foliage	Cut and burn diseased tops. Use resistant varieties. Mancozceb, maneb-zinc
Bean	Anthracnose	Brown or black sunken spots with pink centers on pods, dark red or black cankers on stems and leaf veins	Use diseasefree seed and rotate crops every 2 years. Plow fall stubble. Do not cultivate when plants are wet. Maneb, maneb-zinc, zineb
	Bacterial blight	Large, dry, brown spots on leaves, often encircled by yellow border; water-soaked spots on pods; reddish cankers on stems. Plants may be girdled	Use diseasefree seed. Do not cultivate when plants are wet. Use 3-year rotation. Copper compounds
	Mosaic	Mottled (light and dark green) and curled leaves; stunting; reduced yields	Use mosaic-resistance varieties. Control weeds in areas adjacent to field. Control aphid carrier with insecticides

DISEASE CONTROL FOR VEGETABLES—Continued

Crop	Disease	Description	Control
Bean (Continued)	Powdery mildew	Faint, slightly discolored spots appear first on leaves, later on stems and pods, from which white powdery spots develop and may cover the entire plant	Sulfur
	Rust	Red to black pustules on leaves; leaves yellow and drop	Chlorothalonil, maneb, zineb
	Seed rot	Seed or seedling decay, which results in poor stands. Occurs most commonly in cold, wet soils	Crop rotation. Treat seed with captan or thiram. Metalaxyl
	White mold	Water-soaked spots on plants. White, cottony masses on pods	Benomyl, DCNA, thiophanate-methyl
Beet	Cercospora	Numerous light tan to brown spots with reddish to dark brown borders on leaves	Long rotation. Zineb
	Damping-off	Seed decay in soil; young seedlings collapse and die	Avoid wet soils, rotate crops. Treat seed with thiram
	Downy mildew	Lighter than normal leaf spots on upper surface and white mildew areas on lower side. Roots, leaves, flowers, and seed balls distorted on stecklings	Zineb
Broccoli, Brussels sprouts,	Alternaria leaf spot	Damping-off of seedlings. Small, circular yellow areas that enlarge in concentric	Chlorothalonil, maneb, zineb

cabbage, cauliflower, kale, kohlrabi		circles, and become black and sooty	
	Black leg	Sunken areas on stem near ground line resulting in girdling; gray spots speckled with black dots on leaves and stems	Use hot-water-treated seed and long rotation. Sanitation
	Black rot	Yellowing and browning of the foliage; blackened veins; stems show blackened ring when cross-sectioned	Use hot-water-treated seed and long rotation. Do not work wet fields. Sanitation
	Club root	Yellow leaves or green leaves that wilt on hot days; large, irregular swellings or "clubs" on roots	Start plants in new, steamed or fumigated plant beds. Adjust soil pH to 7.2 with hydrated lime before planting. PCNB.
	Downy mildew	Begins as slight yellowing on upper side of leaves; white mildew on lower side; spots enlarge until plant dies	Chlorothalonil, maneb, metalaxyl, zineb
	Fusarium yellows	Yellowish-green leaves; stunted plants; lower leaves drop	Use yellows-resistant varieties
Carrot	Alternaria leaf blight	Small, brown to black, irregular spots with yellow margins may enlarge to infect the entire top	Chlorothalonil, mancozeb, maneb, maneb-zinc
	Cercospera leaf blight	Small, necrotic spots that may enlarge and infect the entire top	Chlorothalonil, mancozeb, maneb, maneb-zinc
	Yellows	Purpling of tops; yellowed young leaves at center of crown followed by bushiness due to excessive petiole formation. Roots become woody and form numerous adventitious roots	Control leafhopper carrier with insecticides
Celery	Aster yellows	Yellowed leaves; stunting; tissues brittle and bitter in taste	Use resistant varieties. Control leafhopper carrier with insecticides. Control weeds in adjacent areas

DISEASE CONTROL FOR VEGETABLES—Continued

Crop	Disease	Description	Control
Celery (Continued)	Bacterial blight	Bright-yellow leaf spots, center turns brown and a yellow halo appears with enlargement	Seedbed sanitation. Copper compounds
	Early blight	Dead, ash gray, velvety areas on leaves	Anilazine, benomyl, chlorothalonil, copper compounds, mancozeb, maneb, thiophanate-methyl
	Late blight	Yellow spots on old leaves and stalks that turn dark gray speckled with black dots	
	Mosaic	Dwarfed plants with narrow, gray, or mottled leaves	Control weeds in adjacent areas. Control aphid carrier with insecticides
	Pink rot	Water-soaked spots; white- to pink-colored cottony growth at base of stalk leads to rotting	Crop rotation. Flooding for 4–8 weeks. DCNA
Cucumber (*See* Vine crops)			
Eggplant	Anthracnose	Sunken, tan fruit lesions	Use diseasefree seed. Captan, maneb, zineb
	Phomopsis blight	Young plants blacken and die; older plants have brown spots on leaves and fruit covered with brownish-black pustules	Use resistant varieties. Captan, maneb, zineb
	Verticillium wilt	Slow wilting; browning between leaf veins; stunting	Fumigate soil with methyl bromide or 1,3-D. Use verticillium-tolerant varieties. Use long rotation
Endive, escarole, lettuce	Aster yellows	Center leaves bleached, dwarfed, curled or twisted. Heads do not form; young plants particularly affected	Control leafhopper carrier with insecticides

	Big vein	Leaves with light green, enlarged veins developing into yellow, crinkled leaves; stunting; delayed maturity	Avoid cold, wet soils. Use tolerant varieties. Crop rotation
	Bottom rot	Damage begins at base of plants; blades of leaves rot first, then the midrib but the main stem is hardly affected	Avoid wet, poorly drained areas. Plant on raised beds. Practice 3-year rotation. Iprodione
	Downy mildew	Light green spots on upperside of leaves; lesions enlarge and white mycelium appears on opposite side of spots; browning and dwarfing of plant	Maneb, zineb
	Drop	Wilting of outer leaves; watery decay on stems and old leaves	Crop rotation. Deep plowing. Raised beds. DCNA, iprodione, vinclozolin
	Mosaic	Mottling (yellow and green), ruffling, or distortion of leaves; plants have sickly appearance	Use virusfree MTO seed. Plant away from old lettuce beds. Control weeds. Control aphid carrier with insecticide
	Tipburn	Edges of tender leaves brown and die; may interfere with growth; most severe on head lettuce	Use tolerant varieties. Prevent stress by providing good growing conditions
Lima bean	Downy mildew	Purpling and distortion of leaf veins; white downy mold on pods; blackened beans	Use resistant varieties and diseasefree seed. Maneb, zineb
Muskmelon (*See* Vine crops)			
Okra	Southern blight	Mass of pinkish fungus bodies around base of plant; sudden loss of leaves	Crop rotation. Deep plowing of plant stubble
	Verticillium wilt	Stunting; chlorosis; shedding of leaves	Crop rotation. Avoid planting where disease previously present
Onion	Blight (blast)	Papery spots on leaves; browning and death of upper portion of leaves; delayed maturity	Iprodione, mancozeb, maneb, zineb

DISEASE CONTROL FOR VEGETABLES—Continued

Crop	Disease	Description	Control
Onion (Continued)	Downy mildew	Begins as pale-green spot near tip of leaf; purple mold found when moisture present; infected leaves olive-green to black	Mancozeb, maneb, zineb
	Neck rot	Soft, brownish tissue around neck; scales around neck are dry, and black sclerotia may form. Essentially a dry rot if soft rot bacteria not present	Undercut, and windrow plants until inside neck tissues are dry before storage. Cure at 93–95°F for 5 days
	Pink root	Plants are affected from seedling stage onward throughout life cycle. Affected roots turn pink, shrivel, and die	Avoid infected soils. Use tolerant varieties
	Purple blotch	Small, white sunken lesions with purple centers enlarge to girdle leaf or seed stem. Leaves and stems fall over 3–4 weeks after infection in severe cases. Bulb rot at and after harvest	Iprodione, mancozeb, maneb, zineb
	Smut	Black spots on leaves; cracks develop on side of spot revealing black, sooty powder within	Crop rotation. Captan
Parsnip	Canker	Brown discoloration near shoulder or crown of root	Ridge soil over shoulders
	Leaf blight	Leaves and petioles turn yellow and then brown. Entire plant may be killed	Practice 2-year rotation, use well-drained soil with pH 7.0

Pea	Powdery mildew	White, powdery mold on leaves, stems, and pods. Mildewed areas become brown and necrotic	Use diseasefree seed and resistant varieties. Sulfur
	Root rot	Rotted and yellowish-brown or black stems (below ground) and roots; outer layers of root slough off leaving a central core	Early planting and 3-year rotation. Do not double crop with bean. Seed treatment
	Virus	Several viruses affect pea causing mottling, distortion of leaves, rosetting, chlorosis, or necrosis	Use resistant varieties. Control aphid carrier with insecticides
	Wilt	Yellowing leaves; dwarfing, browning of xylem; wilting	Early planting and 3-year rotation. Use resistant varieties
Pepper	Anthracnose	Dark, round spots with black specks on fruits	Captan, maneb, zineb
	Bacterial leaf spot	Yellowish-green spots on young leaves; raised, brown spots on undersides of older leaves, brown, cracked, rough spots on fruit; old leaves turn yellow	Use diseasefree seed, hot-water-treated seed. Copper compounds plus mancozeb or maneb
	Mosaic	Mottled (yellowed and green) and curled leaves; fruits yellow or show green ring spots; stunted; reduced yields	Use resistant varieties. Control insect carriers (particularly aphids) and weed hosts. Stylet oil
Potato	Early blight	Dark brown spots on leaves; foliage injured; reduced yields	For late blight, bury all cull potatoes. Anilazine, chlorothalonil, mancozeb, maneb, maneb-zinc
	Late blight	Dark, then necrotic area on leaves and stem; infected tubers rot in storage. Disease is favored by moist conditions	
	Rhizoctonia	Nectrotic spots, girdling and death of sprouts before or shortly after emergence. Brown to black raised spots on mature tubers	Avoid deep planting to encourage early emergence. Use diseasefree seed. Captan, mancozeb

DISEASE CONTROL FOR VEGETABLES—Continued

Crop	Disease	Description	Control
Potato (Continued)	Scab	Rough, scabby, raised or pitted lesions on tubers	Crop rotation. Use resistant varieties. Keep soil pH about 5.3
	Virus	A large number of viruses infect potato causing leaf mottling, distortion, and dwarfing. Some viruses cause irregularly shaped or necrotic area in tubers	Use certified seed. Control aphid and leafhopper carrier with insecticides
Radish	Downy mildew	Internal discoloration of root crown tissue. Outer surface may become dark and rough at the soil line	Select clean, well-drained soils. Zineb
	Fusarium wilt	Young plants yellow and die rapidly in warm weather. Stunting, unilateral leaf yellowing; vascular discoloration of fleshy roots	Use tolerant varieties. Avoid infected soil
Rhubarb	Crown rot	Wilting of leaf blades; browning at base of leaf stalk leading to decay	Plant in well-drained soil
	Leaf spot	Tiny, greenish-yellow spots (resembling mosaic) on upper side of leaf, eventually browning and forming a white spot surrounded by a red band; these spots may drop out to give a shot-hole appearance	Captan (greenhouse use only)
Rutabaga, turnip	Alternaria	Small, circular, yellow areas that enlarge in concentric circles and become	Use hot-water-treated seed. Turnip: maneb, zineb

		a black sooty color. Roots may become infested in storage	
	Anthracnose	Small, water-soaked spots on all above ground parts, which become light colored and may drop out. Small, sunken, dry spots on turnip roots, which are subject to secondary decay	Turnip: maneb, zineb
	Club root	Tumorlike swellings on taproot. Main root may be distorted. Diseased roots decay prematurely	Avoid soil previously infected with club root. Adjust acid soil to pH 7.3 by liming
	Downy mildew	Small, purplish, irregular spots on leaves, stems, and seedpods, which produce fluffy white growth. Desiccation of roots in storage	Turnip: maneb, zineb
	Mosaic virus	Stunted plants having ruffled leaves. Infected roots store poorly	Destroy volunteer plants. Control aphid carrier with insecticides
Southern pea	Fusarium wilt	Yellowed leaves; wilted plants; interior of stems lemon yellow	Avoid infected soil
Spinach	Blight (CMV)	Yellowed and curled leaves; stunted plants; reduced yields	Use tolerant varieties. Control aphid carrier with insecticides
	Downy mildew	Yellow spots on upper surface of leaves; downy or violet-gray mold on undersides	Use resistant varieties. Maneb, zineb
Squash (*See* Vine crops)			
Strawberry	Anthracnose	Spotting and girdling of stolons and petioles, crown rot, fruit rot, and a black leaf spot; occurs in southeastern United States	Use diseasefree plants and resistant varieties. Benomyl, captan

DISEASE CONTROL FOR VEGETABLES—Continued

Crop	Disease	Description	Control
Strawberry (Continued)	Gray mold	Rot on green or ripe fruit, beginning at calyx or contact with infected fruit; affected area supports white or gray mycelium	Use less susceptible varieties. Benomyl, captan, thiophanate-methyl, vinclozolin
	Leaf scorch	Numerous irregular, purplish blotches with brown centers; entire leaves dry up and appear scorched	Use diseasefree plants and resistant varieties. Renew perennial plantings frequently. Benomyl, captan, thiophanate-methyl, zineb
	Leaf spot	Indefinite-shaped spots with brown, gray, or white centers and purple borders	Use diseasefree plants and resistant varieties. Benomyl, captan, zineb
	Powdery mildew	Characteristic white mycelium on leaves, flower, and fruit	Use resistant varieties. Benomyl, sulfur
	Red stele	Stunted plants having roots with red stele that is seen when root is cut lengthwise	Improve drainage and avoid compaction of soil. Use diseasefree plants and resistant varieties
	Verticillium	Marginal and interveinal necrosis of outer leaves, inner leaves remain green	Preplant soil fumigation. Use resistant varieties
Sweet corn	Bacterial blight	Dwarfing; premature tassels die; yellow bacterial slime oozes from wet stalks; stem dries and dies	Use resistant varieties. Control corn flea beetle with insecticides
	Leaf blight	Canoe-shaped spots on leaves	Use resistant varieties. Chlorothalonil, mancozeb, maneb

	Maize dwarf mosaic	Stunting; mottling of new leaves in whorl and poor ear fill at the base	Use tolerant varieties. Plant tolerant varieties around susceptible ones. Control aphid carrier with insecticides
	Seed rot	Seed decays in soil	Use seed treated with captan or thiram
	Smut	Large, smooth, whitish galls, or outgrowths on ears, tassels, and nodes; covering dries and breaks open to release black, powdery, or greasy spores	Use tolerant varieties. Control corn borers with insecticides
Sweet potato	Black rot	Black depressions on sweet potato; black cankers on underground stem parts	Select diseasefree potato seed. Rotate crops and planting beds. Use vine cuttings rather than slips
	Internal cork	Dark brown to black, hard, corky lesions in flesh developing in storage at high temperature. Yellow spots with purple borders on new growth of leaves	Select diseasefree seed potatoes
	Pox	Plants dwarfed; only one or two vines produced; leaves thin and pale green; soil rot pits on roots	Use diseasefree stock and clean planting beds. Sulfur to lower soil pH to 5.2
	Scurf	Brown to black discoloration of root; uniform rusting of root surface	Rotation of crops and beds. Use diseasefree stock. Use vine cuttings rather than slips
	Stem rot	Yellowing between veins; vines wilt; stems darken inside and may split	Select diseasefree seed potatoes. Rotate fields and plant beds
Tomato	Anthracnose	Begins with circular, sunken spots on fruit; as spots enlarge, center becomes dark and fruit rots	Anilazine, chlorothalonil, mancozeb, maneb
	Bacterial canker	Wilting; rolling, and browning of leaves; pith may discolor or disappear; fruit displays bird's-eye spots	Use hot-water-treated seed. Avoid planting in infected fields for 3 years

DISEASE CONTROL FOR VEGETABLES—Continued

Crop	Disease	Description	Control
Tomato (Continued)	Bacterial spot	Young lesions on fruit appear as dark, raised spots; older lesions blacken and appear sunken with brown centers; leaves brown and dry	Use hot-water-treated seed. Copper compounds plus mancozeb or maneb
	Early blight	Dark brown spots on leaves; brown cankers on stems; girdling; dark, leathery, decayed areas at stem end of fruit	Anilazine, chlorothalonil, mancozeb, maneb, maneb-zinc
	Late blight	Dark, water-soaked spots on leaves; white fungus on undersides of leaves; withering of leaves; water-soaked spots on fruit turn brown. Disease is favored by moist conditions	Anilazine, chlorothalonil, mancozeb, maneb, maneb-zinc
	Fusarium wilt	Yellowing and wilting of lower, older leaves; disease affects whole plant eventually	Use resistant varieties
	Gray leaf spot	Symptoms appear first in seedlings. Small brown to black spots on leaves, which enlarge and have shiny gray centers. The centers may drop out to give shotgun appearance. Oldest leaves affected first	Use resistant varieities. Anilazine, chlorothalonil, mancozeb, maneb
	Leaf mold	Chlorotic spots on upper side of oldest leaves appear in humid weather. Underside of leaf spot may have green	Use resistant varieties. Staking and pruning to provide air movement. Anilazine, benomyl, chlorothalonil,

		mold. Spots may merge until entire leaf is affected. Disease advances to younger leaves	mancozeb, maneb
	Mosaic	Mottling (yellow and green) and roughening of leaves; dwarfing; reduced yields; russeting of fruit	Avoid contact by smokers. Control aphid carrier with insecticides. Stylet oil
	Verticillium wilt	Differs from fusarium wilt by appearance of disease on all branches at the same time; yellow areas on leaves become brown; midday wilting; dropping of leaves beginning at bottom	Use resistant varieties
Vine crops: cucumber, muskmelon, pumpkin, squash, watermelon	Alternaria leaf spot	Circular spots showing concentric rings as they enlarge, appear first on oldest leaves	Field sanitation. Use diseasefree seed. Maneb, maneb-zinc
	Angular leaf spot	Irregular, angular, water-soaked spots on leaves which later turn gray and die. Dead tissue may tear away leaving holes. Nearly circular fruit spots, which become white	Use tolerant varieties. Copper compounds
	Anthracnose	Reddish-black spots on leaves; elongated tan cankers on stems; fruits have sunken spots with flesh-colored ooze in center, later turning black	Use tolerant varieties. Benomyl, chlorothalonil, mancozeb, maneb, maneb-zinc, thiophanate-methyl, zineb
	Bacterial wilt	Vines wilt and die; stem sap produces strings; no yellowing occurs	Control striped cucumber beetles with insecticides. Remove wilting plants from field
	Black rot (squash and pumpkin only)	Water-soaked areas appear on rinds of fruit in storage. Brown or black infected tissue rapidly invades entire plant	Use diseasefree seed. Crop rotation. Cure fruit for storage at 85°F for 2 weeks, store at 50–55°F. Benomyl (squash only), chlorothalonil, maneb

DISEASE CONTROL FOR VEGETABLES—Continued

Crop	Disease	Description	Control
Vine crops: cucumber, muskmelon, pumpkin, squash, watermelon (Continued)	Downy mildew	Angular, yellow spots on older leaves; purple fungus on undersides of leaves when moisture present; leaves wither, die; fruit may be dwarfed with poor flavor	Use tolerant varieties. Benomyl, chlorothalonil, maneb, maneb-zinc
	Fusarium wilt	Stunting and yellowing of vine; water-soaked streak on one side of vine turning yellow eventually cracks and oozes sap	Use resistant varieties. Avoid infected soils
	Gummy stem blight	Lesions may occur on stems, leaves, and fruit from which a gummy exudate may ooze	Use diseasefree seed. Rotate crops. Benomyl, chlorothalonil, mancozeb, maneb, maneb-zinc, thiophanate-methyl
	Mosaic	Mottling (yellow and green) and curling of leaves; mottled and warty fruit; reduced yields; burning and dwarfing of entire plant	Control striped cucumber beetle and aphid with insecticides. Use resistant varieties. Destroy surrounding perennial weeds
	Powdery mildew	White, powdery growth on upper leaf surface and petioles; wilting of foliage	Use tolerant varieties. Benomyl, thiophanate-methyl, triadimefon
	Scab	Water-soaked spots on leaves turning white; sunken cavity on fruit later covered by grayish-olive fungus; fruit destroyed by soft rot	Use resistant varieties. Benomyl, mancozeb, maneb, zineb

Chemical controls from *Guidelines for the Control of Plant Diseases and Nematodes*, USDA Agricultural Handbook 656 (1986) and *Crop Protection Chemicals Reference*, 3rd ed., Wiley, New York (1987).

TOXICITY OF PESTICIDES: INSECTICIDES

Insecticide	Some Trade Names	Acute Oral LD_{50} (mg/kg)	Acute Dermal LD_{50} (mg/kg)
acephate	Orthene	945	10,250
aldicarb	Temik	1	5
azinphos-methyl	Guthion	5–20	220
Bacillis thuringiensis	several	—	—
carbaryl	Sevin	500	850
carbofuran	Furadan	11	10,200
chlorpyrifos	Lorsban	97–276	2,000
cyromazine	Trigard	3,387	3,100
demeton	Systox	2.5–12	8.2–14
diazinon	Diazinon	300–400	3,600
dimethoate	Cygon De-Fend	215	1,000
disulfoton	Di-Syston	2–12	6–25
endosulfan	Thiodan	30–110	359
esfenvalerate	Asana	75	2,000
ethion	Ethion	208	—
ethoprop	Mocap	61	2.4
fensulfothion	Dasanit	2–10	3–30
fenvalerate	Pydrin	451	2,500
fonofos	Dyfonate	8–17	25
malathion	several	1,375	4,100
methamidophos	Monitor	18–21	118
methidathion	Supracide	44	200
methomyl	Lannate Nudrin	17	5,880
methoxychlor	several	6,000	—
mevinphos	Phosdrin	16–33	33
monocrotophos	Azodrin	8–23	354
naled	Dibrom	430	1,100
oxamyl	Vydate	5.4	2,960
oxydemeton-methyl	Metasystox-R	65–75	250
parathion	several	4–13	55
permethrin	Ambush Pounce	4,000	4,000
phorate	Thimet	2–4	20–30
phosalone	Zolone	120	1,250
phosmet	Imidan	147–316	4,640
terbufos	Counter	4–9	1
trichlorfon	Dylox Proxol	150–400	500

Adapted from *Farm Chemicals Handbook*, Meister Publishing Co., Willoughby, OH (1987).

Refer to Toxicity of Pesticides (page 216) for definitions.

INSECT CONTROL FOR VEGETABLES

When using insecticides, read the label and carefully follow the instructions. Do not exceed maximum rates given; observe the interval between application and harvest, and apply only to crops for which use is approved. Make a record of the product used, trade name, formulation, dilution, rate applied per acre, and dates of application. Read and follow all label precautions to protect the applicator and workers from insecticide injury, and environment from contamination. Insecticides listed are for planning purposes. Follow local recommendations for efficacy and label for proper use.

Crop	Insect	Description	Control
Artichoke	Aphid	Small, green, pink, or black soft-body insects that rapidly reproduce tc large populations. Damage results from sucking plant sap; indirectly from virus transmission to crop plants	Endosulfan, mevinphos, parathion, phosalone
	Plume moth	Small wormlike larvae blemish bracts and may destroy the base of the bract	Azinphos-methyl, endosulfan, esfenvalerate, fenvalerate, methidathion, parathion, permethrin
Asparagus	Beetle and 12-spotted beetle	Metallic blue or black beetles (1/4 in.) with yellowish wing markings and reddish, narrow head. Larvae are humpbacked, slate gray. Both feed on shoots and foliage	Carbaryl, chlorpyrifos, malathion, methomyl, permethrin
	Cutworm	Dull-colored moths lay eggs in the soil producing dark-colored smooth	Chlorpyrifos, methomyl, permethrin

		worms, 1–2 in. long, which characteristically curl up when disturbed. May feed belowground, or aboveground at night	
Bean	Aphid	*See* Artichoke	Acephate, azinphos-methyl, demeton, dimethoate, disulfoton, methomyl, mevinphos, parathion
	Corn earworm	Gray-brown moth (1½ in.) with dark wing tips deposits eggs, especially on fresh corn silk. Brown, green, or pink larvae (2 in.) feed on silk, kernels, and foliage	Carbaryl, methomyl, parathion
	Leafhopper	Green wedge-shaped, soft bodies (⅛ in.). When present in large numbers, sucking of plant sap causes plant distortion or burned appearance. Secondary damage results from transmission of yellows disease	Acephate, azinphos-methyl, carbaryl, dimethoate, disulfoton, ethion, malathion, methomyl, mevinphos, oxydemeton-methyl, parathion
	Mexican bean beetle	Copper-colored beetle (¼ in.) with 16 black spots on its back. Orange to yellow spiny larva (⅓ in.). Beetle and larvae feeding on leaf undersides cause a lacework appearance	Acephate, azinphos-methyl, carbaryl, diazinon, dimethoate, disulfoton, endosulfan, ethion, malathion, methomyl, mevinphos, parathion, trichlorfon
	Seed corn maggot	Grayish-brown flies (⅕ in.) deposit eggs in the soil near plants. Cream-colored, wedge-shaped maggots (¼ in.) tunnel into seeds, potato seed pieces, and sprouts	Use fungicide and insecticide-treated seed, planter box, slurry, or band insecticide treatment

INSECT CONTROL FOR VEGETABLES—Continued

Crop	Insect	Description	Control
Bean (Continued)	Spider mite	Reddish, yellow, or greenish, tiny, eight-legged spiders that suck plant sap from leaf undersides causing distortion. Fine webs may be visible when mites are present in large numbers. Mites are not true insects	Azinphos-methyl, demeton, dimethoate, disulfoton, ethion, mevinphos, oxydemeton-methyl, parathion
	Spotted-cucumber beetle	Yellowish, elongated beetle (1/4 in.) with 11 or 12 black spots on its back. Leaf-feeding may destroy young plants when present in large numbers. Transmits bacterial wilt of cucurbits	Azinphos-methyl, carbaryl, diazinon, endosulfan, methomyl, parathion
	Striped-cucumber beetle	Yellow (1/5 in.) with three black stripes on its back; feeds on leaves. White larvae (1/3 in.) feed on roots and stems. Transmits bacterial wilt of cucurbits	Azinphos-methyl, carbaryl, diazinon, endosulfan, parathion
	Tarnish plant bug	Brownish, flattened, oval bugs (1/4 in.) with a clear triangular marking at the rear. Bugs damage plants by sucking plant sap	Lima bean only—acephate, azinphos-methyl, carbaryl, methomyl, parathion
Beet	Aphid	*See* Artichoke	Malathion, mevinphos, parathion
	Flea beetle	Small (1/6 in.) variable-colored, usually dark beetles, often present in large	Carbaryl, methomyl, parathion

		numbers in the early part of the growing season. Feeding results in numerous small holes, giving a shotgun appearance. Indirect damage results from diseases transmitted	
	Leaf miner	Tiny, black and yellow adults. Yellowish-white maggotlike larvae tunnel within leaves and cause white or translucent, irregularly damaged areas	Mevinphos, parathion
	Webworm	Yellow to green worm (1¼ in.) with a black stripe and numerous black spots on its back	*Bacillus thuringiensis*, parathion
Broccoli, Brussels sprouts, cabbage, cauliflower, kale, kohlrabi	Aphid	*See* Artichoke	*See pesticide labels for use on specific cole crops* Azinphos-methyl, dimethoate, disulfoton, endosulfan, malathion, methamidophos, mevinphos, oxydemeton-methyl, parathion, permethrin
	Flea beetle	*See* Beet	Carbaryl, disulfoton, endosulfan, fenvalerate
	Harlequin cabbage bug	Black, shield-shaped bug (⅜ in.) with red or yellow markings	Carbaryl, endosulfan
	Cabbage maggot	Housefly-like adult lays eggs in the soil at the base of plants. Yellowish, legless maggot (¼–⅓ in.) tunnels into roots and lower stem	Azinphos-methyl, chlorpyrifos, diazinon, fonofos

INSECT CONTROL FOR VEGETABLES—Continued

Crop	Insect	Description	Control
Broccoli, Brussels sprouts, cabbage, cauliflower, kale, kohlrabi (Continued)	Worms		
	Cabbage looper	A brownish moth (1½ in.) that lays eggs on upper leaf surfaces. Resulting worms (1½ in.) are green with thin white lines. Easily identified by their looping movement	Azinphos-methyl, *Bacillus thuringiensis*, carbaryl, endosulfan, esfenvalerate, fenvalerate, malathion, methamidophos, methomyl, mevinphos, parathion, permethrin, trichlorfon
	Diamondback moth	Small, slender, gray or brown moths. The folded wings of male moths show three diamond markings. Small (⅓ in.) larvae with distinctive V at rear, wiggle when disturbed	Same as for cabbage looper
	Imported cabbage worm	White butterflies with black wing spots lay eggs on undersides of leaves. Resulting worms (1¼ in.) are sleek, velvety, green	Same as for cabbage looper
Carrot	Leafhopper	*See* Bean	Carbaryl, malathion, methomyl, mevinphos, parathion
	Rust fly	Shiny, dark fly with a yellow head; lays eggs in the soil at the base of plants. Yellowish-white, legless maggot tunnels into roots	Diazinon, parathion
Celery	Aphid	*See* Artichoke	Acephate, azinphos-methyl, demeton, endosulfan, malathion, parathion

	Leaf miner	Adults are small, shiny, black flies with a bright yellow spot on upper thorax. Eggs are laid within the leaf. Larvae mine between upper and lower leaf surfaces	Azinphos-methyl, cyromazine, mevinphos, parathion, permethrin
	Spider mite	*See* Bean	Demeton, malathion, mevinphos, parathion
	Tarnished plant bug	*See* Bean	Azinphos-methyl, carbaryl, parathion
	Loopers and worms	*See* Broccoli, etc.	Acephate, *Bacillis thuringiensis*, carbaryl, endosulfan, methomyl, mevinphos, parathion, permethrin
Cucumber (*See* Vine crops)			
Eggplant	Aphid	*See* Artichoke	Demeton, malathion, methomyl, mevinphos, oxamyl, oxydemeton-methyl, parathion
	Colorado potato beetle	Oval beetle (3/8 in.) with 10 yellow and 10 black stripes lays yellow eggs on undersides of leaves. Brick-red, humpbacked larvae (1/2 in.) have black spots. Beetles and larvae are destructive leaf feeders	Carbaryl, endosulfan, esfenvalerate, fenvalerate, oxamyl, permethrin
	Flea beetle	*See* Beet	Azinphos-methyl, carbaryl, endosulfan, esfenvalerate, fenvalerate, parathion, permethrin
	Leaf miner	*See* Celery	Azinphos-methyl, oxamyl, parathion, permethrin
	Spider mite	*See* Bean	Ethion, malathion, oxamyl, oxydemeton-methyl

Crop	Insect	Description	Control
Endive, escarole, lettuce	Aphid	*See* Artichoke	Acephate, demeton, dimethoate, disulfoton, endosulfan, malathion, methomyl, mevinphos, oxydemeton-methyl, parathion
	Flea beetle	*See* Beet	Carbaryl, parathion
	Leafhopper	*See* Bean	Carbaryl, dimethoate, disulfoton, malathion, methomyl, parathion
	Leaf miner	*See* Beet	Cyromazine, dimethoate, mevinphos, parathion, permethrin
	Looper	*See* Broccoli	Acephate, *Bacillis thuringiensis*, endosulfan, methomyl, mevinphos, parathion, permethrin
Muskmelon (*See* Vine crops)			
Mustard greens	Aphid	*See* Artichoke	Dimethoate, endosulfan, malathion, parathion
	Worms	*See* Broccoli, etc.	*Bacillis thuringiensis*, carbaryl, endosulfan, malathion, methomyl, parathion
Okra	Aphid	*See* Artichoke	Mevinphos, parathion
	Green stinkbug	Large, flattened, shield-shaped, bright green bugs; various-sized nymphs with reddish markings	Carbaryl, mevinphos, parathion
Onion	Maggot	Slender, gray flies (1/4 in.) lay eggs in	Chlorpyrifos, diazinon, fensulfothion,

		soil. Small (1/3 in.) maggots bore into stems and bulbs	fonofos, malathion, parathion
	Thrips	Yellow or brown winged or wingless tiny (1/25 in.) insect. Damages plant by sucking plant sap causing white areas or brown leaf tips	Endosulfan, malathion, methomyl, mevinphos, parathion
Parsnip	Carrot rust fly	*See* Carrot	Diazinon
Pea	Aphid	*See* Artichoke	Diazinon, esfenvalerate, fenvalerate, methomyl, mevinphos, parathion, phosmet and dimethoate
	Seed maggot	Housefly-like gray adults lay eggs that develop into maggots (1/4 in.) with sharply pointed heads	Diazinon
	Weevil	Brown-colored adults marked by white, black, or gray (1/5 in.) lay eggs on young pods. Larvae are small and whitish with a brown head and mouth. Adults feed on blossoms. May infest seed before harvest and remain in hibernation during storage	Carbaryl, endosulfan, fenvalerate, parathion
Pepper	Aphid	*See* Artichoke	Acephate, diazinon, dimethoate, endosulfan, malathion, methomyl, mevinphos, oxamyl, oxydemeton-methyl
	Corn borer	*See* Sweet corn	Acephate, azinphos-methyl, *Bacillis thuringiensis*, esfenvalerate, fenvalerate, permethrin
	Flea beetle	*See* Beet	Azinphos-methyl, carbaryl, endosulfan, esfenvalerate, fenvalerate, permethrin

INSECT CONTROL FOR VEGETABLES—Continued

Crop	Insect	Description	Control
Pepper (Continued)	Leaf miner	*See* Beet	Azinphos-methyl, diazinon, dimethoate, ethion, parathion, permethrin, oxamyl, trichlorfon
	Maggot	Housefly-sized adults have yellow stripes on body and brown stripes on wings. Larvae are typical maggots with pointed heads	Dimethoate, endosulfan, malathion, trichlorfon
	Weevil	Black-colored, gray or yellow marked, snout beetle, with the snout about one-half the length of the body. Grayish-white larvae are legless and have a pale brown head. Both adults and larvae feed on buds and pods; adults also feed on foliage	Esfenvalerate, fenvalerate, oxamyl, permethrin
Potato	Aphid	*See* Artichoke	Aldicarb, demeton, diazinon, dimethoate, disulfoton, endosulfan, esfenvalerate, fenvalerate, malathion, methamidophos, methomyl, mevinphos, monocrotophos, oxydemeton-methyl, parathion, permethrin, phorate
	Colorado potato beetle	*See* Eggplant	Aldicarb, azinphos-methyl, carbaryl, carbofuran, diazinon, disulfoton,

		endosulfan, esfenvalerate, fenvalerate, methamidophos, monocrotophos, parathion, permethrin, phosmet
Cutworm	*See* Asparagus	Diazinon, esfenvalerate, fenvalerate, methamidophos, methomyl, parathion, permethrin
Flea beetle	*See* Beet	Azinphos-methyl, carbaryl, carbofuran, diazinon, disulfoton, endosulfan, esfenvalerate, fenvalerate, methamidophos, methomyl, monocrotophos, oxydemeton-methyl, parathion, permethrin, phorate
Leafhopper	*See* Bean	Aldicarb, azinphos-methyl, carbaryl, demeton, dimethoate, disulfoton, endosulfan, esfenvalerate, fenvalerate, malathion, methamidophos, methomyl, mevinphos, monocrotophos, oxydemeton-methyl, parathion, permethrin, phorate
Leaf miner	*See* Beet	Azinphos-methyl, carbofuran, diazinon, parathion
Tuberworm	Small, narrow-winged, grayish-brown moths (1/2 in.) lay eggs on foliage and exposed tubers in evening. Purplish or green caterpillars (3/4 in.) with brown heads burrow into exposed tubers in the field or in storage	Azinphos-methyl, endosulfan, esfenvalerate, fenvalerate, methamidophos, methomyl, monocrotophos, permethrin. Prevent soil cracking

INSECT CONTROL FOR VEGETABLES—Continued

Crop	Insect	Description	Control
Potato (Continued)	Wireworm	Adults are dark-colored, elongated beetles (click beetles). Yellowish, tough-bodied, segmented larvae feed on roots and tunnel through fleshy roots and tubers	Diazinon, ethoprop, fensulothion, fonofos, phorate
Radish	Maggot	*See* Broccoli, etc.	Chlorpyrifos, diazinon
Rhubarb	Curculio	Yellow-dusted snout beetle that damages plants by puncturing stems	Destroy yellow-dock plants (alternate host) in vicinity of rhubarb plantings
Rutabaga, turnip	Flea beetle	*See* Beet	Carbaryl, diazinon
	Maggot	*See* Broccoli, etc.	Chlorpyrifos, fensulfothion (rutabaga), diazinon (turnip)
Squash (*See* Vine crops)			
Southern pea	Curculio	Black, humpbacked snout beetle. Eats small holes in pods and peas. Larvae are white with yellowish head and no legs	Azinphos-methyl, carbaryl, endosulfan
	Leafhopper	*See* Bean	Carbaryl, malathion, methomyl
	Leaf miner	*See* Beet	Azinphos-methyl, parathion, trichlorfon
Spinach	Aphid	*See* Artichoke	Azinphos-methyl, dimethoate, malathion, mevinphos, parathion
	Leaf miner	*See* Beet	Azinphos-methyl, dimethoate, mevinphos, parathion, permethrin

Strawberry	Aphid	*See* Artichoke	Azinphos-methyl, demeton, diazinon, disulfoton, endosulfan, malathion, methomyl, mevinphos, naled, parathion
	Mites	Several mite species attack strawberry	Demeton, diazinon, disulfoton, endosulfan, ethion, malathion, mevinphos, naled, parathion
		See Bean	
	Tarnished plant bug	*See* Bean	Endosulfan
	Thrips	*See* Onion	Malathion, methomyl, parathion
	Weevils	Several weevil species attack strawberry	Azinphos-methyl, carbaryl, chlorpyrifos, malathion, methoxychlor
	Worms	Several worm species attack strawberry	Azinphos-methyl, *Bacillis thuringiensis*, carbaryl, methomyl, methoxychlor, parathion
Sweet corn	Armyworms	Moths (1½ in.) with dark gray front wings and light-colored hind wings lay eggs on leaf undersides. Tan, green, or black worms (1¼ in.) feed on plant leaves and corn ears	Carbaryl, chlorpyrifos, diazinon, esfenvalerate, fenvalerate, methomyl, parathion, permethrin, trichlorfon
	Earworm	*See* Bean	Carbaryl, endosulfan, esfenvalerate, fenvalerate, methomyl, parathion, permethrin
	European corn borer	Pale, yellowish moths (1 in.) with dark bands lay eggs on undersides of leaves. Caterpillars hatch, feed on leaves briefly, and tunnel into stalk and to the ear	*Bacillis thuringiensis*, carbaryl, carbofuran, chlorpyrifos, diazinon, esfenvalerate, fenvalerate, methomyl, parathion, permethrin

INSECT CONTROL FOR VEGETABLES—Continued

Crop	Insect	Description	Control
Sweet corn (Continued)	Flea beetle	*See* Beet	Carbaryl, carbofuran, chlorpyrifos, esfenvalerate, fenvalerate, methomyl, parathion, permethrin, terbufos
	Japanese beetle	Shiny, metallic green with coppery-brown wing covers, oval beetles (½ in.). Severe leaf feeding results in a lacework appearance. Larvae are grubs that feed on grass roots	Carbaryl, malathion, parathion
	Seed-corn maggot	*See* Bean	Carbofuran, diazinon, fensulfothion, phorate, terbufos
	Stalk borer	Grayish moths (1 in.) lay eggs on weeds in the fall. Small, white, brown-striped caterpillars hatch in spring and tunnel into weed and crop stalks. Most damage is usually at edges of fields	Chlorpyrifos, esfenvalerate, fenvalerate, terbufos
Sweet potato	Flea beetle	*See* Beet	Carbaryl, endosulfan, ethoprop
	Weevil	Blue-black and red adult (¼ in.) feeds on leaves and stems, grublike larva tunnels into roots in the field and storage	Destroy volunteer plants in field. Clean out storage; destroy old plant material. Carbaryl
	Wireworm	*See* Potato	Chlorpyrifos, diazinon, ethoprop, fensulfothion

Tomato	Aphid	*See* Artichoke	Azinphos-methyl, dimethoate, methomyl, mevinphos, parathion
	Colorado potato beetle	*See* Eggplant	Azinphos-methyl, carbaryl, endosulfan, esfenvalerate, fenvalerate, parathion
	Corn earworm (tomato fruitworm)	*See* Bean	Azinphos-methyl, *Bacillis thuringiensis*, carbaryl, esfenvalerate, fenvalerate, methomyl, parathion
	Flea beetle	*See* Beet	Carbaryl, endosulfan, esfenvalerate, fenvalerate, parathion
	Fruit fly	Small, dark-colored flies usually associated with overripe or decaying vegetables	Sanitation. Azinphos-methyl, diazinon
	Hornworm	Large (4–5 in.) moths lay eggs that develop into large (3–4 in.) green fleshy worms with prominent white lines on sides and a distinct horn at the rear. Voracious leaf feeders	Azinphos-methyl, *Bacillis thuringiensis*, carbaryl, esfenvalerate, fenvalerate, methomyl, parathion, trichlorfon
	Leaf miner	*See* Beet	Dimethoate, ethion, oxamyl, parathion, trichlorfon
	Pinworm	Tiny yellow, gray, or green, purple-spotted, brown-headed caterpillars cause small fruit lesions, mostly near calyx. Presence detected by large white blotches near folded leaves	Azinphos-methyl, carbaryl, esfenvalerate, fenvalerate, methomyl, parathion
	Mite	*See* Bean	Ethion, mevinphos, parathion
	Stink bug	*See* Okra	Azinphos-methyl, carbaryl, parathion
	White fly	Small, white flies that move when disturbed	Azinphos-methyl, esfenvalerate, fenvalerate, parathion

INSECT CONTROL FOR VEGETABLES—Continued

Crop	Insect	Description	Control
Vine crops: cucumber, muskmelon, pumpkin, squash, watermelon	Aphid	*See* Artichoke	Diazinon, endosulfan, methomyl, mevinphos, oxydemeton-methyl, parathion
	Cucumber beetle (spotted or striped)	*See* Bean	Azinphos-methyl, carbaryl, endosulfan, esfenvalerate, fenvalerate, methomyl, parathion
	Leafhopper	*See* Bean	Carbaryl, diazinon, esfenvalerate, fenvalerate, mevinphos
	Leaf miner	*See* Beet	Diazinon, ethion, oxamyl
	Mite	*See* Bean	Diazinon, ethion, mevinphos, oxydemeton-methyl
	Pickleworm	White moths (1 in.), later become greenish with black spots, with brown heads and brown-tipped wings with white centers, and a conspicuous brush at the tip of the body, lay eggs on foliage. Brown-headed, white, later becoming greenish with black spots. Larvae ($^3/_4$ in.) feed on blossoms, leaves, and fruit	Carbaryl, endosulfan, esfenvalerate, fenvalerate
	Squash bug	Brownish, flat stinkbug ($^5/_8$ in.). Nymphs ($^3/_8$ in.) are gray to green.	Carbaryl, endosulfan, esfenvalerate, fenvalerate

	Plant damage is due to sucking of plant sap	
Squash vine borer	Black, metallic moth (1½ in.) with transparent hind wings and abdomen ringed with red and black; lays eggs at the base of the plant. White caterpillars bore into the stem and tunnel throughout	Endosulfan, esfenvalerate, fenvalerate, parathion

Chemical controls referenced from *Crop Protection Chemicals Reference*, 3rd ed., Wiley, New York (1987).

IDENTIFICATION OF VEGETABLE INSECTS

Effective insect management requires accurate identification, and a thorough knowledge of the insect's habits and life cycle.

Aphid
Winged adult (*l.*), Wingless adult (*r.*)
(1.6–2.4 mm long)

Asparagus beetle
Common (*l.*), Spotted (*r.*)
(6.0–9.5 mm long)

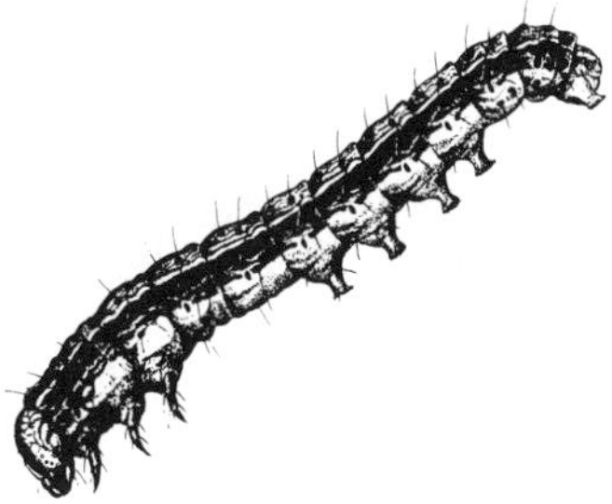

Armyworm
(30–40 mm long)

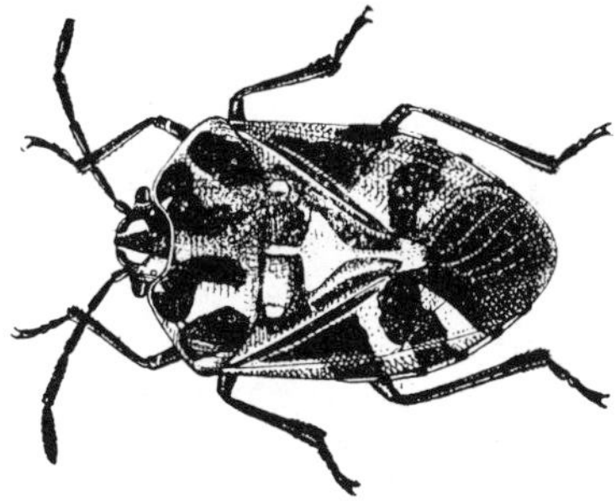

Cabbage harlequin bug
(7–10 mm long)

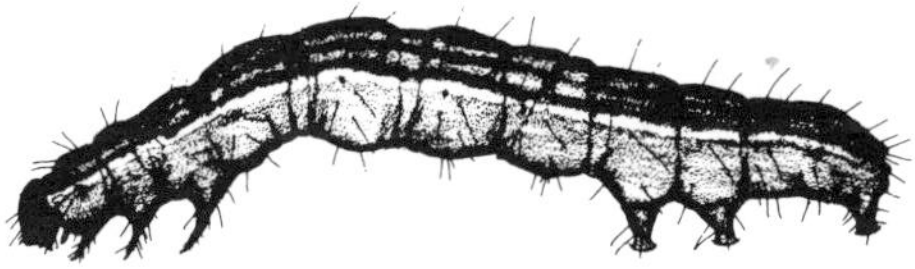

Cabbage looper
(30 mm long)

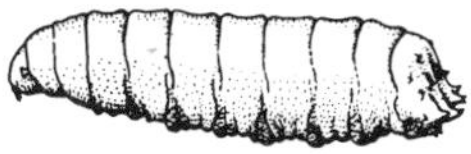

Cabbage maggot
(6 mm long)

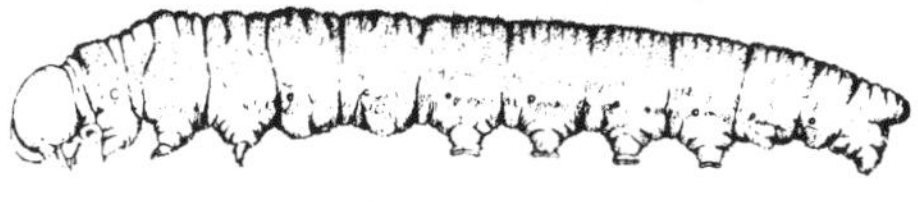

Cabbage worm
(32 mm long)

Carrot rust fly larva
(9 mm long)

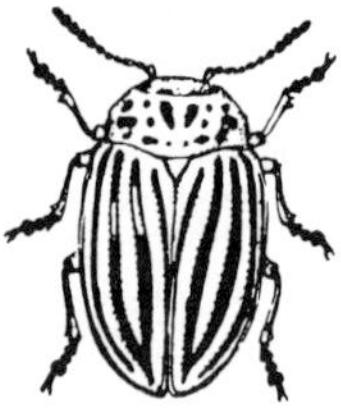

Colorado potato beetle
Adult (*l.*) Larva (*r.*)
(9–14 mm long) (10 mm long)

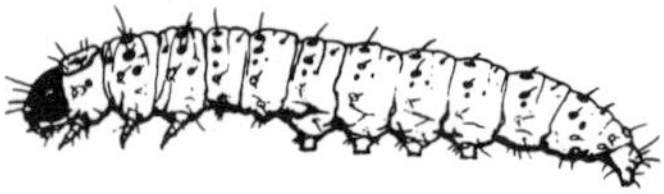

Corn borer
(25 mm long)

Corn seed maggot
(5–7 mm long)

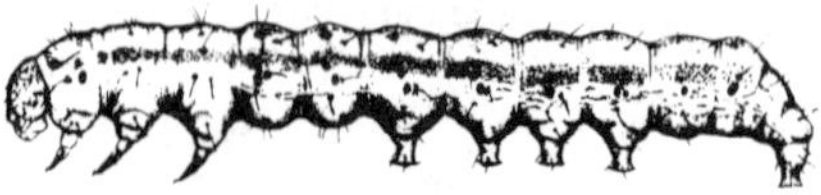

Corn earworm
(44 mm long)

Cutworm
(28–50 mm long)

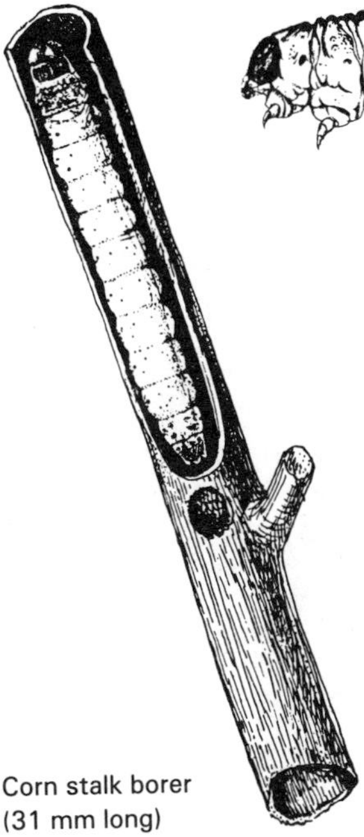

Corn stalk borer
(31 mm long)

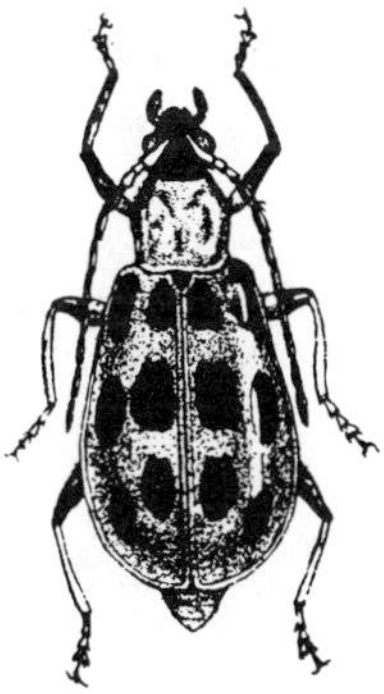

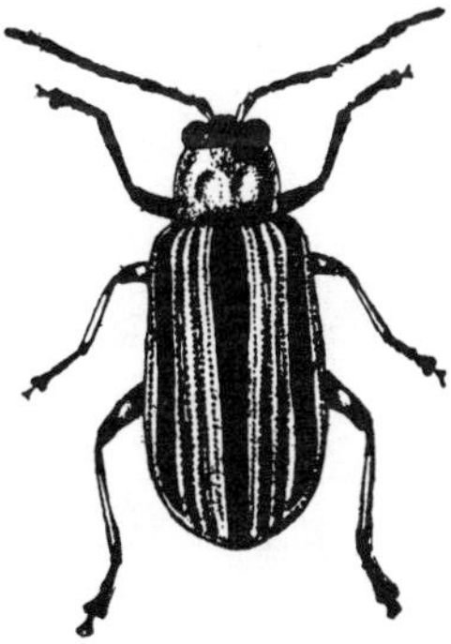

Cucumber beetles
Spotted (*l.*) Striped (*r.*)
(6 mm long) (5 mm long)

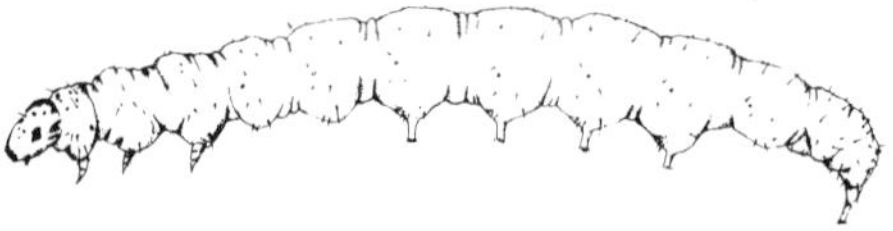

Diamondback moth larva
(7 mm long)

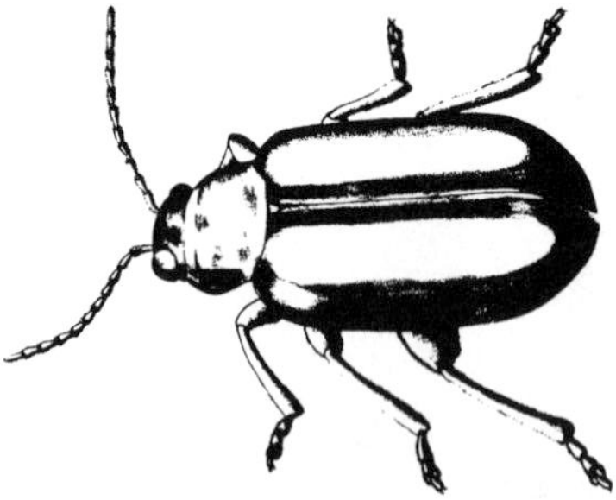

Flea beetle
(2.5 mm long)

Fruit fly
(3 mm long)

Hornworm
(75–85 mm long)

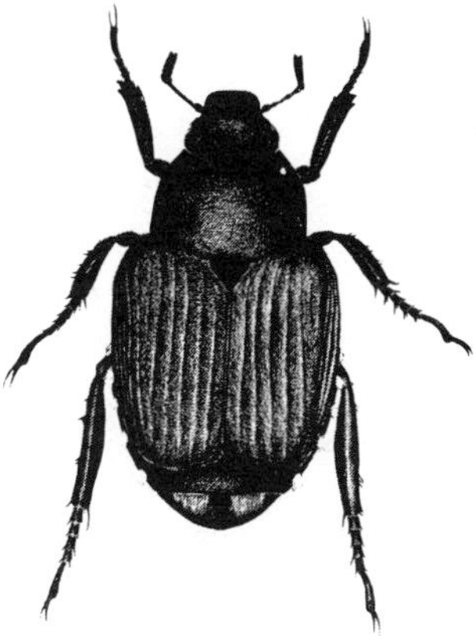

Japanese beetle
(13 mm long)

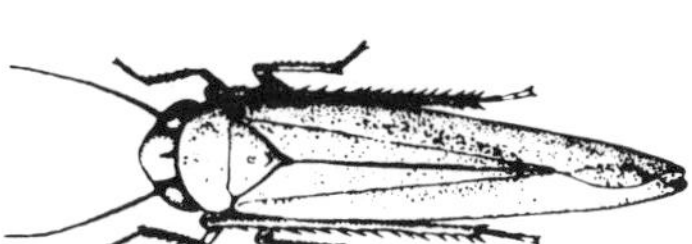

Leafhopper
(3 mm long)

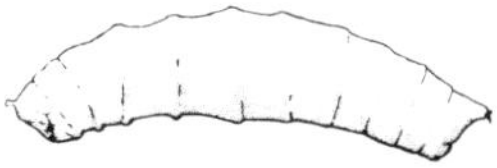

Leaf miner
(3 mm long)

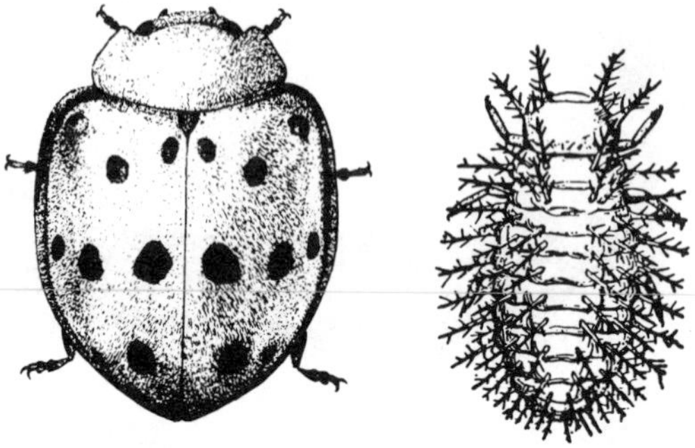

Mexican bean beetle
Adult (*l.*) Larva (*r.*)
(6–8.5 mm long) (8.5 mm long)

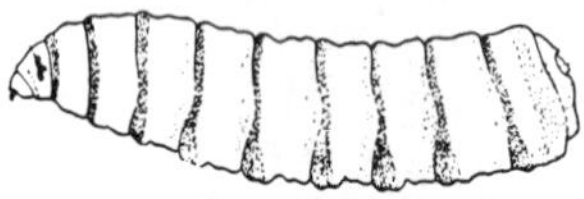

Pepper maggot
(10–12 mm long)

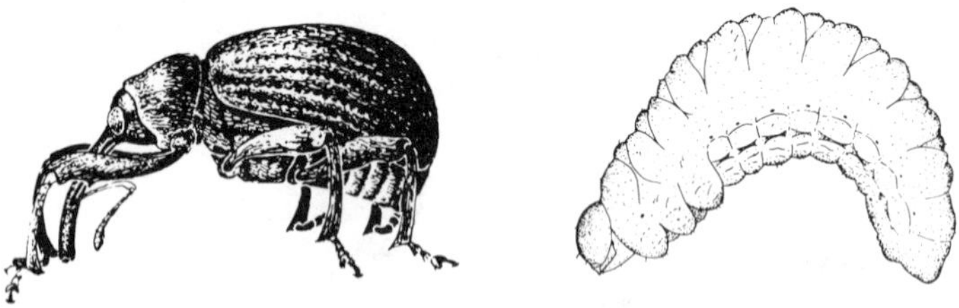

Pepper weevil
Adult (*l.*) Larva (*r.*)
(3 mm long) (6 mm long)

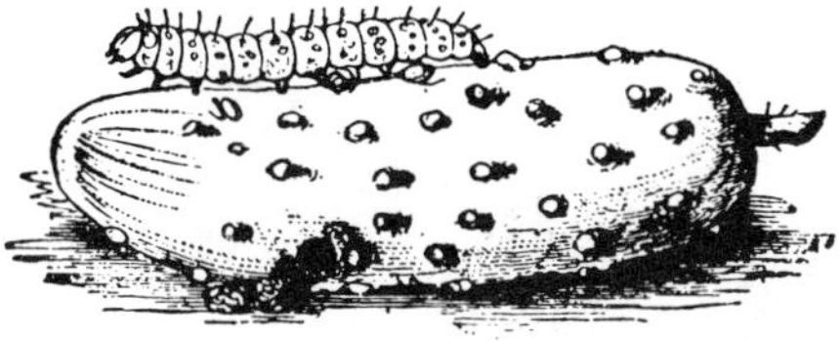

Pickleworm
(25–30 mm long)

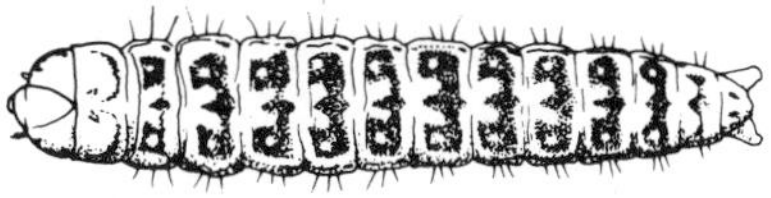

Pinworm
(0.8 mm long)

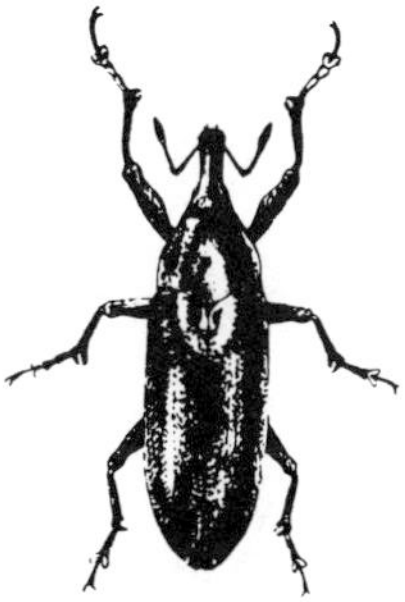

Rhubarb curculio
(12 mm long)

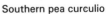

Southern pea curculio
Adult (*l.*) Larva (*r.*)
(6–7 mm long) (6–7 mm long)

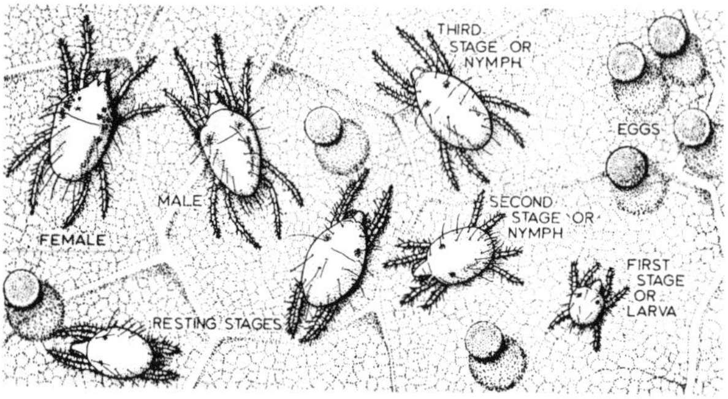

Spider mite
(0.3–0.5 mm long)

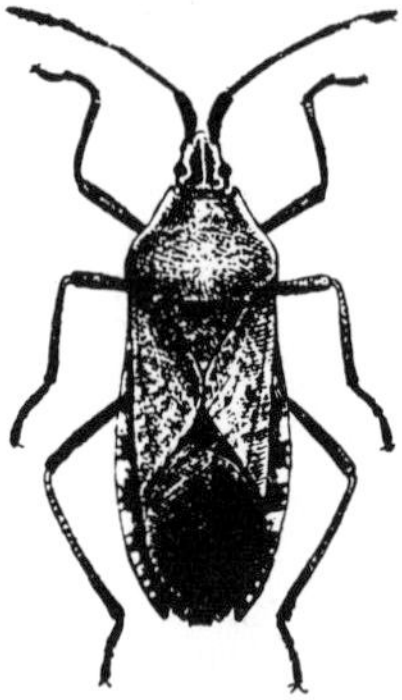

Squash bug
(16 mm long)

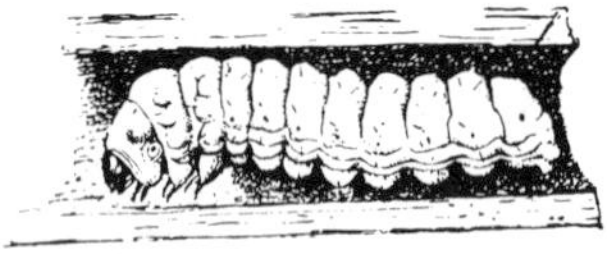

Squash vine borer
(25 mm long)

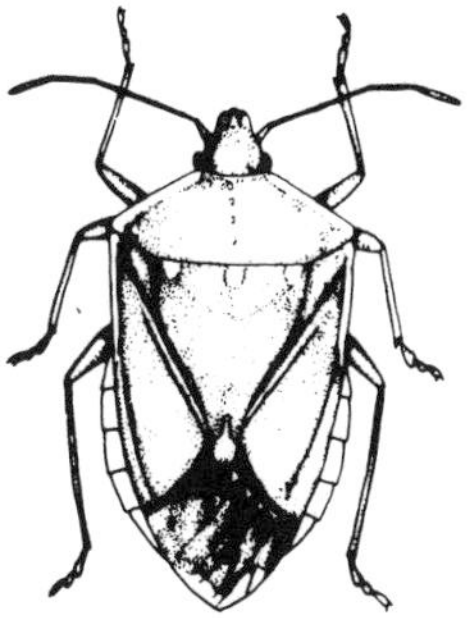

Stinkbug
(14–19 mm long)

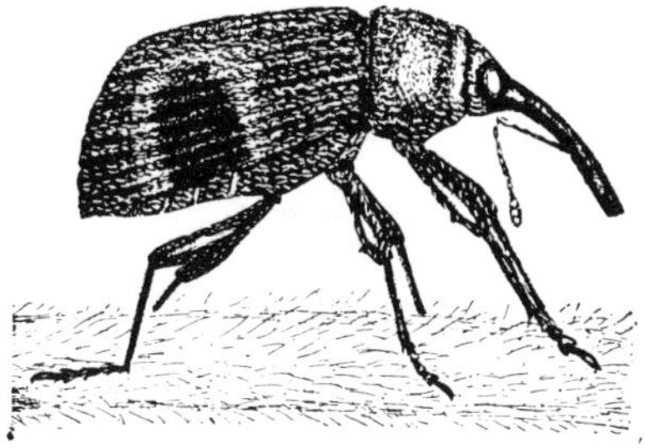

Strawberry bud weevil
(3 mm long)

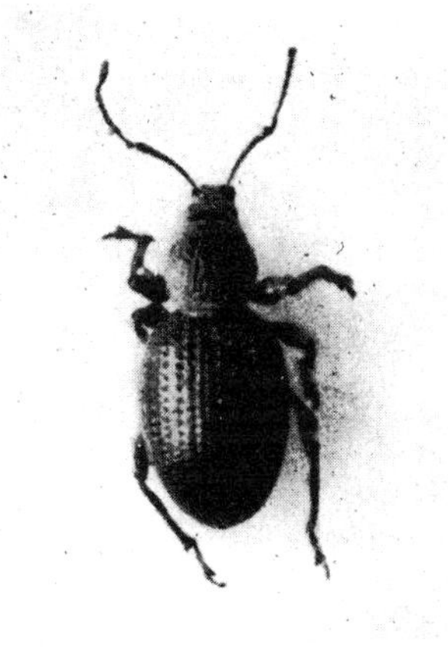

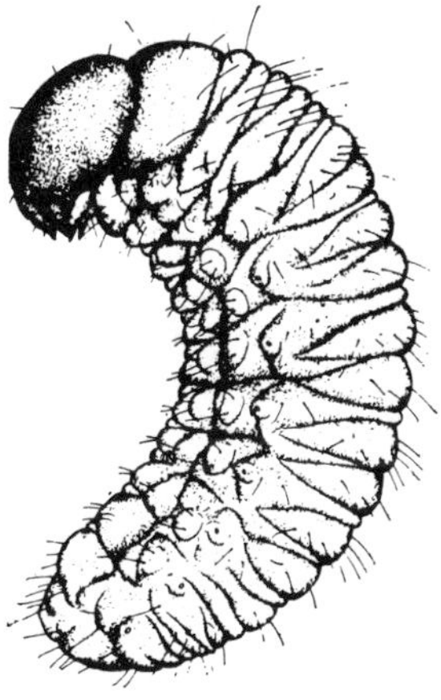

Strawberry root weevil
Adult (*l.*) (5–10 mm long)
Larva (*r.*) (10 mm long)

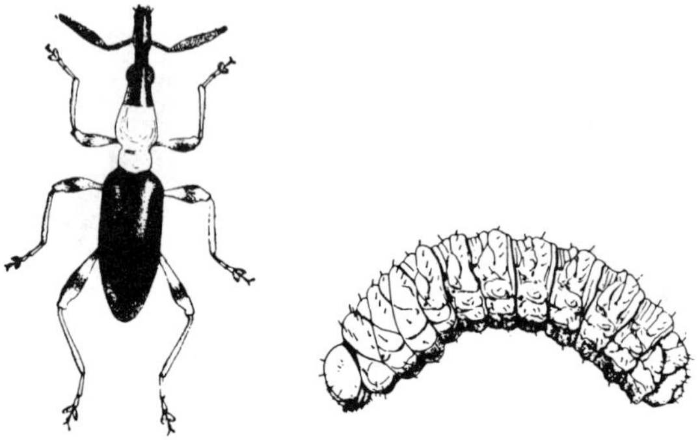

Sweet potato weevil
Adult (*l.*) (6 mm long)   Larva (*r.*) (9 mm long)

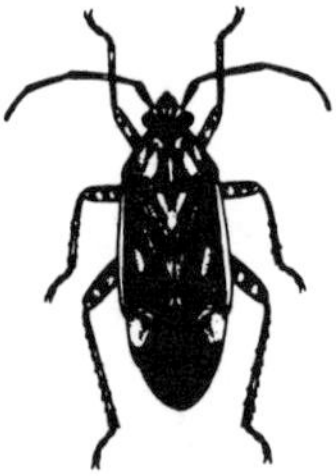

Tarnished plant bug
(6.4 mm long)

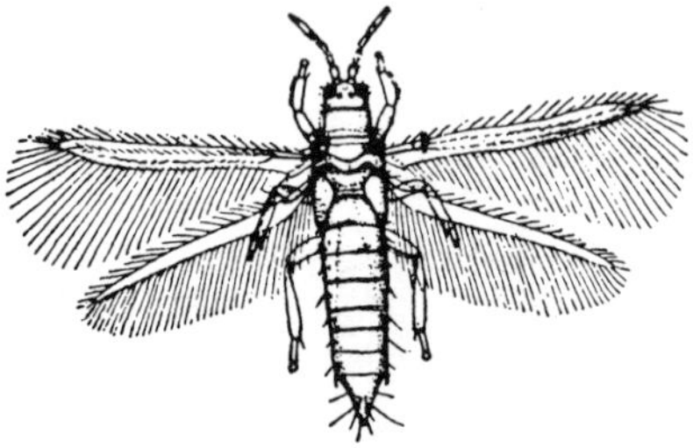

Thrips
(2 mm long)

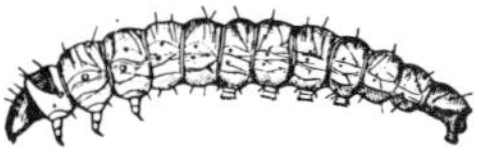

Tuberworm
(13–19 mm long)

Webworm
(13–15 mm long)

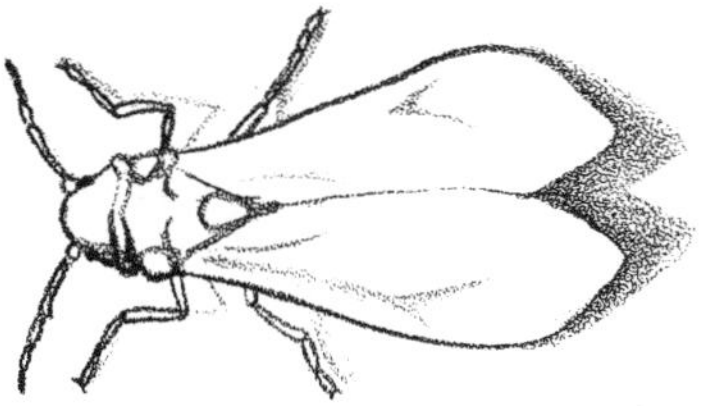

Whitefly
(1.5 mm long)

Wireworm
(21–25 mm long)

Adapted from K. A. Sorenson and J. R. Baker (eds.), Insects and related pests of vegetables, North Carolina Agricultural Extension Service AG-295 (1983) and reprinted with permission from R. H. Davidson and W. F. Lyon, *Insect Pests of Farm, Garden, and Orchard*, 8th ed., Wiley, New York (1987).

PART 7
WEED CONTROL

HERBICIDES

EQUIPMENT AND APPLICATION

WEED-CONTROL PRACTICES

EFFECTIVENESS AND LONGEVITY OF HERBICIDES

WEED CONTROL WITH HERBICIDES

Chemical weed control minimizes labor and is effective if used with care. The following precautions should be observed:

1. Do not use a herbicide unless the label states that it is registered for that particular crop. Be sure to use as directed by the manufacturer.
2. Use herbicides so that no excessive residues remain on the harvested product, which may otherwise be confiscated. Residue tolerances are established by the Environmental Protection Agency.
3. Note that some herbicides will kill only certain weeds.
4. Make certain that the soil is sufficiently moist for effective action of preemergence sprays. Do not expect good results in dry soil.
5. Keep in mind that postemergence herbicides are most effective when conditions favor rapid weed germination and growth.
6. Avoid using too much herbicide. Overdoses can injure the vegetable crop. Few crops, if any, are entirely resistant.
7. Use less herbicide on light sandy soils than on heavy clay soils. Muck soils require somewhat greater rates than do heavy mineral soils.
8. When using wettable powders, be certain the liquid in the tank is agitated constantly as spraying proceeds.
9. Use a boom and nozzle arrangement that will fan out the material close to the ground in order to avoid drift.
10. Thoroughly clean spray tank after use.

CLEANING SPRAYERS AFTER USE WITH HERBICIDES

Sprayers must be kept clean to avoid injury to the crop on which they are to be used for applying insecticides or fungicides, as well as to prevent possible deterioration of the sprayers after use of certain materials.

1. Rinse all parts of sprayer with water before and after any special cleaning operation is undertaken.
2. If in doubt about the effectiveness of water alone to clean tank, pump, boom, hoses, and nozzles of the herbicide, use a cleaner. In some cases, it is desirable to use activated carbon to reduce contamination.
3. Fill tank with water. Use one of the following materials for each 100 gal of water: 5 lb of paint cleaner (trisodium phosphate), 1 gal of household ammonia, or 5 lb of sal soda.
4. If hot water is used, let the solution stand in the tank for 18 hr. If cold water is used, leave it for 36 hr. Pump solution through sprayer.
5. Rinse tank and parts several times with clear water.
6. If copper has been used in the sprayer before a weed control operation is to be performed, put 1 gal of vinegar in 100 gal of water and let the solution stay in the sprayer for 2 hr. Drain the solution and rinse thoroughly. Copper will interfere with the effectiveness of some herbicides.

DETERMINING RATES OF APPLICATION OF WEED-CONTROL MATERIALS

Commercially available herbicide formulations differ in their content of the active ingredient. The label will indicate the amount of the active ingredient (lb/gal). By referring to this amount in the table, it is possible to determine how much of the formulation you need in order to supply the recommended amount of the active ingredient per acre. For calibration of herbicide application equipment see pages 226–232.

HERBICIDE DILUTION TABLE: QUANTITY OF LIQUID CONCENTRATES TO USE TO GIVE DESIRED DOSAGE OF ACTIVE CHEMICAL

Active Ingredient Needed (lb/acre):	0.125	0.25	0.50	1	2	3	4
Active Ingredient Content of Liquid Concentrate (lb/gal)	Liquid Concentrate to Use (pint/acre)						
1	1.0	2.0	4.0	8.0	16.0	24.0	32.0
1½	0.67	1.3	2.6	5.3	10.6	16.0	21.3
2	0.50	1.0	2.0	4.0	8.0	12.0	16.0
3	0.34	0.67	1.3	2.7	5.3	8.0	10.7
4	0.25	0.50	1.0	2.0	4.0	6.0	8.0
5	0.20	0.40	0.80	1.6	3.2	4.8	6.4
6	0.17	0.34	0.67	1.3	2.6	4.0	5.3
7	0.14	0.30	0.60	1.1	2.3	3.4	4.6
8	0.125	0.25	0.50	1.0	2.0	3.0	4.0
9	0.11	0.22	0.45	0.9	1.8	2.7	3.6
10	0.10	0.20	0.40	0.8	1.6	2.4	3.2

Adapted from Spraying Systems Co., Catalog 36, Wheaton, IL (1978).

SELECTION OF NOZZLE HEIGHTS

To ensure that the herbicide is applied to the area at the proper rate, both the boom height and the angle of the nozzle fan must be known. Many spray rigs have the nozzles spaced 20 in. on the boom. The tables below show the height of the nozzles required for different fan angles and bandwidths.

Nozzle Height for Uniform Coverage

	Nozzle Height (in.)		
Nozzle Type	18-in. Spacing	20-in. Spacing	24-in. Spacing
65° fan	19–21	21–23	25–27
73° fan	16–18	20–22	22–24
80° fan	14–16	17–19	19–21

Boom Height for Band Applications of Various Widths

Bandwidth (in.):	8	10	12	14
Fan	Boom Height (in.)			
80°	5	6	7	8
90°	4	5	6	7

Adapted from R. W. Akesson and W. E. Yates, The safe application of agricultural chemicals—equipment and calibration, University of California Extension Publication No. 4048 (1983).

SUGGESTED CHEMICAL WEED CONTROL PRACTICES

State recommendations for herbicides vary, because the effect of herbicides is influenced by growing area, soil type, temperature, and soil moisture. Growers should consult local authorities for specific recommendations. The Environmental Protection Agency has established residue tolerances for those herbicides that may leave injurious residues in or on a harvested vegetable and has approved certain materials, rates, and methods of application. Laws regarding vegetation and herbicides are constantly changing. Growers and commercial applicators should not use a chemical on a crop for which the compound is not registered. Herbicides should be used exactly as stated on the label, regardless of information presented here. The information presented here is for planning purposes and not as a guide for use. Growers are advised to give special attention to any plant-back restrictions.

Crop	Material[1]	Time of Application	Rate of Application of Active Ingredient[1] (lb/acre)	Comments	Weeds Controlled
Artichoke	Diuron (Karmex)	After last fall tillage	1.6–3.2	Allow 2 years before replanting land	Annuals
	Napropamide (Devrinol)	Late fall	4	Moisture required for activation	Annuals
	Oxyfluorfen (Goal)	Late fall or winter	1–2	Do not spray directly on plants	Annuals
	Simazine (Princep)	After last fall tillage	2–4	Do not use on sandy soils	Annuals
Asparagus (mature beds)	Dalapon (Dowpon)	Postemergence	10–20	Treat weeds under fern	Bermuda grass, quack grass

	Dicamba (Banvel)	After cutting	0.25–0.50	Only one application per season	Pigweed, thistle
	Diuron (Direx, Karmex)	Before weeds established. When fern develops	0.75–3		Annuals
	2,4-D	When fern develops following harvest	1–2	Direct spray to base of plants	Bindweed, broad-leaved
	Fluazifop (Fusilade)	Postemergence	0.25–0.50	Consult label. Nonbearing plants only, cannot harvest 12 months after application	Grasses
	Glyphosate (Roundup)	After last harvest before spears appear	0.25–5	Rate depends on weed species	Annuals, perennials
	Metribuzin (Sencor)	Before spears emerge	1–2	Apply at least 14 days before emergence	Broad-leaved
	Napropamide (Devrinol)	Late fall	4	Moisture required to activate	Annual grasses
	Paraquat (Gramoxone Super)	Before spears appear	0.5–1	Apply to emerged weeds	Most
	Simazine (Princep)	Preemergence	2–4	May cause crop injury on light soils	Annuals
	Trifluralin (Treflan)	Preemergence or postharvest	0.5–2.5	Incorporate	Annuals
Bean	Bentazon (Basagran)	After emergence	0.75–1		Broad-leaved
	Chloramben (Amiben)	Preemergence	1.8–2.7	Use for dry beans	Broad-leaved

SUGGESTED CHEMICAL WEED CONTROL PRACTICES—Continued

Crop	Material[1]	Time of Application	Rate of Application of Active Ingredient[1] (lb/acre)	Comments	Weeds Controlled
Bean (Continued)	Chlorpropham (Furloe)	Preemergence	4	Plant seed at least 1 in. deep	Grasses, broad-leaved
	DCPA (Dacthal)	At planting	4.5–10.5	Incorporate	Broad-leaved, grasses
	Dalapon (Dowpon)	Preplanting	8–15	Use higher rate for fall application	Grasses
	EPTC (Eptam)	Preplanting	3	Incorporate. Not to be used for all types of beans	Broad-leaved, grasses
	Glyphosate (Roundup)	Preemergence	0.25–5	Rate depends on weed species	Annuals, perennials
	Metolachlor (Dual)	Preemergence	1.5–3		Annuals
	Paraquat (Gramoxone Super)	Preemergence	0.5–1	Apply to emerged weeds	Annuals
	Pendimethalin (Prowl)	Preplanting	0.5–1.5	Incorporate	Grasses, broad-leaved
	Trifluralin (Treflan)	Preplanting	0.5–0.75	Incorporate after application	Broad-leaved, grasses

Beet	Cycloate (Ro-Neet)	Preplanting	4	Incorporate immediately	Annual grasses, sedges
	EPTC (Eptam)	Preplanting	2	Incorporate in soil. Use in northwestern states only	Broad-leaved, grasses, sedges
	Phenmedipham (Spin-Aid)	Apply after beets are in 4-leaf stage	0.5–1	Do not apply later than 60 days before harvest	Broad-leaved
	Chloridazon (Pyramin)	Preemergence and postemergence	3–3.5	Applied to top of bed before weeds are 1 in. high	Broad-leaved
Broccoli, Brussels sprouts, cabbage, cauliflower	Bensulide (Prefar)	Preplanting or preemergence	5–6	Incorporate 1–2 in. Southeast and southwest only	Grasses, broad-leaved
	DCPA (Dacthal)	At planting	4.5–10.5	Can be incorporated before planting	Grasses, broad-leaved
	Glyphosate (Roundup)	Preemergence	0.25–5	Rate depends on weed species	Annuals, perennials
	Napropamide (Devrinol)	Preemergence	1–2	Incorporate soon after applied	Grasses, pigweed
	Paraquat (Gramoxone) Super	Preemergence	0.5–1	Apply to emerged weeds	Annuals
	Trifluralin (Treflan)	Preplanting	0.5–1	Must be incorporated	Annuals
Carrot, dill, fennel, parsley	Glyphosate (Roundup)	Preemergence	0.25–5	Rate depends on weed species	Annuals, perennials

SUGGESTED CHEMICAL WEED CONTROL PRACTICES—Continued

Crop	Material[1]	Time of Application	Rate of Application of Active Ingredient[1] (lb/acre)	Comments	Weeds Controlled
Carrot, dill, fennel, parsley (Continued)	Linuron (Lorox)	After planting but before crop emerges. Postemergence when plants are 3 in. tall	0.5–1.5	Plant seed at least ½ in. deep	Annuals
	Paraquat (Gramaxone Super)	Preemergence	0.5–1	Apply to emerged weeds	Annuals
	Trifluralin (Treflan)	Preemergence	0.5–1	Must be incorporated. Carrots only	Annual grasses, many broad-leaved
Celery	Glyphosate (Roundup)	Preemergence	0.2–5	Date depends on weed species	Annuals, perennials
	Linuron (Lorox)	After transplanting before crop reaches 8 in. height	0.75–1.5	Do not plant other crops until 4 months after application	Annual grasses, broad-leaved

	Prometryn (Caparol)	After transplanting before weeds reach 2 in. height	0.8–3.2	Do not apply later than 6 weeks after transplanting	Annual broad-leaved, grasses
	Trifluralin (Treflan)	Preplanting	0.5–1	Must be incorporated 1–2 in. deep	Annual grasses, some broad-leaved
Lettuce	Benefin (Balan)	Preplanting	1–1.5	Must be incorporated 1–2 in. deep immediately after application	Annual grasses, some broad-leaved
	Bensulide (Prefar)	Preplanting	5–6	Incorporated 1–2 in. deep or applied to surface and sprinkle irrigated	Grasses, broad-leaved
	Glyphosate (Roundup)	Preemergence	0.25–5	Rate depends on weed species	Annuals, perennials
	Propham (Chem Hoe)	Preemergence, or postemergence	4–6	Irrigate within few days of application. If before planting, incorporate 1–2 in. deep	Annual grasses
	Paraquat (Gramoxone Super)	Preplanting or preemergence	0.5–1	Prepare seedbeds ahead of planting so that weeds will emerge	Emerged annuals and broad-leaved
	Pronamide (Kerb)	Preplanting or preemergence	1–2	Incorporate shallowly. Do not apply within 55 days of harvest	Many grasses and annual broad-leaved

SUGGESTED CHEMICAL WEED CONTROL PRACTICES—Continued

Crop	Material[1]	Time of Application	Rate of Application of Active Ingredient[1] (lb/acre)	Comments	Weeds Controlled
Onion	Bensulide (Prefar)	Preplanting or preemergence	5–6	Incorporate for preplanting application. Texas and New Mexico only	Grasses, few broad-leaved
	Bromoxynil (Brominal)	Postemergence, 2–5 true leaves	0.25–0.375	Use large volume of spray	Mostly broad-leaved
	Chlorpropham (Furloe)	Preemergence	4–8	Not to be used within 1 month of harvest	Annual grasses, purslane, chickweed
	DCPA (Dacthal)	Preemergence or at lay-by	4.5–10.5	Do not incorporate	Annual grasses, broad-leaved, purslane
	Glyphosate (Roundup)	Preemergence	0.25–5	Rate depends on weed species	Annuals, perennials
	Oxyfluorfen (Goal)	Postemergence, 3 true leaves	0.03–0.06	Use only on dry bulb onions	Annual broad-leaved

	Paraquat (Gramoxone Super)	Preemergence	0.5–1	Do not apply within 60 days of harvest	Emerged annuals and perennials
	Trifluralin (Treflan)	After planting	0.37–0.62	Spray weeds between rows of onions	Annual grasses, broad-leaved
Pea	Barban (Carbyne)	Second-leaf stage of wild oats	0.25–0.375	Not to be used after peas past 6-leaf stage	Wild oats
	Bentazon (Basagran)	Postemergence	0.75–1	—	Broad-leaved
	Propham (Chem Hoe)	Preplanting or postemergence	4	Irrigate within 3 days of application	Grasses, wild oats
	Dalapon (Dowpon, etc.)	Postemergence	1	When plants are 2–6 in. tall	Annual grasses
	Diallate (Avadex)	Preemergence	1.25	Incorporate	Wild oats
	Glyphosate (Roundup)	Preemergence	0.25–5	Rate depends on weed species	Annuals, perennials
	MCPA (Weedar)	Plants 4–6 in. tall	0.25–0.38	Do not spray on plants in bloom	Broad-leaved
	MCPB (Thistrol)	Postemergence	0.5–1.5	Apply before flowering	Broad-leaved
	Metolachlor (Dual)	Preplanting	1.5–3	Incorporate 1–2 in.	Grasses, broad-leaved
	Paraquat (Gramoxone Super)	Preplanting	0.5–1	Apply to emerged weeds	Annuals

SUGGESTED CHEMICAL WEED CONTROL PRACTICES—Continued

Crop	Material[1]	Time of Application	Rate of Application of Active Ingredient[1] (lb/acre)	Comments	Weeds Controlled
Pea (Continued)	Propachlor (Ramrod)	Preemergence	3.9–4.9	—	Annual grasses, pigweed, purslane
	Triallate (Avadex)	Preplanting	1.25	Incorporate	Wild oats
	Trifluralin (Treflan)	Preplanting	0.5–0.75	Incorporate	Annual grasses, broad-leaved
Pepper	Bensulide (Prefar)	Preplanting or preemergence	5–6	Incorporate 1–2 in. deep. May injure subsequent crops	Grasses, some broad-leaved
	Chloramben (Amiben)	At transplanting or at lay-by	3–4	Do not use on light, sandy soils	Broad-leaved, annual grasses
	DCPA (Dacthal)	When plants are 4–6 in. tall	4.5–10.5	Use lower rate on sandy soils	Annual grasses, broad-leaved
	Diphenamid (Dymid, Enide)	Seeding or postemergence	3–5	Apply before weeds emerge	Annual grasses, some broad-leaved

	Napropamide (Devrinol)	Preplanting	1–2	Incorporate	Grasses, some broad-leaved
	Paraquat (Gramoxone Super)	Preplanting or preemergence	0.5–1	—	Grasses, emerged broad-leaved
	Trifluralin (Treflan)	Before transplanting	0.5–1	Incorporate 2 in. deep	Annual grasses, broad-leaved
Potato	Ametryn (Evik)	Preharvest	1–2.4	To kill vines and weeds preharvest	All
	Dalapon (Dowpon)	Preemergence	3–10	Not recommended for all varieties	Annual grasses
	DCPA (Dacthal)	At planting or at lay-by	4.5–10.5	Not for California. Use lower rates on sandy soils	Annual grasses, broad-leaved
	Diphenamid (Enide, Dymid)	Preemergence or early lay-by	4–6	Apply to moist soil	Germinating annuals
	Endothall (Desicate)	14 days preharvest	0.78–1	Vine killing	All
	EPTC (Eptam)	Preplanting or at lay-by	3–6	Incorporate	Annual grasses, broad-leaved
	Glyphosate (Roundup)	Preemergence	0.25–5	Rate depends on weed species	Annuals, perennials
	Linuron (Linex, Lorox)	Preemergence	0.5–1.25	Use limited to certain states	Grasses, broad-leaved

SUGGESTED CHEMICAL WEED CONTROL PRACTICES—Continued

Crop	Material[1]	Time of Application	Rate of Application of Active Ingredient[1] (lb/acre)	Comments	Weeds Controlled
Potato (Continued)	Metolachlor (Dual)	Preemergence	1.5–3	Not for peat soils	Grasses, broad-leaved
	Metribuzin (Lexone, Sencor)	Preemergence	0.5–1	Not for sandy low organic matter soils	Broad-leaved, grasses
	Oryzalin (Surflan)	Preemergence	0.75–1	—	Broad-leaved, grasses
	Paraquat (Gramoxone Super)	Preemergence	0.25–0.50	Apply to young weeds	Most vegetation
	Pendimethalin (Prowl)	Preemergence	0.75–1.5	Not for peat or muck soils	Broad-leaved, grasses
	Trifluralin (Treflan)	Preemergence	0.5–1	Incorporate	Annual grasses, broad-leaved
Pumpkin, squash	Bensulide (Prefar)	Preplanting	5–6	Incorporate	Annual grasses
	Chloramben (Amiben)	At planting	3–4	Use lower rate on light soils	Broad-leaved, grasses

	DCPA (Dacthal)	When plants are at 4- or 5-leaf stage	4.5–10.5	Not for use on peat or muck soils	Annual grasses, broad-leaved
	Paraquat (Gramoxone Super)	Preemergence	0.5–1	For emerged weeds	Grasses, broad-leaved
	Propachlor (Ramrod)	Preemergence	4–6	Not for low organic matter soils	Grasses, broad-leaved
Spinach and other greens such as collard, mustard, and turnip	Chlorpropham (Furloe)	Preemergence	1–2	Some states only	Grasses, broad-leaved
	Cycloate (Ro-Neet)	Preplanting	3–4	Use only on mineral soils. Spinach only	Annual grasses, broad-leaved
	DCPA (Dacthal)	At seeding	4.5–10.5	Do not use on spinach	Annual grasses, broad-leaved
	Diethatyl ethyl (Antor)	Preemergence	2–4	Spinach	Grasses, broad-leaved
	Glyphosate (Roundup)	Preemergence	0.25–5	Rate depends on weed species	All emerged weeds
	Phenmedipham (Spin-Aid)	Postemergence	0.5–1	Processing spinach only	Broad-leaved
	Propham (Chem Hoe)	Postemergence	4.5	Spinach. Moisture required	Most annuals
	Paraquat (Gramoxone Super)	Preemergence	0.5–1	Collard	Grasses, broad-leaved
	Trifluralin (Treflan)	Preemergence	0.5–0.75	Turnip, kale, mustard. Incorporate	Annual grasses, broad-leaved

SUGGESTED CHEMICAL WEED CONTROL PRACTICES—Continued

Crop	Material[1]	Time of Application	Rate of Application of Active Ingredient[1] (lb/acre)	Comments	Weeds Controlled
Strawberry	DCPA (Dacthal)	Prebloom or postharvest	9	Do not apply during harvest	Annual grasses, some broad-leaved
	Diphenamid (Dymid, Enide)	Postharvest	4–6	Established plants	Annual grasses, some broad-leaved
	Napropramide (Devrinol)	Postharvest	4	Late fall applications	Annual grasses
	Paraquat (Gramoxone Super)	Weeds 1–6 in. high	0.5	Apply to emerged weeds	Emerged annuals
	Terbacil (Sinbar)	Postharvest	0.4–1	Lower rates on sandy soils	Annual grasses, broad-leaved
Sweet corn	Alachlor (Lasso)	Preplanting or preemergence	2–4	Incorporate. Effective over a wide range of conditions	Grasses, purslane, pigweed. Will suppress nut sedge

Ametryn (Evik)	Postemergence	0.6–2	Apply when corn 12 in. tall. Direct spray to weeds	Grasses, annual broad-leaved
Atrazine (AAtrex)	Before or at planting	2–3	Crops following corn may be injured. Often used in combination with other herbicides	Grasses, broad-leaved
Bentazon (Basagran)	Soon after emergence	0.75–1	Rate depends on growth of weeds to be controlled	Nut sedge, broad-leaved
Butylate (Sutan +)	Preplanting	3–4	Incorporate	Annual grasses, broad-leaved
EPTC (Eradicane)	Preplanting	3–6	Incorporate	Grasses, nut sedge
Glyphosate (Roundup)	Preemergence	0.25–5	Rate depends on weed species	Emerged vegetation
Linuron (Lorox)	Postemergence	0.63–1.5	Spray when corn 14 in. tall	Annual grasses, broad-leaved
Metolachlor (Dual)	Preemergence	1.5–3	Incorporate preplanting	Annual grasses, broad-leaved, nut sedge
Pendimethalin (Prowl)	Preemergence	0.75–2	Not registered in some states	Grasses, broad-leaved
Propachlor (Ramrod)	Preemergence or early postemergence	4–6	Can be used on heavy soils and soils with high organic matter	Annual grasses, ragweed

SUGGESTED CHEMICAL WEED CONTROL PRACTICES—Continued

Crop	Material[1]	Time of Application	Rate of Application of Active Ingredient[1] (lb/acre)	Comments	Weeds Controlled
Sweet corn (Continued)	Simazine (Princep)	Preemergence	3–4	May be harmful to other crops in rotation	Annual grasses, broad-leaved
	2,4-D (Dacamine)	Pre- or postemergence	0.023	Spray after corn 8 in. tall	Broad-leaved
Sweet potato	Chloramben (Amiben)	At transplanting	4	—	Most broad-leaved, grasses
	DCPA (Dacthal)	Before transplanting or at lay-by	4.5–10.5	Use lower rates at lay-by	Annual grasses, purslane, carpetweed
	Diphenamid (Enide)	At transplanting	4–6	—	Annual grasses, broad-leaved
	EPTC (Eptam)	Pretransplanting	3	Incorporate	Annual grasses, broad-leaved
	Glyphosate (Roundup)	Preemergence	0.025–5	Rate depends on weed species	Emerged weeds

Tomato	Bensulide (Prefar)	Preplanting	4–5	Incorporate. May injure sensitive crops planted within 18 months of application	Grasses, purslane, some broad-leaved
	Chloramben (Amiben)	Post-transplanting or at lay-by	3–4	May cause plant injury on sandy soils	Annual grasses, broad-leaved
	DCPA (Dacthal)	Plants 4–6 in. tall	4.5–10.5	Not for use on established weeds	Annual grasses, broad-leaved
	Diphenamid (Dymid, Enide)	At or after seeding or transplanting	4–6	May injure subsequent crops	Annual grasses, broad-leaved
	EPTC (Eptam)	At lay-by	3	Certain areas only	Grasses, broad-leaved
	Metribuzin (Sencor, Lexone)	Preplanting	0.25–0.50	Not for all areas	Broad-leaved
	Napropramide (Devrinol)	Preplanting	1–2	Incorporate	Annual grasses
	Paraquat (Gramoxone Super)	Preemergence	0.25–1	Effective on emerged weeds	All vegetation
	Pebulate (Tillam)	Preplanting or at lay-by	3–6	Incorporate	Grasses, broad-leaved
	Trifluralin (Treflan)	Pretransplanting	0.5–1	Incorporate	Annual grasses, broad-leaved

SUGGESTED CHEMICAL WEED CONTROL PRACTICES—Continued

Crop	Material[1]	Time of Application	Rate of Application of Active Ingredient[1] (lb/acre)	Comments	Weeds Controlled
Muskmelon, cucumber, watermelon	Bensulide (Prefar)	Preemergence	4–6	Incorporate. May injure subsequent crops	Grasses chiefly
	DCPA (Dacthal)	When plants have 4–6 true leaves	4.5–10.5	Use higher rates on heavy soils	Annual grasses, some broad-leaved
	Naptalam (Alanap)	Preemergence	3–4	Incorporate. Varietal responses	Annual grasses, broad-leaved
	Paraquat (Gramoxone Super)	Preemergence	0.125–1	Use for emerged weeds	Emerged weeds
	Trifluralin (Treflan)	When plants have 3 or 4 true leaves	0.5–1	Incorporate immediately	Annual grasses, broad-leaved

The suggested weed control practices are based on information from Cooperative Extension Service publications from various states.

[1]These rates apply on the basis of active ingredients and on a broadcast basis. The user must adjust for the amount (lb) of commercial product needed and adjust further for band application. Most materials can be applied in 20–60 gal of water/acre with good results. Trade names that are commonly used in the United States and Canada are given (in parentheses) for some of the herbicides. Some herbicides have more than one trade name. Various combinations of herbicides are registered for use on certain crops.

EFFECTIVENESS OF HERBICIDES ON SEVERAL WEED SPECIES[1]

Knowing what weeds are in your field will help you choose the most effective chemical among those registered for your crop.

Herbicide (Trade Names)	Redroot pigweed	Common lamb's-quarter	Galinsoga	Mustards	Nightshade	Common purslane	Common ragweed	Smartweed	Crabgrass	Foxtails	Barnyard grass	Fall *Panicum*	Stink grass	Quack grass	Yellow Nut sedge
Preplanting Incorporated Herbicides															
Balan	G	F	P	P	P	G	P	P	E	E	E	E	E	P	P
Devrinol	G	P	P	P	P	G	P	P	E	E	E	E	E	P	P
Dual	G	F	G	P	G	F	P	F	E	E	E	E	E	P	F
Eptam	G	G	F	F	F	P	F	F	E	E	E	E	E	G	G
Prefar	G	P	P	P	P	P	P	P	E	E	E	E	E	P	P
Ro-Neet	G	F	F	P	P	F	P	P	E	E	E	F	E	P	F
Sutan +	F	P	F	P	P	P	P	P	E	E	E	E	E	P	G
Tillam	F	F	F	P	P	P	P	P	E	E	E	F	F	P	G
Treflan	G	F	P	P	P	F	P	P	E	E	E	E	E	P	P

EFFECTIVENESS OF HERBICIDES ON SEVERAL WEED SPECIES[1]—Continued

Herbicide (Trade Names)	Redroot pigweed	Common lamb's-quarter	Galinsoga	Mustards	Nightshade	Common purslane	Common ragweed	Smartweed	Crabgrass	Foxtails	Barnyard grass	Fall *Panicum*	Stink grass	Quack grass	Yellow Nut sedge
Preemergence Surface-Applied Herbicides															
AAtrex	E	E	G	E	E	E	E	E	G	G	G	P	G	G	G
Alanap	G	G	F	F	P	F	F	G	P	P	P	P	P	P	P
Amiben	E	E	F	F	G	G	G	G	F	F	F	P	F	P	P
Antor	G	F	G	F	G	F	P	F	G	G	G	G	G	P	P
Bladex	F	E	G	G	G	E	E	E	G	G	G	F	G	P	P
Caparol	E	E	F	G	G	G	G	F	G	F	F	F	F	P	P
Dacthal	F	F	P	P	P	P	P	P	P	E	E	G	E	P	P
Dual	G	F	G	P	G	F	P	F	E	E	E	E	E	P	F
Enide	G	F	P	P	P	G	P	F	E	E	E	E	E	P	P
Furloe Chloro IPC	F	F	P	P	P	G	P	E	F	F	F	F	F	P	P
Karmex	E	E	G	G	G	E	E	E	F	E	E	F	E	P	P
Kerb	P	F	P	P	P	G	F	F	F	F	F	P	F	G	P
Lasso	E	F	G	P	G	G	F	F	E	E	E	E	E	P	F
Lexone, Sencor	G	E	E	E	P	E	E	E	F	G	G	G	G	P	P
Lorox	E	E	G	G	G	E	E	G	F	E	G	F	E	P	P
Premerge	E	G	G	G	G	E	E	G	F	P	P	P	F	P	P

Princep	E	E	G	E	E	E	E	E	F	E	E	F	E	F	P
Pyramin RB	G	F	P	G	G	G	G	G	F	F	F	F	F	P	P
Ramrod	G	F	G	P	G	G	F	F	E	E	E	E	E	P	P
Sinbar	G	G	G	G	G	G	G	G	G	G	G	G	G	F	P
Sonalan	G	G	P	F	F	G	P	G	E	E	E	E	E	P	P
Surflan	G	G	F	F	F	G	F	F	E	E	E	E	E	P	P
Herbicides with Postemergence Activity															
AAtrex	E	E	G	E	G	E	E	E	G	G	G	F	G	G	G
Basagran	P	G	G	F	F	G	G	E	P	P	P	P	P	P	G
Bladex	F	G	G	G	G	G	G	G	G	G	G	G	G	P	P
Brominal	F	E	G	G	G	G	G	E	P	P	P	P	P	P	P
Caparol	E	E	G	G	G	G	E	F	F	F	F	F	F	P	P
Dowpon	P	P	P	P	P	P	P	P	F	G	G	G	G	G	P
Formula 40	E	E	G	G	E	P	E	E	P	P	P	P	P	P	P
Goal	E	F	G	G	G	E	G	G	F	F	F	F	G	P	P
Lexone, Sencor	G	E	E	E	P	E	E	E	F	G	F	F	F	P	P
Lorox	E	E	G	G	G	G	E	E	P	P	F	P	F	P	P
Paraquat	E	E	G	E	E	E	E	E	E	E	E	E	E	E[2]	E[2]
Roundup	E	E	E	E	E	E	E	E	E	E	E	E	E	E	F
Spin-aid	P	G	G	G	F	G	G	G	P	P	P	P	P	P	P
Stoddard Solvent	E	E	F	E	E	E	P	E	E	E	E	E	E	F	F
Tenoran	E	G	G	E	G	G	F	F	F	F	F	P	F	P	P

Adapted from B. H. Zandstra and A. R. Putnam, Weed control guide for vegetable crops, Michigan Extension Bulletin E433 (1985).

[1]E = excellent, G = good, F = fair, P = poor.

[2]Kill of top growth only.

LONGEVITY OF PHYTOTOXIC EFFECTS OF HERBICIDES IN SOILS[1]

Common Name	Trade Name	Phytotoxic Soil Residual (months)
alachlor	Lasso	2–4
atrazine	AAtrex 4L	6–18
	Atrazine 4L	6–18
	AAtrex 80W	6–18
	Atrazine 80W	6–18
	AAtrex Nine-0	6–18
bensulide	Prefar 4-E	6–12
bentazon	Basagran	<1
bromoxynil	Brominal ME-4	1–2
butylate	Sutan +	1.5–2
	Sutan + 10-G	1–1.5
chloramben	Amiben	1–2
	Amiben DS	1–2
chloroxuron	Tenoran	1–3
chlorpropham	Furloe	1–3
cycloate	Ro-Neet	2–4
dalapon	Dalapon 85	<1
DCPA	Dacthal	4–8
diphenamid	Enide 90 WP	4–8
diuron	Karmex	4–12
EPTC	Eptam 7-E	2–2.5
EPTC + safener + extender	Eradicane Extra 6E	2.5–3
glyphosate	Roundup	0
linuron	Lorox	2–4
MCPB	Thistrol	1–2
metolachlor	Dual 8E	2–4
metribuzin	Sencor DF	2–4
	Sencor 50 WP	2–4
	Lexone 50 WP	2–4
napropamide	Devrinol 50 WP	4–12
	Devrinol 2-E	4–12
naptalam (sodium salt)	Alanap	1–2
oxyfluorfen	Goal 1.6E	2–4
paraquat	Gramoxone Super	0
pebulate	Tillam 6-E	1–2
petroleum solvents	—	<1
pronamide	Kerb	4–8

LONGEVITY OF PHYTOTOXIC EFFECTS OF HERBICIDES IN SOILS[1]—Continued

Common Name	Trade Name	Phytotoxic Soil Residual (months)
pyrazon	Pyramin RB	2–3
simazine	Princep 80W	12–18
	Caliber 90	6–12
terbacil	Sinbar	8–12
trifluralin	Treflan	6–12
2,4-D		
amine	Dacamine	1
amine salt	Formula 40	1

Adapted from Pennsylvania vegetable production guide, Pennsylvania State University Cooperative Extension Service (1987).

[1] The longevity of phytotoxic effects varies considerably, depending on such factors as rate applied, moisture, temperature, soil type, and soil pH.

PART 8
HARVESTING AND STORAGE

APPROXIMATE TIME FROM PLANTING TO MARKET MATURITY UNDER OPTIMUM GROWING CONDITIONS

Vegetable	Time to Market Maturity (days)		
	Early Variety	Late Variety	Common Variety
Bean, broad	—	—	120
Bean, bush	48	60	—
Bean, pole	62	68	—
Bean, Lima, bush	65	78	—
Bean, Lima, pole	78	88	—
Beet	56	70	—
Broccoli[1]	55	78	—
Broccoli raab	60	70	—
Brussels sprouts[1]	90	100	—
Cabbage	62	120	—
Cardoon	—	—	120
Carrot	50	95	—
Cauliflower[1]	50	125	—
Celeriac	—	—	110
Celery[1]	90	125	—
Chard, Swiss	50	60	—
Chervil	—	—	60
Chicory	65	150	—
Chinese cabbage	70	80	—
Chive	—	—	90
Collard	70	85	—
Corn, sweet	64	95	—
Corn salad	—	—	60
Cress	—	—	45
Cucumber, pickling	48	58	—
Cucumber, slicing	62	72	—
Dandelion	—	—	85
Eggplant[1]	50	80	—
Endive	85	100	—
Florence fennel	—	—	100
Kale	—	—	55
Kohlrabi	50	60	—
Leek	—	—	150
Lettuce, butterhead	55	70	—
Lettuce, cos	70	75	—
Lettuce, head	70	85	—
Lettuce, leaf	40	50	—

APPROXIMATE TIME FROM PLANTING TO MARKET MATURITY UNDER OPTIMUM GROWING CONDITIONS—Continued

Vegetable	Time to Market Maturity (days)		
	Early Variety	Late Variety	Common Variety
Melon, casaba	—	—	110
Melon, honeydew	—	—	110
Melon, Persian	—	—	110
Muskmelon	85	95	—
Mustard	35	55	—
New Zealand spinach	—	—	70
Okra	50	60	—
Onion, dry	90	150	—
Onion, green	45	60	—
Parsley	70	80	—
Parsley root	—	—	90
Parsnip	—	—	120
Pea	56	75	—
Pea, edible-podded	60	70	—
Pepper, hot[1]	65	80	—
Pepper, sweet[1]	65	80	—
Potato	90	120	—
Pumpkin	100	120	—
Radish	22	30	—
Radish, winter	50	60	—
Roselle	—	—	175
Rutabaga	—	—	90
Salsify	—	—	150
Scolymus	—	—	150
Scorzonera	—	—	150
Sorrel	—	—	60
Southern pea	65	85	—
Spinach	37	45	—
Squash, summer	40	50	—
Squash, winter	85	110	—
Sweet potato	120	150	—
Tomato[1]	60	90	—
Turnip	40	75	—
Watercress	—	—	180
Watermelon	75	95	—

[1] Time from transplanting. See page 37.

APPROXIMATE TIME FROM POLLINATION TO MARKET MATURITY UNDER WARM GROWING CONDITIONS

Vegetable	Time to Market Maturity (days)
Bean	7–10
Corn,[1] market	18–23
Corn,[1] processing	21–27
Cucumber, pickling (¾–1⅛ in. in diameter)	4–5
Cucumber, slicing	15–18
Eggplant (⅔ maximum size)	25–40
Muskmelon	42–46
Okra	4–6
Pepper, green stage (about maximum size)	45–55
Pepper, red stage	60–70
Pumpkin, Connecticut Field	80–90
Pumpkin, Dickinson	90–110
Pumpkin, Small Sugar	65–75
Squash, summer, Crookneck	6–7[2]
Squash, summer, Early Prolific Straightneck	5–6[2]
Squash, summer, Scallop	4–5[2]
Squash, summer, Zucchini	3–4[2]
Squash, winter, Banana	70–80
Squash, winter, Boston Marrow	60–70
Squash, winter, Buttercup	60–70
Squash, winter, Butternut	60–70
Squash, winter, Golden Delicious	60–70
Squash, winter, Hubbard	80–90
Squash, winter, Table Queen or Acorn	55–60
Strawberry	25–42
Tomato, mature green stage	35–45
Tomato, red ripe stage	45–60
Watermelon	42–45

[1] Days from 50% silking.
[2] For a weight of ¼–½ lb.

ESTIMATING YIELDS OF CROPS

The prediction of crop yields before the harvest aids in the scheduling of harvests of various fields for total yields, as well as harvest to obtain highest yields of a particular grade or stage of maturity. To estimate yields, follow these steps:

1. Select and measure a typical 10-ft section of a row. If the field is variable or large, you may want to select several 10-ft sections.
2. Harvest the crop from the measured section or sections.
3. Weigh the entire sample for total yields or grade the sample and weigh the graded sample for yield of a particular grade.
4. If you have harvested more than one 10-ft section, divide the yield by the number of sections harvested.
5. Multiply the sample weight by the conversion factor in the table for your row spacing. The value obtained will equal hundred-weight (cwt) per acre.

Conversion Factors for Estimating Yields

Row Spacing (in.)	Multiply Sample Weight (lb) by Conversion Factor to Obtain cwt/acre
12	43.6
15	34.8
18	29.0
20	26.1
21	24.9
24	21.8
30	17.4
36	14.5
40	13.1
42	12.4
48	10.9

Example 1: A 10-ft sample of carrots planted in 12-in. rows yields 9 lb of No. 1 carrots.

$$9 \times 43.6 = 392.4 \text{ cwt/acre}$$

Example 2: The average yield of three 10-ft samples of No. 1 potatoes planted in 36-in. rows is 26 lb.

$$26 \times 14.5 = 377 \text{ cwt/acre}$$

YIELDS OF VEGETABLE CROPS

Vegetable	Approximate Average Yield in the United States (cwt/acre)	Good Yield (cwt/acre)
Artichoke	95	120
Asparagus	25	40
Bean, market	35	100
Bean, processing	60	100
Bean, Lima, processing	30	40
Beet, market	140	200
Beet, processing	300	350
Broccoli	95	120
Brussels sprouts	140	175
Cabbage, market	235	300
Cabbage, processing	480	600
Carrot, topped	260	350
Cauliflower	105	150
Celeriac	—	200
Celery	535	700
Chard, Swiss	—	150
Corn, market	80	120
Corn, processing	115	150
Cucumber, market	115	250
Cucumber, processing	120	250

Vegetable	Approximate Average Yield in the United States (cwt/acre)	Good Yield (cwt/acre)
Eggplant	190	250
Endive, escarole	130	180
Garlic	130	160
Horseradish	—	80
Lettuce	280	400
Melon, Persian	120	150
Melon, honeydew	175	250
Muskmelon	145	200
Okra	—	150
Onion	340	500
Pea, market	40	60
Pea, processing (shelled)	30	40
Pepper, bell	100	200
Pepper, chili (dried)	40	60
Pepper, pimiento	40	60
Potato	290	400
Pumpkin	—	400
Rhubarb	—	200
Rutabaga	—	400
Spinach, market	80	150
Spinach, processing	150	200
Squash, summer	—	300
Squash, winter	—	400
Sweet potato	125	250
Strawberry	225	400
Tomato, market	230	270
Tomato, processing	500	700
Turnip	—	300
Watermelon	125	300

COOLING METHODS FOR VEGETABLES

Method[1]	Vegetable	Comments
Room cooling	All vegetables	Too slow for many perishable commodities. Cooling rates vary extensively within loads, pallets, and containers
Forced-air cooling (pressure cooling)	Strawberry, fruit-type vegetables, tubers, cauliflower	Much faster than room cooling; cooling rates very uniform if properly used. Container venting and stacking requirements are critical to effective cooling
Hydrocooling	Stems, leafy vegetables, some fruit-type vegetables	Very fast cooling; uniform cooling in bulk if properly used, but may vary extensively in packed shipping containers; daily cleaning and sanitation measures essential; product must tolerate wetting; water-tolerant shipping containers may be needed
Package-icing	Roots, stems, some flower-type vegetables, green onion, Brussels sprouts	Fast cooling; limited to commodities that can tolerate water–ice contact; water-tolerant shipping containers are essential
Vacuum cooling	Leafy vegetables; some stem and flower-type vegetables	Commodities must have a favorable surface-to-mass ratio for effective cooling. Causes about 1% weight loss for each 6°C cooled. A procedure that adds water during cooling prevents this weight loss but equipment is more expensive, and water-tolerant shipping containers are needed

Transit Cooling:		
Mechanical refrigeration	All vegetables	
Top-icing and channel-icing	Some roots, stems, leafy vegetables, muskmelon	Cooling in most available equipment is too slow and variable; generally not effective. Slow and irregular, top-ice weight reduces net pay load; water-tolerant shipping containers needed

Adapted from A. A. Kader et al., Postharvest technology of horticultural crops, California Cooperative Extension Special Publication 3311 (1985).

[1] For these methods to be effective, cold-storage rooms are needed to hold the vegetables after cooling.

HALF-COOLING TIMES[1] FOR SOME VEGETABLES

Vegetable	Coolant	Conditions during Cooling	Half-Cooling Time
Artichoke	Water	Single buds, size 36	8 min
		In crate, uncovered	12 min
Asparagus	Water	Single spear	1.1 min
		In lidded pyramid crate	2.2 min
Broccoli	Water	Single head	2.1 min
		In crate with liner, three-quarters filled with water, four layers deep	2.2 min
		In crate without liners, four layers deep	3.1 min
Brussels sprouts	Water	Single sprout	4.4 min
		In carton, 9 in. deep, filled with water	4.8 min
Cabbage	Water	Single head	1.1 hr
		In carton, two layers, lid open, filled with water	1.3 hr
Carrot	Water	Single root, 1½ in. diameter	3.2 min
		In 50-lb mesh bag, lying flat	4.4 min
Cauliflower	Water	Single head, trimmed	7.2 min
	Air-forced	In single-layer cartons; head film wrapped	1.5 hr
Celery	Water	Single stalk	5.8 min
		In "Sturdy" crate, lidded on edge, paper liner	9.1 min
	Air-forced	In wirebound crates, air movement side to side	35 min

HALF-COOLING TIMES[1] FOR SOME VEGETABLES—Continued

Vegetable	Coolant	Conditions during Cooling	Half-Cooling Time
Celery (Continued)		In ⅔-size cartons	60 min
Muskmelon	Water	Single fruit, size 36 or 27	15 min
	Air	In crate, tunnel cooler, airflow unknown	1.3 hr
Pea	Water	Single pod	1.9 min
		In bushel basket, lid off	2.8 min
Potato	Water	Single tuber or stacked 9 in. deep	11 min
Radish, bunched	Water	Single bunch	1.1 min
		In crate, 9 in. deep	1.9 min
		In carton, 9 in. deep, filled with water	1.4 min
Radish, topped	Water	Stack, 9 in. deep	2.2 min
Sweet corn	Water	Single ear, in husk	20 min
		In wirebound crates, five ears deep	28 min
Tomato	Water	Single fruit	10 min
		Stack 5 fruit (10 in.) deep	11 min
	Air	Forced air, pressure difference 0.1 in., water cartons	47 min

Reprinted with permission from A. L. Ryall and W. J. Lipton, *Handling Transportation and Storage of Fruits and Vegetables*, Vol. 1, 2nd ed., AVI Publishing Co. Westport, CT (1979).

[1] Half-cooling time is the interval during which the initial temprature difference between product and coolant is halved. For example, if muskmelons are at 92°F and water is at 32°F, a difference of 60°, the time required to cool the melons by 30° is the half-cooling time.

OPTIMUM CONDITIONS FOR CURING ROOT, TUBER, AND BULB VEGETABLES PRIOR TO STORAGE

Vegetable	Temperature (°F)	Relative Humidity (%)	Duration of Curing (days)
Cassava	86–104	90–95	2–5
Onion and garlic	95–113	60–75	0.5–1[1]
Potato	59–68	85–90	5–10
Sweet potato	85–90	85–90	4–7
Yam	90–104	90–100	1–4

Adapted from A. A. Kader et al., Postharvest technology of horticultural crops, California Cooperative Extension Special Publication 3311 (1985).

[1]With warm forced air.

RECOMMENDED TEMPERATURE AND RELATIVE HUMIDITY, APPROXIMATE STORAGE LIFE AND HIGHEST FREEZING POINT OF FRESH VEGETABLES

	Storage Conditions			
Vegetable	Temperature (°F)	Relative Humidity (%)	Storage Life	Highest Freezing Temperature (°F)
Artichoke, globe	32	95–100	2–3 weeks	29.9
Artichoke, Jerusalem	31–32	90–95	4–5 months	28.0
Asparagus	32–35	95–100	2–3 weeks	30.9
Bean, Lima	37–41	95	5–7 days	31.0
Bean, snap	40–45	95	7–10 days	30.7
Beet, bunched	32	98–100	10–14 days	31.3
Beet, topped	32	98–100	4–6 months	30.3
Broccoli	32	95–100	10–14 days	30.9
Brussels sprouts	32	95–100	3–5 weeks	30.5
Cabbage, early	32	98–100	3–6 weeks	30.4
Cabbage, late	32	98–100	5–6 months	30.4
Cabbage, Chinese	32	95–100	2–3 months	—
Carrot, bunched	32	95–100	2 weeks	—
Carrot, mature	32	98–100	7–9 months	29.5

RECOMMENDED TEMPERATURE AND RELATIVE HUMIDITY, APPROXIMATE STORAGE LIFE AND HIGHEST FREEZING POINT OF FRESH VEGETABLES—Continued

Vegetable	Storage Conditions: Temperature (°F)	Storage Conditions: Relative Humidity (%)	Storage Life	Highest Freezing Temperature (°F)
Carrot, immature	32	98–100	4–6 weeks	29.5
Cassava	32–41	85–90	1–2 months	—
Cauliflower	32	95–98	3–4 weeks	30.6
Celeriac	32	97–99	6–8 months	30.3
Celery	32	98–100	2–3 months	31.1
Chard	32	95–100	10–14 days	—
Chicory, witloof	32	95–100	2–4 weeks	—
Collard	32	95–100	10–14 days	30.6
Cucumber	50–55	95	10–14 days	31.1
Eggplant	46–54	90–95	1 week	30.6
Endive, escarole	32	95–100	2–3 weeks	31.9
Garlic	32	65–70	6–7 months	30.5
Ginger	55	65	6 months	—
Greens	32	95–100	10–14 days	—
Horseradish	30–32	98–100	10–12 months	28.7
Jicama	55–65	65–70	1–2 months	—
Kale	32	95–100	2–3 weeks	31.1
Kohlrabi	32	98–100	2–3 months	30.2
Leek	32	95–100	2–3 months	30.7
Lettuce	32	98–100	2–3 weeks	31.7
Melon				
Casaba	50	90–95	3 weeks	30.1
Crenshaw	45	90–95	2 weeks	30.1
Honeydew	45	90–95	3 weeks	30.3
Muskmelon, ¾ slip	36–41	95	15 days	29.9
Muskmelon, full slip	32–36	95	5–14 days	29.9
Persian	45	90–95	2 weeks	30.5
Watermelon	50–60	90	2–3 weeks	31.3
Mushroom	32	95	3–4 days	30.4
Okra	45–50	90–95	7–10 days	28.7
Onion, dry	32	65–70	1–8 months	30.6
Onion, green	32	95–100	3–4 weeks	30.4
Parsley	32	95–100	8–10 weeks	30.0
Parsnip	32	98–100	4–6 months	30.4

RECOMMENDED TEMPERATURE AND RELATIVE HUMIDITY, APPROXIMATE STORAGE LIFE AND HIGHEST FREEZING POINT OF FRESH VEGETABLES—Continued

Vegetable	Storage Conditions: Temperature (°F)	Storage Conditions: Relative Humidity (%)	Storage Life	Highest Freezing Temperature (°F)
Pea, English	32	95–98	1–2 weeks	30.9
Pea, southern	40–41	95	6–8 days	—
Pepper, chili (dry)	32–50	60–70	6 months	—
Pepper, sweet	45–55	90–95	2–3 weeks	30.7
Potato, early	—[1]	90–95	—[1]	30.9
Potato, late	—[2]	90–95	5–10 months	30.9
Pumpkin	50–55	50–70	2–3 months	30.5
Radish, spring	32	95–100	3–4 weeks	30.7
Radish, winter	32	95–100	2–4 months	—
Rhubarb	32	95–100	2–4 weeks	30.3
Rutabaga	32	98–100	4–6 months	30.0
Salisfy	32	95–98	2–4 months	30.0
Spinach	32	95–100	10–14 days	31.5
Squash, summer	41–50	95	1–2 weeks	31.1
Squash, winter	50	50–70	—[4]	30.5
Strawberry	32	90–95	5–7 days	30.6
Sweet corn	32	95–98	5–8 days	30.9
Sweet potato	55–60[3]	85–90	4–7 months	29.7
Tamarillo	37–40	85–95	10 weeks	—
Taro	45–50	85–90	4–5 months	—
Tomato, mature green	55–70	90–95	1–3 weeks	31.0
Tomato, firm ripe	46–50	90–95	4–7 days	31.1
Turnip	32	95	4–5 months	30.1
Turnip greens	32	95–100	10–14 days	31.7
Water chestnut	32–36	98–100	1–2 months	—
Watercress	32	95–100	2–3 weeks	31.4
Yam	61	70–80	6–7 months	—

Adapted from R. E. Hardenburg, A. E. Watada, and C. Y. Wang, *The Commercial Storage of Fruits, Vegetables, and Florist and Nursery Stocks*, USDA Agriculture Handbook 66 (1986).

[1] Spring- or summer-harvested potatoes are usually not stored. However, they can be held 4–5 months at 40°F if cured 4 or more days at 60–70°F before storage. Potatoes for chips should be held at 70°F or conditioned for best chip quality.

[2] Fall-harvested potatoes should be cured at 50–60°F and high relative humidity for 10–14 days. Storage temperatures for table stock or seed should be lowered gradually to 38–40°F. Potatoes intended for processing should be stored at 50–55°F; those stored at lower temperatures or with a high reducing sugar content should be conditioned at 70°F for 1–4 weeks, or until cooking tests are satisfactory.

[3] Sweet potatoes should be cured immediately after harvest by holding at 85°F and 90–95% relative humidity for 4–7 days.

[4] Winter squash varieties differ in storage life.

POSTHARVEST HANDLING OF FRESH CULINARY HERBS

Herb	Storage Conditions		Relative Ethylene Sensitivity
	Temperature (°F)	Relative Humidity (%)	
Basil	40–42	95–98	Slightly sensitive
Marjoram	33–35	95–98	Sensitive
Mint	33–35	95–98	Sensitive
Oregano	33–35	95–98	Slightly sensitive
Parsley	33–35	95–98	Sensitive
Rosemary	33–35	95–98	Insensitive
Sage	33–35	95–98	Insensitive
Savory	33–35	95–98	Slightly sensitive
Thyme	33–35	95–98	Slightly sensitive

Adapted from D. Joyce and M. Reid, Postharvest handling of fresh culinary herbs, University of Massachusetts Cooperative Extension, *The Herb, Spice, and Medicinal Plant Digest* 4(2):1–2, 5–7 (1986).

RESPIRATION RATES OF VEGETABLES AT VARIOUS TEMPERATURES[1]

Vegetable	Respiration Rate (mg/kg/hr of CO_2)					
	32°F	40–41°F	50°F	59–60°F	68–70°F	77–80°F
Artichoke, globe	15–45	26–60	55–98	76–145	135–233	145–300
Asparagus	27–80	55–136	90–304	160–327	275–500	500–600
Bean, Lima	10–30	20–36	—	100–125	133–179	—
Bean, snap	20	35	58	93	130	193
Beet, topped	5–7	9–10	12–14	17–23	—	—
Beet, with tops	11	14	22	25	40	—
Broccoli	19–21	32–37	75–87	161–186	278–320	—
Brussels sprouts	10–30	22–48	63–84	64–136	86–190	—
Cabbage	4–6	9–12	17–19	20–32	28–49	49–63
Carrot, topped	10–20	13–26	20–42	26–54	46–95	—
Carrot, with tops	18–35	25–51	33–62	55–106	87–121	—
Cauliflower	16–19	19–22	32–36	43–49	75–86	84–140
Celery	5–7	9–11	24	30–37	64	—
Celeriac	7	15	25	39	50	—
Cucumber	—	—	23–29	24–33	14–48	19–55
Endive	45	52	73	100	133	200
Garlic	4–14	9–33	9–10	14–29	13–25	—
Kale	16–27	34–47	72–84	120–155	186–265	—
Kohlrabi	10	16	31	49	—	—
Leek	10–20	20–29	50–70	75–117	110	107–119
Lettuce, head	6–17	13–20	21–40	32–35	51–60	73–91

Lettuce, leaf	19–27	24–35	32–46	51–74	82–119	120–173
Lettuce, romaine	—	18–23	31–40	39–50	60–77	95–121
Melon						
Honeydew	—	3–5	7–9	12–16	20–27	26–35
Muskmelon	5–6	9–10	14–16	34–39	45–65	62–71
Watermelon	—	3–4	6–9	—	17–25	—
Mushroom	28–44	71	100	—	264–316	—
Onion, dry	3	3–4	7–8	10–11	14–19	27–29
Onion, green	10–32	17–39	36–62	66–115	79–178	98–210
Okra	—	53–59	86–95	138–153	248–274	328–362
Parsley	30–40	53–76	85–164	144–184	196–225	291–324
Parsnip	8–15	9–18	20–26	32–46	—	—
Pea	30–47	55–76	68–117	179–202	245–361	343–377
Pea, shelled	47–75	79–97	—	—	349–556	—
Pepper, sweet	—	10	14	23	44	55
Potato, immature	—	12	14–21	14–31	18–45	—
Potato, mature	—	3–9	7–10	6–12	8–16	—
Radish, topped	3–9	6–13	15–16	22–42	44–58	60–89
Radish, with tops	14–17	19–21	31–36	70–78	124–136	158–193
Rhubarb	9–13	11–18	25	31–48	40–57	—
Rutabaga	2–6	5–10	15	11–28	41	—
Spinach	19–22	35–58	82–138	134–223	172–287	—
Squash, butternut	—	—	—	—	—	66–121
Squash, summer	12–13	14–19	34–36	75–90	85–97	—
Strawberry	12–18	16–23	49–95	71–92	102–196	169–211
Sweet corn, in husk	30–51	43–83	104–120	151–175	268–311	282–435
Sweet potato, uncured	—	—	—	29	—	54–73
Sweet potato, cured	—	—	14	20–24	—	—

RESPIRATION RATES OF VEGETABLES AT VARIOUS TEMPERATURES[1]—Continued

	Respiration Rate (mg/kg/hr of CO_2)					
Vegetable	32°F	40–41°F	50°F	59–60°F	68–70°F	77–80°F
Tomato, mature green	—	5–8	12–18	16–28	28–41	35–51
Tomato, ripening	—	—	13–16	24–29	24–44	30–52
Turnip, topped	6–9	10	13–19	21–24	24–25	—
Watercress	15–26	44–49	91–121	136–205	302–348	348–438

Adapted from R. E. Hardenburg, A. E. Watada, and C. Y. Wang, *The Commercial Storage of Fruits, Vegetables, and Florist and Nursery Stocks*, USDA Agriculture Handbook 66 (1986).

[1]Some data is included for low temperatures which may cause injury to chilling-sensitive vegetables; these low temperatures are potentially dangerous and should be avoided for these vegetables.

GENERATION OF HEAT BY VEGETABLES AT VARIOUS TEMPERATURES

	Heat Generated (1000 Btu/ton/day)					
Vegetable	32°F	40–41°F	50°F	59–60°F	68–70°F	77–80°F
Artichoke, globe	3.3–9.9	5.7–13.2	12.1–21.6	16.7–31.9	29.7–51.3	31.9–66.0
Asparagus	5.9–17.6	12.1–29.9	19.8–66.9	35.2–71.9	60.5–110.0	110.0–132.0
Bean, Lima	2.2–6.6	4.4–7.9	—	22.0–27.5	29.3–39.4	—
Bean, snap	4.4	7.7	12.8	20.5	28.6	37.2
Beet, topped	1.0–1.4	1.7–2.2	2.3–2.7	3.3–5.1	—	—
Beet, with tops	2.4	3.1	4.8	5.5	8.8	—
Broccoli	4.2–4.6	7.0–8.1	16.5–19.1	35.4–40.9	61.2–70.4	—
Brussels sprouts	2.2–6.6	4.8–10.6	13.9–18.5	14.1–29.9	18.9–41.8	—
Cabbage	0.9–1.3	2.0–2.6	3.7–4.2	4.4–7.0	6.2–10.8	10.8–13.9
Carrot, topped	2.2–4.4	2.9–5.7	4.4–9.2	5.7–11.9	10.1–20.9	—
Carrot, with tops	4.0–7.7	5.5–11.2	7.3–13.6	12.1–23.3	19.1–26.6	—
Cauliflower	3.5–4.2	4.2–4.8	7.0–7.9	9.5–10.8	16.5–18.9	18.5–30.8
Celery	1.1–1.5	2.0–2.4	5.3	6.6–8.1	14.1	—
Celeriac	1.5	3.3	5.5	8.6	11.0	—
Cucumber	—	—	5.1–6.4	5.3–7.3	3.1–10.6	4.2–12.1
Endive	9.9	11.4	16.1	22.0	29.3	44.0
Garlic	0.9–3.1	2.0–7.3	2.0–2.2	3.1–6.4	3.9–5.5	—
Kale	3.5–5.9	7.5–10.3	15.8–18.5	26.4–34.1	40.9–58.3	—
Kohlrabi	2.2	3.5	6.8	10.8	—	—
Leek	2.2–4.4	4.4–6.4	11.0–15.4	16.5–25.7	24.2	23.5–26.2
Lettuce, head	1.3–3.7	2.9–4.4	4.6–8.8	7.0–7.7	11.2–13.2	16.1–20.0

GENERATION OF HEAT BY VEGETABLES AT VARIOUS TEMPERATURES—Continued

Vegetable	Heat Generated (1000 Btu/ton/day)					
	32°F	40–41°F	50°F	59–60°F	68–70°F	77–80°F
Lettuce, leaf	4.2–5.9	5.3–7.7	7.0–10.1	11.2–16.3	18.0–26.2	26.4–38.1
Lettuce, romaine	—	4.0–5.1	6.8–8.8	8.6–11.0	13.2–16.9	20.9–26.6
Melon						
Honeydew	—	0.7–1.1	1.5–2.0	2.6–3.5	4.4–5.9	5.7–7.7
Muskmelon	1.1–1.3	2.0–2.2	3.1–3.5	7.5–8.6	9.9–14.3	13.6–15.6
Watermelon	—	0.7–0.9	1.3–2.0	—	3.7–5.5	—
Mushroom	6.7–9.7	15.6	22.0	—	58.1–69.5	—
Onion, dry	0.7	0.7–0.9	1.5–1.8	2.2–2.4	3.1–4.2	5.9–6.4
Onion, green	2.2–7.0	3.7–8.6	7.9–13.6	14.5–25.3	17.4–39.2	21.6–46.2
Okra	—	11.7–13.0	18.9–20.9	30.4–33.7	54.6–60.3	72.2–79.6
Parsley	6.6–8.8	11.7–36.1	18.7–36.1	31.7–40.1	43.1–49.5	64.0–71.3
Parsnip	1.8–3.3	2.0–4.0	4.4–5.7	7.0–10.1	—	—
Pea	6.6–10.3	12.1–16.7	15.0–25.7	39.4–44.4	53.9–79.4	75.5–82.9
Pea, shelled	10.3–16.5	17.4–21.3	—	—	76.8–122.3	—
Pepper, sweet	—	2.2	3.1	5.1	9.7	12.1
Potato, immature	—	2.6	3.1–4.6	3.1–6.8	4.0–9.9	—
Potato, mature	—	0.7–2.0	1.5–2.2	1.3–2.6	1.8–3.5	—
Radish, topped	0.7–2.0	1.3–2.9	3.3–3.5	4.8–9.2	9.7–12.8	13.2–19.6
Radish, with tops	3.1–3.7	4.2–4.6	6.8–7.9	15.4–17.2	27.3–29.9	34.8–42.5
Rhubarb	2.0–2.9	2.4–4.0	5.5	6.8–10.6	8.8–12.5	—

Rutabaga	0.4–1.3	1.1–2.2	3.3	2.4–6.2	9.0	—
Spinach	4.2–4.8	7.7–12.8	18.0–30.4	29.5–49.1	37.8–63.1	—
Squash, butternut	—	—	—	—	—	14.5–26.6
Squash, summer	2.6–2.9	3.1–4.2	7.5–7.9	16.5–19.8	18.7–21.3	—
Strawberry	2.6–4.0	3.5–5.1	10.8–20.9	15.6–20.2	22.4–43.1	37.2–46.4
Sweet corn, in husk	6.6–11.2	9.5–18.3	22.9–26.4	33.2–38.5	59.0–68.4	62.0–95.7
Sweet potato, uncured	—	—	—	6.4	—	11.9–16.1
Sweet potato, cured	—	—	3.1	4.4–5.3	—	—
Tomato, mature green	—	1.1–1.8	2.6–4.0	3.5–6.2	6.2–9.0	7.7–11.2
Tomato, ripening	—	—	2.9–3.5	5.3–6.4	5.3–9.7	6.6–11.4
Turnip, topped	1.3–2.0	2.2	2.9–4.2	4.6–5.3	5.3–5.5	—
Watercress	3.3–5.7	9.7–10.8	20.0–26.6	29.9–45.1	66.4–76.6	76.6–96.4

Adapted from R. E. Hardenburg, A. E. Watada, and C. Y. Wang, *The Commercial Storage of Fruits, Vegetables, and Florist and Nursery Stocks*, USDA Agriculture Handbook 66 (1986).

SUMMARY OF RECOMMENDED CONTROLLED ATMOSPHERE OR MODIFIED ATMOSPHERE CONDITIONS DURING TRANSPORT AND/OR STORAGE OF SELECTED VEGETABLES

Vegetable	Temperature (°F)[1]	Controlled Atmosphere[2] (%) O_2	Controlled Atmosphere[2] (%) CO_2	Potential for Benefit	Remarks[3]
Artichoke	32–41	2–3	3–5	Good	No commercial use
Asparagus	32–41	Air	5–10	Good	Limited commercial use
Bean, snap	41–50	2–3	5–10	Fair	Potential for use by processors
Beet	32–41	None	None	None	98–100% relative humidity is best
Broccoli	32–41	1–2	5–10	Good	Limited commercial use
Brussels sprouts	32–41	1–2	5–7	Good	No commercial use
Cabbage	32–41	3–5	5–7	Good	Some commercial use for long-term storage of certain cultivars
Carrot	32–41	None	None	None	98–100% relative humidity is best
Cauliflower	32–41	2–5	2–5	Fair	No commercial use
Celery	32–41	2–4	0	Fair	Limited commercial use in mixed loads with lettuce
Corn, sweet	32–41	2–4	10–20	Good	Limited commercial use
Cucumber	46–54	3–5	0	Fair	No commercial use
Honeydew melon	50–54	3–5	0	Fair	No commercial use

Leek	32–41	1–2	3–5	Good	No commercial use
Lettuce	32–41	2–5	0	Good	Some commercial use with 2–3% CO_2 added
Mushroom	32–41	Air	10–15	Fair	Limited commercial use
Muskmelon	37–45	3–5	10–15	Good	Limited commercial use
Okra	46–54	3–5	0	Fair	No commercial use; 5–10% CO_2 is beneficial at 41–46°F
Onion, dry	32–41	1–2	0	Good	No commercial use; 75% relative humidity
Onion, green	32–41	1–2	10–20	Fair	Limited commercial use
Pepper, bell	46–54	3–5	0	Fair	Limited commercial use
Pepper, chili	46–54	3–5	0	Fair	No commercial use; 10–15% CO_2 is beneficial at 41–46°F
Potato	39–54	None	None	None	No commercial use
Radish	32–41	None	None	None	98–100% relative humidity is best
Spinach	32–41	Air	10–20	Fair	No commercial use
Strawberry	32–41	10	15–20	Excellent	Increasing use during transit
Tomato					
Mature, green	54–68	3–5	0	Good	Limited commercial use
Partially ripe	46–54	3–5	0	Good	Limited commercial use

Adapted from A. A. Kader et al., Postharvest technology of horticultural crops, California Cooperative Extension Special Publication 3311 (1985).

[1] Usual and/or recommended temperature range. A relative humidity of 85–95% is recommended.

[2] Best controlled atmosphere combination may vary among varieties and according to storage temperature and duration.

[3] Comments about use refer to domestic marketing only; many of these commodities are shipped under modified atmospheres for export marketing.

SUSCEPTIBILITY OF VEGETABLES TO CHILLING INJURY[1]

Vegetable	Approximate Lowest Safe Temperature (°F)	Appearance when Stored Between 32°F and Safe Temperature
Asparagus	32–36	Dull, gray-green, and limp tips
Bean, Lima	34–40	Rusty-brown specks, spots, or areas
Bean, snap	45	Pitting and russeting
Cucumber	45	Pitting, water-soaked spots, decay
Eggplant	45	Surface scald, alternaria rot, blackening of seeds
Jicama	55–65	Surface decay, discoloration
Melon		
Casaba	45–50	Pitting, surface decay, failure to ripen
Crenshaw	45–50	Pitting, surface decay, failure to ripen
Honeydew	45–50	Reddish-tan discoloration, pitting, surface decay, failure to ripen
Muskmelon	36–41	Pitting, surface decay
Persian	45–50	Pitting, surface decay, failure to ripen
Watermelon	40	Pitting, objectionable flavor
Okra	45	Discoloration, water-soaked areas, pitting, decay
Pepper, sweet	45	Sheet pitting, alternaria rot on fruit and calyx, darkening of seed
Potato	38	Mahogany browning (Chippewa and Sebago), sweetening

Pumpkin and hard-shell squash	50	Decay, especially alternaria rot
Sweet potato	55	Decay, pitting, hardcore when cooked
Tamarillo	37–40	Surface pitting, discoloration
Tomato, ripe	45–50	Watersoaking and softening, decay
Tomato, mature green	55	Poor color when ripe, alternaria rot

Adapted from R. E. Hardenburg, A. E. Watada, and C. Y. Wang, *The Commercial Storage of Fruits, Vegetables, and Florist and Nursery Stock*, USDA Agriculture Handbook 66 (1986).

[1] Severity of injury is related to temperature and time.

RELATIVE SUSCEPTIBILITY OF VEGETABLES TO FREEZING INJURY

Most Susceptible	Moderately Susceptible	Least Susceptible
Asparagus	Broccoli	Beet
Bean, snap	Cabbage, new	Brussels sprouts
Cucumber	Carrot, topped	Cabbage, old and savoy
Eggplant	Cauliflower	Kale
Lettuce	Celery	Kohlrabi
Okra	Onion, dry	Parsnip
Pepper, sweet	Parsley	Rutabaga
Potato	Pea	Salsify
Squash, summer	Radish, topped	Turnip, topped
Strawberry	Spinach	
Sweet potato	Squash, winter	
Tomato		

Adapted from R. E. Hardenburg, A. E. Watada, and C. Y. Wang, *The Commercial Storage of Fruits, Vegetables, and Florist and Nursery Stocks*, USDA Agriculture Handbook 66 (1986).

SYMPTOMS OF FREEZING INJURY ON SOME VEGETABLES

Vegetable	Symptoms
Artichoke	Epidermis becomes detached and forms whitish to light-tan blisters. When blisters are broken, underlying tissue turns brown
Asparagus	Tip becomes limp and dark, the rest of the spear is water soaked. Thawed spears become mushy
Beet	External and internal water soaking and sometimes blackening of conducting tissue
Broccoli	The youngest florets in the center of the curd are most sensitive to freezing injury. They turn brown and give strong off-odors upon thawing
Cabbage	Leaves become water-soaked, translucent, and limp upon thawing; separated epidermis
Carrot	A blistered appearance; jagged lengthwise cracks. Interior becomes water soaked and darkened upon thawing
Cauliflower	Curds turn brown and have a strong off-odor when cooked
Celery	Leaves and petioles appear wilted and water soaked upon thawing. Petioles freeze more readily than leaves
Garlic	Thawed cloves appear water soaked, grayish-yellow
Lettuce	Blistering, dead cells of the separated epidermis on outer leaves become tan; increased susceptibility to physical damage and decay
Onion	Thawed bulbs are soft, grayish-yellow, and water soaked in cross section; often limited to individual scales
Pepper, bell	Dead, water-soaked tissue in part of or all pericarp surface; pitting, shriveling, and decay follow thawing
Potato	Freezing injury may not be externally evident, but shows as gray or bluish-gray patches beneath the skin. Thawed tubers become soft and watery
Radish	Thawed tissues appear translucent; roots soften and shrivel
Sweet potato	A yellowish-brown discoloration of the vascular ring, and a yellowish-green water-soaked appearance of other tissues. Roots soften and become very susceptible to decay
Tomato	Water-soaked and soft upon thawing. In partially frozen fruits, the margin between healthy and dead tissue is distinct, especially in green fruits
Turnip	Small water-soaked spots or pitting on the surface. Injured tissues appear tan or gray and give off an objectionable odor

Adapted from A. A. Kader, J. M. Lyons, and L. L. Morris, Postharvest responses of vegetables to preharvest field temperature, *HortScience* 9:523–527 (1974).

SOME POSTHARVEST PHYSIOLOGICAL DISORDERS OF VEGETABLES, ATTRIBUTABLE DIRECTLY OR INDIRECTLY TO PREHARVEST FIELD TEMPERATURES

Vegetable	Disorder	Symptoms and Development
Asparagus	Feathering	Bracts of the spears are partly spread as a result of high temperature
Brussels sprouts	Black leaf speck	Becomes visible after storage for 1–2 weeks at low temperature. Has been attributed in part to cauliflower mosaic virus infection in the field, which is influenced by temperature and other environmental factors
	Tip burn	Leaf margins turn light tan to dark brown
Garlic	Waxy breakdown	Enhanced by high temperature during growth; slightly sunken, light-yellow areas in fleshy cloves, then the entire clove becomes amber, slightly translucent, and waxy but still firm
Lettuce	Tip burn	Light-tan to dark-brown margins of leaves. Has been attributed to several causes, including field temperature; it can lead to soft rot development during postharvest handling
	Rib discoloration	More common in lettuce grown when day temperatures exceed 81°F or when night temperatures are between 55 and 64°F than in lettuce grown during cooler periods
	Russet spotting	Small tan, brown, or olive spots randomly distributed over the affected leaf; a postharvest disorder of lettuce induced by ethylene. Lettuce is more susceptible to russet spotting when harvested after high field temperatures (above 86°F) for 2 days or more during the 10 days before harvest

SOME POSTHARVEST PHYSIOLOGICAL DISORDERS OF VEGETABLES, ATTRIBUTABLE DIRECTLY OR INDIRECTLY TO PREHARVEST FIELD TEMPERATURES—Continued

Vegetable	Disorder	Symptoms and Development
Lettuce (Continued)	Rusty-brown discoloration	On 'Climax' lettuce rusty-brown discoloration has been related to internal rib necrosis associated with lettuce mosaic virus infection, which is influenced by field temperature and other environmental factors
Muskmelon	Vein tract browning	Discoloration of unnetted longitudinal stripes; related partly to high temperature and virus diseases
Onion	Translucent scale	Grayish water-soaked appearance of the outer two or three fleshy scales of the bulb; translucency makes venation very distinct. In severe cases, the entire bulb softens and off-odors may develop
Potato	Blackheart	May occur in the field during excessively hot weather in waterlogged soils. Internal symptom is dark-gray to purplish or black discoloration usually in the center of the tuber
Radish	Pithiness	Textured white spots or streaks in cross section, large air spaces near the center, tough and dry roots. Results from high temperature

Adapted from A. A. Kader, J. M. Lyons, and L. L. Morris, Postharvest responses of vegetables to preharvest field temperature, *HortScience* 9:523–527 (1974).

SYMPTOMS OF SOLAR INJURY ON SOME VEGETABLES

Vegetable	Symptoms
Bean, snap	Very small brown or reddish spots on one side of the pod coalesce and become water soaked and slightly shrunken
Cabbage	Blistering of some outer leaves which leads to a bleached papery appearance. Desiccated leaves are susceptible to decay
Cauliflower	Discoloration of curds from yellow to brown to black (solar browning)
Lettuce	Papery areas on leaves, especially the cap leaf, develop during clear weather when air temperatures are higher than 77°F; affected areas become focus for decay
Honeydew melon	White to gray area at or near the top, may be slightly wrinkled, undesirable flavor or brown blotch, which is tan to brown discolored areas caused by death of epidermal cells due to excessive ultraviolet radiation
Muskmelon	Sunburn: dry, sunken, and white to light tan areas. In milder sunburn, ground color is green or spotty brown
Onion and garlic	Sunburn: dry scales are wrinkled and this may extend to one or two fleshy scales, injured area may be bleached depending on the color of the bulb
Pepper, bell	Dry and papery areas, yellowing and sometime wilting
Potato	Sunscald: water and blistered areas on the tuber surface. Injured areas become sunken and leathery and subsurface tissue rapidly turns dark-brown to black when exposed to air
Tomato	Sunburn (solar yellowing): affected areas on the fruit become whitish, translucent, thin walled; a netted appearance may develop. Mild solar injury might not be noticeable at harvest, but becomes more apparent after harvest as uneven ripening

Adapted from A. A. Kader, J. M. Lyons, and L. L. Morris, Postharvest responses of vegetables to preharvest field temperature, *HortScience* 9:523–527 (1974).

CLASSIFICATION OF HORTICULTURAL COMMODITIES ACCORDING TO ETHYLENE PRODUCTION RATES

Very Low Rate	Low Rate	Moderate Rate	High Rate	Very High Rate
Artichoke	Blueberry	Banana	Apple	Cherimoya
Asparagus	Cranberry	Fig	Apricot	Mamey sapote
Cauliflower	Cucumber	Guava	Avocado	Passion fruit
Cherry	Eggplant	Honeydew melon	Feijoa	Sugar apple
Citrus	Okra	Mango	Kiwi fruit (ripe)	
Grape	Olive	Plantain	Muskmelon	
Jujube	Pepper	Tomato	Nectarine	
Leafy vegetables	Persimmon		Papaya	
Most cut flowers	Pineapple		Peach	
Potato	Pumpkin		Pear	
Root vegetables	Raspberry		Plum	
Strawberry	Tamarillo			
	Watermelon			

Adapted from A. A. Kader et al., Postharvest technology of horticultural crops, California Cooperative Extension Special Publication 3311 (1985).

COMPATIBILITY OF FRESH PRODUCE IN MIXED LOADS UNDER VARIOUS RECOMMENDED TRANSIT CONDITIONS

Shippers or receivers of fresh fruits and vegetables frequently prefer to handle shipments that consist of more than one commodity. In mixed loads, it is important to combine only those commodities that are compatible in their requirements for temperature, modified atmosphere, relative humidity, protection from odors, and protection from physiologically active gases such as ethylene.

Recommended Transit Conditions

Temp.: 55–60°F; Relative humidity: 85–95%. Ice: No contact with commodity	Temp.: 36–41°F; Relative humidity: 90–95%. Ice: Contact muskmelon only	Temp.: 40–45°F; Relative humidity: about 95%. Ice: No contact with commodity	Temp.: 40–55°F; Relative humidity: 85 to 90%. Ice: No contact with commodity
Avocado	Cranberry	Snap bean	Cucumber
Banana	Lemon	Lychee	Eggplant
Grapefruit (AZ and CA, FL before Jan. 1)	Muskmelon	Okra	Ginger (not with eggplant)
Guava	Orange	Pepper, green (not with bean)	Grapefruit (FL after Jan. 1 and TX)
Mango	Tangerine	Pepper, red	Lime
Casaba melon		Summer squash	Potato
Crenshaw melon		Tomato, pink	Pumpkin
Honeydew melon		Watermelon	Watermelon
Persian melon			Winter squash
Olive			

Papaya Pinapple (not with avocado) Tomato, green Tomato, pink Watermelon			
Temp.: 32–34°F; Relative humidity: 95–100%. Ice: No contact with asparagus, fig, grape, mushroom	Temp.: 32–34°F; Relative humidity: 95–100%. Ice: Contact acceptable with all commodities	Temp.: 55–65°F; Relative humidity: 85–90%. Ice: No contact with any commodity	Temp.: 32–34°F; Relative humidity: 65–75%. Ice: No contact with any commodity
Artichoke Asparagus Beet Carrot Endive, escarole Fig Grape Greens Leek (not with fig or grape) Lettuce Mushroom	Broccoli Brussels sprouts Cabbage Cauliflower Celeriac Celery Horseradish Kohlrabi Onion, green (not with rhubarb, fig, or grape; probably not with mushroom or sweet corn)	Ginger Sweet potato	Garlic Onion, dry

COMPATIBILITY OF FRESH PRODUCE IN MIXED LOADS UNDER VARIOUS RECOMMENDED TRANSIT CONDITIONS—Continued

Temp.: 32–34°F; Relative humidity: 95–100%. Ice: No contact with asparagus, fig, grape, mushroom	Temp.: 32–34°F; Relative humidity: 95–100%. Ice: Contact acceptable with all commodities	Temp.: 55–65°F; Relative humidity: 85–90%. Ice: No contact with any commodity	Temp.: 32–34°F; Relative humidity: 65–75%. Ice: No contact with any commodity
Parsley	Radish		
Parsnip	Rutabaga		
Pea	Turnip		
Rhubarb			
Salsify			
Spinach			
Sweet corn			
Watercress			

Adapted from W. J. Lipton, Compatibility of fruits and vegetables during transport in mixed loads, USDA, ARS, Marketing Research Report 1070 (1977).

VEGETABLE QUALITY

Quality is defined as *any of the features that make something what it is* or *the degree of excellence or superiority.* The word *quality* is used in various ways in reference to fresh fruits and vegetables such as *market* quality, *edible* quality, *dessert* quality, *shipping* quality, *table* quality, *nutritional* quality, *internal* quality, and *appearance* quality.

Quality of fresh vegetables is a combination of characteristics, attributes, and properties that give the vegetables value to humans for food and enjoyment. Producers are concerned that their commodities have good appearance and few visual defects, but for them a useful cultivar must score high on yield, disease resistance, ease of harvest, and shipping quality. To receivers and market distributors, appearance quality is most important; they are also keenly interested in firmness and long storage life. Consumers consider good-quality vegetables to be those that look good, are firm, and offer good flavor and nutritive value. Although consumers buy on the basis of appearance and feel, their satisfaction and repeat purchases depend on good edible quality.

QUALITY COMPONENTS OF FRESH VEGETABLES

Main Factors	Components
Appearance (visual)	*Size:* dimensions, weight, volume *Shape and form:* diameter/depth ratio, smoothness, compactness, uniformity *Color:* uniformity, intensity *Gloss:* nature of surface wax *Defects,* external and internal: morphological, physical and mechanical, physiological, pathological, entomological
Texture (feel)	Firmness, hardness, softness Crispness Succulence, juiciness Mealiness, grittiness Toughness, fibrousness
Flavor (taste and smell)	Sweetness Sourness (acidity) Astringency Bitterness

QUALITY COMPONENTS OF FRESH VEGETABLES—Continued

Main Factors	Components
Flavor (taste and smell) (Continued)	Aroma (volatile compounds)
	Off-flavors and off-odors
Nutritive value	Carbohydrates (including dietary fiber)
	Proteins
	Lipids
	Vitamins
	Minerals
Safety	Naturally occurring toxicants
	Contaminants (chemical residues, heavy metals)
	Mycotoxins
	Microbial contamination

Adapted from A. A. Kader et al., Postharvest technology of horticultural crops, California Cooperative Extension Special Publication 3311 (1985).

U.S. STANDARDS FOR FRESH VEGETABLES

Grade standards issued by the U.S. Department of Agriculture are currently in effect for most vegetables for fresh market and for processing. Some standards have been unchanged since they became effective whereas others have been revised quite recently.

A publication—U.S. Standards and Inspection Instructions for Fresh Fruits and Vegetables and Other Special Products—lists the crops for which standards have been established and their effective date. This publication can be obtained free of charge from Fresh Products Branch, AMS, FV; U.S. Department of Agriculture, Room 2056, South Building, Washington, DC 20250.

STORAGE SPROUT INHIBITORS

Sprout inhibitors are most effective when used in conjunction with good storage; their use cannot substitute for poor storage or poor storage management. However, storage temperatures may be somewhat higher when sprout inhibitors are used than when they are not. Follow label directions.

Vegetable	Material	Application
Potato (do not use on seed potatoes)	Maleic hydrazide	When most tubers are 2 in. in diameter. Vines must remain green for several weeks after application
	Chloro-IPC (do not use herbicide formulation)	In storage, 2–3 weeks after harvest as an aerosol treatment. Do not store seed potatoes in a treated storage. During washing, as an emulsifiable concentrate added to wash water to prevent sprouting during marketing
	TCNB	Apply as a dust as potatoes are going into storage. Provides short-term sprout inhibition
Onion	Maleic hydrazide	Apply when 50% of the tops are down, the bulbs are mature, the necks soft, and 5–7 leaves are still soft

CHARACTERISTICS OF SOME WHOLESALE MARKETING ALTERNATIVES FOR FRESH VEGETABLES

Grower Consideration	Terminal Market	Cooperative and Private Packing Facilities	Peddling to Grocer or Restaurant	Wholesale/Broker
Harvesting cost	Usual cost	Sometimes harvesting equipment is provided	Usual cost	Usual cost
Transportation cost	Depends on distance to market	Sometimes transportation is provided	Depends on distance traveled	Depends on prior arrangements for delivery or pick up
Prices received for produce	Grower is usually the price taker	Prices received by growers depend on market prices, costs, and revenues	Buyer and grower may compromise on price or grower fixes price	Grower is usually the price taker
Required volume	Usually large quantities are needed	Depends on the products to be sold	Depends on the size of outlets and route	Usually large quantities are needed
Market investment	Truck or some transportation arrangements. Specialized containers are required	Relatively low on a per unit basis	Truck. Containers	Depends on arrangements. Usually minimal costs to grower. Specialized containers are required

Quality	Must meet buyer's standards or U.S. grades	Must meet buyer's standards or U.S. grades	High quality is needed	Must meet standards or U.S. grades so that produce can be handled in bulk
Other	Good source of market information. Can move very large quantities at one time. Many buyers are located at terminal markets	May provide technical assistance to growers. Firms help in planning of growing and selling. Equipment may be shared by growers	Long-term outlet for consistent quality. Good price for quality produce. Difficult to enter market and develop customers	Good wholesaler/broker can sell produce quickly at good prices. A long-term buyer/seller relationship is desirable. Broker does not necessarily take title of produce

Adapted from Cucurbit production and pest management, Oklahoma Cooperative Extension Circular E-853 (1986).

CHARACTERISTICS OF DIRECT MARKETING ALTERNATIVES FOR FRESH VEGETABLES

Grower Characteristic	Pick-Your-Own	Roadside Market	Farmer's Market
Harvesting cost	Customer assumes the cost	Usual cost	Usual cost
Transportation cost	Customer assumes the cost	Usually very minimal for produce	Depends on grower's distance to market
Selling cost	Field attendant is needed. Harvesting instructions should be provided. Advertising	Checkout attendant is needed. Advertising	Checkout attendant is needed
Grower liability	Liable for accidents. Absorbs damages to property and crop	Liable for accidents at market	Owner of market is responsible
Market investment	Containers. Locational signs. Available parking	Building or stand. Available parking. Containers	Usually parking or building space is rented. Containers
Volume of produce desired	Enough for customer traffic demands	Enough to visibly attract customers to stop. Variety is helpful	Enough to justify transportation and other costs
Prices received for produce	Often lower than other alternatives because transportation and harvesting cost is assumed by the customer. Producer sets the price	Producer sets the price given perceived demand and competitive conditions	Producer sets the price. There may be competition from other sellers

Quality	Can sell whatever the customers will pick	Can classify produce and sell more than one grade	Ability to sell may depend on the competing qualities available from other growers
Other	Balance between number of pickers and amount needing to be harvested sometimes is difficult to achieve	Sometimes other items besides produce are sold to supplement income. Produce spoilage can be minimized if adequate cooling facilities are used	Sometimes other items besides produce are sold to supplement income. Bulk sales are sometimes recommended

Adapted from Cucurbit production and pest management, Oklahoma Cooperative Extension Circular E-853 (1986).

SHIPPING CONTAINERS FOR FRESH VEGETABLES

Vegetable	Container[1]	Approximate Net Weight (lb)[2]
Anise	15½-in. wirebound crate	40–50
	Carton and crate packed, 1½ to 2½ dozen	25
	Crate	60–70
Artichoke	Carton or box by count or loose pack	20–25
Asparagus	Pyramid crate	30–36
	½-pyramid crate or carton	15–17
	Carton holding sixteen 1½-lb packages	24–25
Bean, snap and Lima	Bushel crate, hamper, or basket	28–32
	Carton	28–32
Beet		
Bunched	1⅗-bushel crate, 24's	36–40
	⅘-bushel crate, 12's	15–20
Topped	Sack, as marked	25–50
Broccoli	Carton holding 14–18 bunches	20–24
Brussels sprouts	Carton	25
	Flat or carton holding twelve 10-oz cups	7½–8
Cabbage	Sack, crate, or carton	50–55
Savoy	Sack, crate, or carton	37
Carrot		
Bunched	Carton holding 2 dozen bunches	23–27
Topped	48 1-lb bags or 24 2-lb bags in master container	48

	Mesh bag, loose, as marked	25–55
Mini	20 12-oz. film bags	15–17
Cauliflower	Flat or 2-layer carton holding 9–16 trimmed heads	18–24
	Long Island type crate	45–55
Celery		
California	15½-in. crate, flatpack	60–65
Florida	14½-in. crate	55–60
Celery hearts		
California	Carton holding 12–18 film bags (2 or 3 stalks each)	24–28
Florida	Carton holding 12–18 film bags (2 or 3 stalks each)	32–38
Chinese cabbage	15½-in. wirebound crate	50–53
	1⅑-bushel wirebound crate	40–45
Chive	Flat holding 12 pots	10
Corn, sweet	Wirebound crate 4½–5 dozen	42–50
	Sacks	35–40
Cucumber	Bushel carton or wirebound crate	50–55
	1⅑-bushel carton or wirebound	50–55
	Los Angeles lug	28–32
	Carton holding 24	22–28
Cucumber, greenhouse	Carton holding 1-layer pack	8–10
	Carton	16
Eggplant	Carton packed 18's and 24's	20–23
	Bushel carton, 1⅑-bushel carton, or wirebound crate	30–35
Escarole, endive	Carton or wirebound crate holding 24 heads	30–36
	1⅑-bushel wirebound crate	25–28

SHIPPING CONTAINERS FOR FRESH VEGETABLES—Continued

Vegetable	Container[1]	Approximate Net Weight (lb)[2]
Endive, Belgian	Carton	10
Garlic	Carton or crate, bulk	20
	Carton or crate, bulk	30
	Carton of 12 packages of 2 cloves each	10
Greens	Bushel basket, crate, or carton	20–25
	$1\frac{2}{5}$- or $1\frac{3}{5}$-bushel wirebound crate	30–35
Ginger	Carton	30
Horseradish	Sack	50–60
Leek	$\frac{4}{5}$-bushel crate	20
Lettuce		
Iceberg	Western iceberg carton of 18–30 heads	45–50
Romaine	$1\frac{1}{9}$-bushel wirebound crate	20–25
Big Boston	Carton and eastern carton holding 24 heads	20–24
Bibb	Carton	5–8
Leaf	Carton	10–13
Melon		
Casaba	Carton, bliss style, packed 4, 5, 6, or 8	32–34
Crenshaw	Carton, bliss style, packed 4, 5, 6, or 8	30–33
Honeydew	Carton, various counts	29–32
	Flat crate standard	40
Muskmelon	$\frac{1}{2}$-carton or crate packed 12, 15, 18, 23	35–40
	Jumbo crate packed 18 to 45	70–80
	$\frac{2}{3}$-carton packed 15, 18, 24, 30	53–55

Persian	Carton packed 4, 5, or 6	35–50
Watermelon		
Western and New Mexico	Bulk	40,000
Florida, Texas, and other states	Bulk	45,000
	Bulk bin, small size	800–1,000
	Bulk bin, medium size	1,400–1,800
	Carton holding 3–5 melons	65–80
Texas and Mexico	Carton holding 3 or 4 melons	65–80
Mushroom	Carton holding eight 1-lb packages	8
	Carton holding nine 8-oz packages	4½
	Carton, loose pack	10
	4-qt basket	3–5
Okra	Bushel hamper or crate	30
	5/9-bushel crate	18
	Carton	18
	12-qt basket	15–18
Mexico	Crate or carton	15–18
Onion		
Dry	Sack	50
	Sack	25
	Carton holding fifteen 3-lb bags	45
	Carton holding twenty 2-lb bags	40
Green	Carton or crate holding 4 dozen bunches	15–25
	Carton or crate holding 2 dozen bunches	20
	Carton	13
Pearl	Carton holding twelve 10-oz containers	8
Oriental vegetables	Lug	25–28

SHIPPING CONTAINERS FOR FRESH VEGETABLES—Continued

Vegetable	Container[1]	Approximate Net Weight (lb)[2]
Oriental vegetables (Continued)	Crate	75–80
	Carton	20–22
	Wirebound crate	45
Parsley	Carton, bushel basket, or crate holding 5 dozen bunches	20–25
Parsnip	Film bags	25
	Carton holding twelve 1-lb film bags	12
Pea		
Greeen	Bushel basket or wirebound crate	28–32
Snow pea	Carton	10
Pepper	Bushel carton	25–30
Green: California	1 1/9-bushel wirebound crate	25–30
	Carton	27–34
Chili: California	Lugs or carton, loose pack	16–25
Texas and Mexico	3/4-bushel carton	20
Potato	100-lb sack	100
	50-lb sack or carton	50
	20-lb film or paper bags	20
	five 10-lb film or paper bags	50
	ten 5-lb film or paper bags	50
Radish		
Bunched	Carton holding 4-dozen bunches	25

Topped	Carton holding twenty-four 8-oz film bags	12
	Carton holding thirty 6-oz film bags	11–12
	Film bag	40
Rhubarb	Carton or lug	20
	Carton	5
Rutabaga	Bag or carton	25
	Sack or carton	50
Salad mix	Carton holding eight 5-lb film bags	40
Shallot, dry	Bag	5
	Carton holding 16 qt	32
Southern pea	Carton holding twelve 11-oz film bags	9¼
	Bushel crate	24
Spinach	Carton or wirebound crate holding 2 dozen	20–22
	Carton holding twelve 10-oz film bags	7½–8
	Bushel basket or crate	20–25
Squash		
Winter	1⅑-bushel crate	40–50
	Bulk bin carton, collapsible and reusable	800–900
	Various bulk bins	900–2,000
Summer	5/9-bushel crate or carton	21
	½-bushel basket or carton	21
	Carton or Los Angeles lug	24–28
	¾ lug	18–22
	1⅑-bushel crate	42–45
Strawberry	Tray holding 12 pints	10–12
	Crate holding 16 qt	32
Sunchoke (Jerusalem artichoke)	Carton holding twelve 1-lb film bags	12
Sweet potato	Carton, crate, or bushel basket	50

SHIPPING CONTAINERS FOR FRESH VEGETABLES—Continued

Vegetable	Container[1]	Approximate Net Weight (lb)
Sweet potato (Continued)	Carton, California	40
Tomatillo	Carton	30
Tomato		
Cherry	Carton holding 12 pints	16–18
Mature green	Carton	25
Pinks and ripes	2-layer flat, carton, or tray pack	20
	3-layer lug or carton	30
	Carton, loose pack	20
Greenhouse	Basket	8–10
Turnip		
Topped	Film bag	25
	Film and mesh bag or bushel basket	50
	Carton holding twenty-four 1-lb film bags	24
Watercress	Carton holding 25 bunches	8

Adapted from Conversion factors and weights and measures for agricultural commodities and their products, USDA Statistical Bulletin 616 (1979).

[1] Other containers are being developed and used in the marketplace. The requirements of each market should be determined.

[2] Weight ranges are shown for most vegetables. Actual weights larger and smaller than the ranges shown may be found. The midpoint of the range should be used if a single value is desired.

CONVENIENT HEAT AND ENERGY EQUIVALENTS AND DEFINITIONS[1]

1 calorie = heat needed to change 1 gram (1 cubic centimeter) of water at maximum density by 1 °C

temperature of maximum density of water = 3.98 °C (about 39 °F)

1 British thermal unit (Btu) = heat needed to change 1 pound of water at maximum density of 1 °F

1 Btu = 252 calories

1 kilogram-calorie = 1000 calories

1 Btu per minute = 0.02356 horsepower

1 Btu per minute = 0.01757 kilowatts

1 Btu per minute = 17.57 watts

1 horsepower = 42.44 Btu per minute

1 horsepower-hour = 2547 Btu

1 kilowatt-hour = 3415 Btu

1 kilowatt = 56.92 Btu per minute

1 pound of water at 32 °F changed to solid ice requires removal of 144 Btu

1 pound of ice in melting takes up 144 Btu

1 ton of ice in melting takes up 288,000 Btu

---

[1]See page 205 for other power and energy equivalents.

PART 9
SEED PRODUCTION AND STORAGE

SEED PURITY AND GERMINATION STANDARDS

SEED PRODUCTION

SEED YIELDS

SEED STORAGE

STANDARDS OF SEED PURITY AND GERMINATION

Seeds entering into interstate commerce must meet the requirements of the Federal Seed Act. Most state seed laws conform to the federal standards. The kinds of primary noxious weeds, sometimes subject to tolerances, and the secondary noxious weeds listed by the laws of the individual states differ to a considerable extent. The weed seed regulations and the tolerances allowed, if any, may be ascertained by writing to the State Seed Laboratory of any state.

Each container of vegetable seeds must bear or have attached to it a label that gives the following information:

1. Name of kind, variety, or hybrid of the seed. The representation of kind and variety shall be confined to the recognized name of the kind and variety. It shall not have affixed thereto words or terms that create a misleading impression about the history or characteristics of the kind or variety.
2. Full name and address of the person who transports the seed in interstate commerce or the person to whom the seed is shipped.
3. Germination information:
    a. Percentage of germination, exclusive of hard seed.
    b. Percentage of hard seed, if present.
    c. Date of test.
    d. Statement as to any seed treatment including the name of substance or process.

MINIMUM OFFICIAL FEDERAL GERMINATION PERCENTAGES

Seed	%	Seed	%
Artichoke	60	Kohlrabi	75
Asparagus	70	Leek	60
Bean, asparagus	75	Lettuce	80
Bean, garden	70	Muskmelon	75
Bean, Lima	70	Mustard	75
Bean, runner	75	Mustard, spinach	75
Beet	65	Mustard, vegetable	75
Broccoli	75	Okra	50
Brussels sprouts	70	Onion	70
Cabbage	75	Onion, Welsh	70
Cardoon	60	Pak-choi	75
Carrot	55	Parsley	60
Cauliflower	75	Parsnip	60
Celery and celeriac	55	Pea	80
Chard, Swiss	65	Pepper	55
Chicory	65	Pumpkin	75
Chinese cabbage	75	Radish	75
Citron	65	Rhubarb	60
Collard	80	Rutabaga	75
Corn, sweet	75	Salsify	75
Corn salad	70	Sorrel	65
Cowpea (southern pea)	75	Soybean	75
Cress, garden	75	Spinach	60
Cress, upland	60	Spinach, New Zealand	40
Cress, water	40	Squash	75
Cucumber	80	Tomato	75
Dandelion	60	Tomato, husk	50
Eggplant	60	Turnip	80
Endive	70	Watermelon	70
Kale	75		

Adapted from USDA Federal Seed Act Regulations (1986).

EUROPEAN ECONOMIC COMMUNITY STATUTORY MINIMUM LEVELS OF GERMINATION FOR SOME VEGETABLE SEEDS

Minimum not Specified	65%	70%	75%	80%
Parsnip	Carrot	Asparagus	Bean, French	Bean, broad
	Chicory	Beetroot	Brussels sprouts	Bean, runner
	Endive	Cauliflower	Cabbage	Pea
	Leek	Celery	Lettuce	Turnip
	Parsley	Maize	Marrow	
		Onion	Spinach	
		Radish	Tomato	

VEGETABLE CROPS NEEDING EXPOSURE TO COOL WEATHER IN ORDER TO PRODUCE SEEDSTALKS

Generally, the biennial vegetables listed below should be partly developed before they are exposed to cold. Those that are too small may not be greatly affected by the cold; cabbage stems, for example, should be at least as large as a lead pencil in diameter. The average chilling temperature should be below 45°F, and the chilling should continue for 1–2 months. Cooler temperatures may shorten the period of exposure. In seed production it is important to obtain close to 100% of the plants developing seedstalks. Every effort should therefore be made to have them large enough to react to the cold stimulus.

Beet	Kohlrabi
Brussels sprouts	Leek
Cabbage	Onion
Carrot	Parsley
Celeriac	Parsnip
Celery	Radish, winter type
Chard, Swiss	Rutabaga
Collard	Salsify
Florence fennel	Turnip
Kale	

DESIRABLE ISOLATION DISTANCES BETWEEN PLANTINGS OF VEGETABLES FOR SEED PRODUCTION

Self-Pollinated Vegetables

Self-pollinated crops show little outcrossing. Consequently, the only isolation necessary is to have plantings spaced far enough apart to prevent mechanical mixture at planting or harvest. Seedmen often plant a tall growing crop between different varieties. Canada requires 150 ft of separation for stock seed sources of most self-pollinated crops.

Bean	Bean, Lima	Chicory	Endive
Lettuce	Pea	Tomato	

Vegetables Pollinated by Airborne Pollen

One mile between varieties is recommended:

Beet	Spinach
Corn	Swiss chard

Vegetables Pollinated by Insect-Borne Pollen

Allow at least ¼ mile between plantings and avoid having fields of several varieties of the same species or group planted in the line of flight of wild or domestic bees to a colony. Isolation of 1 mile is necessary in some cases.

- Asparagus
- Cabbage group:
  - Broccoli
  - Brussels sprouts
  - Cabbage
  - Cauliflower
  - Collard
  - Kale
  - Kohlrabi
- Carrot
- Celeriac
- Celery
- Cucumber
- Eggplant
- Gherkin
- Miscellaneous Brassica group:
  - Chinese cabbage
  - Mustard
  - Radish
  - Rutabaga
  - Turnip
- Melon group:
  - Casaba
  - Crenshaw
  - Honeydew
  - Muskmelon
  - Persian
  - Watermelon
- Onion
- Parsley
- Pepper
- Pumpkin
- Squash

STECKLINGS FOR SEED PRODUCTION

Crop	Spacing between Rows (in.)	Spacing between Plants (in.)	Root Bed Seed Requirement (lb/acre)	Area (acres) to Be Set from 1 acre of Seedbed
Beet	32–36	12–24	8–10	5–15
Carrot	30–36	8–12	6–8	8–20
Onion	36	Practically touching	4–6	2–5
Parsnip	36–48	12–24	3–4	10–20
Rutabaga and turnip	24–36	8–18	3–4	6–10

SEED-TO-SEED PRODUCTION

Whenever the seed-to-seed method is used for producing the commercial seed crop, it is important to use stock seed for very high quality. Roguing is difficult with root crops because there is less opportunity for selection than with stecklings.

Vegetable	Row Spacing (in.)	Spacing between Plants in Row (in.)	Rate of Seeding (lb/acre)
Beet	20–36	1	7–20
Cabbage	20–36	10–12	2–3
Carrot	20–36	1	2–3
Chard, Swiss	36	12–18	6–8
Lettuce	20–36	4–6	1–2
Onion	20–36	1	4–6
Parsnip	36–46	8–12	3–4
Radish, summer and winter types	20–36	2–12	3–4
Rutabaga and turnip	20–36	1	3–4
Salsify	20–36	12	8–10

YIELDS OF VEGETABLE SEEDS

Vegetable	Average U.S. Yields, 1976–1977 (lb/acre)	Very Good Yield (lb/acre)
Asparagus	—	1000
Bean, snap	1510	2000
Bean, Lima	1965	2500
Beet	1188	2000
Broccoli	444	800
Brussels sprouts	—	1000
Cabbage	693	1000
Carrot	611	1000
Cauliflower	397	500
Celeriac	—	1000
Celery	578	1000
Chard, Swiss	1351	2000
Chicory	—	600
Chinese cabbage	—	1000
Corn, sweet	1726	2500
Cucumber	427	700
Eggplant	132	200
Endive, curled or smooth	580	800
Florence fennel	—	2000
Kale	1034	1200
Kohlrabi	706	1000
Leek	450	600
Lettuce	356	600
Muskmelon	313	500
Mustard	1168	1500
New Zealand spinach	—	2000
Okra	1211	2000
Onion	318	800
Parsley	607	1200
Parsnip	698	1300
Pea	1694	2500
Pepper	127	200
Pumpkin	534	800
Radish	982	2000
Rutabaga	2000	2500
Salsify	300	1000
Southern pea	—	1500

YIELDS OF VEGETABLE SEEDS—Continued

Vegetable	Average U.S. Yields, 1976–1977 (lb/acre)	Very Good Yield (lb/acre)
Spinach	1560	2500
Squash, summer	640	1000
Squash, winter	404	800
Tomato	121	200
Turnip	1380	2000
Watermelon	251	400

U.S. yields adapted from Vegetable Crop Reporting Board ESCS, USDA (1978).

STORAGE OF VEGETABLE SEEDS

Both high moisture and high temperature will cause rapid deterioration in the viability of vegetable seeds. The longer seeds are held, the more important becomes the control of the moisture and temperature conditions. Low moisture in the seeds means longer life, especially if they must be held at warm temperatures. Kinds of seeds vary in their responses to humidity (page 387).

The moisture content of seeds can be lowered by drying them in moving air at 120°F. This may be injurious to seeds with an initial moisture content of 25–40%. With such seeds 110°F is better. It may take less than 1 hr to reduce sufficiently the moisture content of small seeds or up to 3 hr for large seeds. This will depend on the depth of the layer of seeds, the volume of air, dryness of air, and original moisture content of seed. When you cannot dry seeds in this way, seal them in airtight containers over, but not touching, some calcium chloride. Use enough of the chemical so that the moisture absorbed from the seeds will produce no visible change in the calcium chloride. Dried silica gel can be used in place of the calcium chloride.

Bean and okra may develop hard seeds if their moisture content is lowered to 7% or below. White-seeded beans are likely to become hard if the moisture content is reduced to about 10%. Dark-colored beans can be dried to less than 10% moisture before they become hard. Hard seeds will not germinate satisfactorily.

The moisture content of seed will reach an equilibrium with the atmosphere after a period of time. This takes about 3 weeks for small seeds and 3–6 weeks for large seeds.

Storage temperatures near 32°F are not necessary. Between 40 and 50°F is quite satisfactory when the moisture content of the seed is low.

If you reduce the moisture content to 4–5% and put the seeds in sealed containers, you can use a storage temperature of about 70°F for more than 1 year.

EQUILIBRIUM MOISTURE CONTENTS OF VEGETABLE SEEDS AT VARIOUS RELATIVE HUMIDITIES AND APPROXIMATELY 25°C—WET BASIS

Relative Humidity (%):	10	20	30	45	60	75	80
Vegetable				Seed Moisture (%)			
Bean, Lima	4.6	6.6	7.7	9.2	11.0	13.8	15.0
Bean, snap	3.0	4.8	6.8	9.4	12.0	15.0	16.0
Beet, garden	2.1	4.0	5.8	7.6	9.4	11.2	15.0
Broadbean	4.2	5.8	7.2	9.3	11.1	14.5	17.2
Cabbage	3.2	4.6	5.4	6.4	7.6	9.6	10.0
Cabbage, Chinese	2.4	3.4	4.6	6.3	7.8	9.4	—
Carrot	4.5	5.9	6.8	7.9	9.2	11.6	12.5
Celery	5.8	7.0	7.8	9.0	10.4	12.4	13.5
Corn, sweet	3.8	5.8	7.0	9.0	10.6	12.8	14.0
Cucumber	2.6	4.3	5.6	7.1	8.4	10.1	10.2
Eggplant	3.1	4.9	6.3	8.0	9.8	11.9	—
Lettuce	2.8	4.2	5.1	5.9	7.1	9.6	10.0
Mustard, leaf	1.8	3.2	4.6	6.3	7.8	9.4	—
Okra	3.8	7.2	8.3	10.0	11.2	13.1	14.5
Onion	4.6	6.8	8.0	9.5	11.2	13.4	13.6
Onion, Welsh	3.4	5.1	6.9	9.4	11.8	14.0	—
Parsnip	5.0	6.1	7.0	8.2	9.5	11.2	—
Pea	5.4	7.3	8.6	10.1	11.9	15.0	15.5
Pepper	2.8	4.5	6.0	7.8	9.2	11.0	12.0
Radish	2.6	3.8	5.1	6.8	8.3	10.2	—
Spinach	4.6	6.5	7.8	9.5	11.1	13.2	14.5
Squash, winter	3.0	4.3	5.6	7.4	9.0	10.8	—
Tomato	3.2	5.0	6.3	7.8	9.2	11.1	12.0
Turnip	2.6	4.0	5.1	6.3	7.4	9.0	10.0
Watermelon	3.0	4.8	6.1	7.6	8.8	10.4	11.0

Adapted from O. L. Justice and L. N. Bass, *Principles and Practices of Seed Storage*, USDA Agricultural Handbook 506 (1978).

ESTIMATED MAXIMUM SAFE SEED-MOISTURE CONTENTS FOR STORAGE FOR 1 YEAR AT DIFFERENT TEMPERATURES

	40–50°F	70°F	80°F
Vegetable	Seed Moisture (%)		
Bean	15	11	8
Bean, Lima	15	11	8
Beet	14	11	9
Cabbage	9	7	5
Carrot	13	9	7
Celery	13	9	7
Corn, sweet	14	10	8
Cucumber	11	9	8
Lettuce	10	7	5
Okra	14	12	10
Onion	11	8	6
Pea	15	13	9
Pepper	10	9	7
Spinach	13	11	9
Tomato	13	11	9
Turnip	10	8	6
Watermelon	10	8	7

Adapted from E. H. Toole, Storage of vegetable seeds, USDA Leaflet 220 (1958).

RELATIVE LIFE EXPECTANCY OF VEGETABLE SEEDS STORED UNDER FAVORABLE CONDITIONS

Vegetable	Years	Vegetable	Years
Asparagus	3	Kohlrabi	3
Bean	3	Leek	2
Beet	4	Lettuce	6
Broccoli	3	Martynia	2
Brussels sprouts	4	Muskmelon	5
Cabbage	4	Mustard	4
Cardoon	5	New Zealand spinach	3
Carrot	3	Okra	2
Cauliflower	4	Onion	1
Celeriac	3	Parsley	1
Celery	3	Parsnip	1
Chard, Swiss	4	Pea	3
Chervil	3	Pepper	2
Chicory	4	Pumpkin	4
Chinese cabbage	3	Radish	5
Ciboule	2	Roselle	3
Collard	5	Rutabaga	4
Corn, sweet	2	Salsify	1
Corn salad	5	Scorzonera	2
Cress, garden	5	Sea kale	1
Cress, water	5	Sorrel	4
Cucumber	5	Southern pea	3
Dandelion	2	Spinach	3
Eggplant	4	Squash	4
Endive	5	Tomato	4
Fennel	4	Turnip	4
Kale	4	Watermelon	4

Adapted from J. F. Harrington and P. A. Minges, Vegetable seed germination, University of California Agricultural Extension Leaflet, unnumbered (1954).

STORAGE OF VEGETABLE SEEDS IN HERMETICALLY SEALED CONTAINERS

Seeds stored in sealed containers should not exceed these moisture percentages on a wet weight basis.

Vegetable	Moisture (%)	Vegetable	Moisture (%)
Bean, garden	7.0	Leek	6.5
Bean, Lima	7.0	Lettuce	5.5
Beet	7.5	Muskmelon	6.0
Broccoli	5.0	Mustard, India	5.0
Brussels sprouts	5.0	Onion	6.5
Cabbage	5.0	Onion, Welsh	6.5
Carrot	7.0	Parsley	6.5
Cauliflower	5.0	Parsnip	6.0
Celeriac	7.0	Pea	7.0
Celery	7.0	Pepper	4.5
Chard, Swiss	7.5	Pumpkin	6.0
Chinese cabbage	5.0	Radish	5.0
Chive	6.5	Rutabaga	5.0
Collard	5.0	Spinach	8.0
Corn, sweet	8.0	Squash	6.0
Cucumber	6.0	Tomato	5.5
Eggplant	6.0	Turnip	5.0
Kale	5.0	Watermelon	6.5
Kohlrabi	5.0	All others	6.0

Adapted from USDA Federal Seed Act Regulations (1976).

PART 10

APPENDIX

SOURCES OF VEGETABLE INFORMATION

SOURCES OF VEGETABLE SEEDS

PERIODICALS FOR VEGETABLE GROWERS

U.S. UNITS OF MEASUREMENT

CONVERSION FACTORS FOR U.S. UNITS

METRIC UNITS OF MEASUREMENT

CONVERSION FACTORS FOR U.S. AND METRIC UNITS

USEFUL CONVERSIONS FOR RATES OF APPLICATION

SOURCES OF INFORMATION AND PUBLICATIONS ON VEGETABLES

Requests for information should be addressed to the Agricultural Extension Service or Agricultural Experiment Station in your state.

State	Post Office
Alabama	Auburn 36849
Alaska	Fairbanks 99701
Arizona	Tucson 85721
Arkansas	Fayetteville 72701
California	Berkeley 94720
	Davis 95616
	Riverside 92521
Colorado	Fort Collins 80523
Connecticut	New Haven 06504
	Storrs 06268
Delaware	Newark 19711
Florida	Gainesville 32611
Georgia	Athens 30602
Hawaii	Honolulu 96822
Idaho	Moscow 83843
Illinois	Urbana 61801
Indiana	Lafayette 47907
Iowa	Ames 50011
Kansas	Manhattan 66506
Kentucky	Lexington 40506
Louisiana	University Station, Baton Rouge 70893
Maine	Orono 04469
Maryland	College Park 20742
Massachusetts	Amherst 01003
Michigan	East Lansing 48824
Minnesota	St. Paul 55108
Mississippi	State College 39762
Missouri	Columbia 65211
Montana	Bozeman 59717
Nebraska	Lincoln 68583
Nevada	Reno 89557
New Hampshire	Durham 03824
New Jersey	New Brunswick 08903
New Mexico	State College 88003

SOURCES OF INFORMATION AND PUBLICATIONS ON VEGETABLES—Continued

State	Post Office
New York	Geneva 14456
	Ithaca 14853
North Carolina	Raleigh 27650
North Dakota	Fargo 58105
Ohio	Columbus 43201
	Wooster 44961
Oklahoma	Stillwater 74078
Oregon	Corvallis 97331
Pennsylvania	University Park 16802
Puerto Rico	Mayaguez 00708
Rhode Island	Kingston 02881
South Carolina	Clemson 29631
South Dakota	Brookings 57007
Tennessee	Knoxville 37901
Texas	College Station 77843
Utah	Logan 84322
Vermont	Burlington 05405
Virginia	Blacksburg 24061
	Norfolk 23501
Washington	Pullman 99164
West Virginia	Morgantown 26506
Wisconsin	Madison 53706
Wyoming	Laramie 82071

A List of Available Publications can be obtained from the Office of Governmental and Public Affairs, U.S. Department of Agriculture, Washington, DC 20250. "For sale only" publications of the USDA can be obtained from the Superintendent of Documents, Government Printing Office, Washington, DC 20402.
Many state and USDA publications are available from County Extension Offices. This may be the easiest and quickest way of obtaining needed information on vegetables.

SOURCES OF VEGETABLE INFORMATION IN CANADA

For bulletins published in Canada write to Information Services, Agriculture Canada, Ottawa, Canada K1A 0C7, or to the Ministry of Agriculture in a particular province.

Province	Post Office
Alberta	Edmonton
British Columbia	Victoria
Manitoba	Winnipeg
New Brunswick	Fredericton
Newfoundland	St. Johns
Nova Scotia	Halifax
Ontario	Toronto
Prince Edward Island	Charlottetown
Quebec	Quebec
Saskatchewan	Regina

SOME PERIODICALS FOR VEGETABLE GROWERS

American Fruit Grower
37841 Euclid Ave.
Willoughby, OH 44094

American Vegetable Grower
37841 Euclid Ave.
Willoughby, OH 44094

Citrus and Vegetable Magazine
PO Box 2349
Tampa, FL 33601

Florida Grower & Rancher
723 E. Colonial Dr.
Orlando, FL 32803

Great Lakes Vegetable Growers News
343 S. Union St.
Sparta, MI 49345

Greenhouse Grower
37841 Euclid Ave.
Willoughby, OH 44094

The Grower
50 Doughty St.
London, England WC1N 2LP

The Grower
7950 College Blvd.
PO Box 2939
Shawnee Mission, KS 66201

The Packer
7950 College Blvd.
PO Box 2939
Shawnee Mission, KS 66201

Western Grower and Shipper
PO Box 2130
Newport Beach, CA 92658

SOME SOURCES OF VEGETABLE SEED[1]

Company	Address
Abbott & Cobb, Inc.	PO Box 307, Feasterville, PA 19047
Agway, Inc., Seed Division	Box 4741, Syracuse, NY 13221
American Takii Inc.	301 Natividad Rd., Salinas, CA 93906
Asgrow Florida Co.	Plant City, FL 33566
Asgrow Seed Co.	7000 Portage Rd., Kalamazoo, MI 49001
Ball Seed Co.	Box 335, West Chicago, IL 60185
Bejo Seeds	PO Box 9, 1722ZG Noordscharwoude, Netherlands
Brawley Seed Co., Inc.	PO Box 180, Mooreville, NC 28115
Bruinsma Hybrid Seed Co.	6346 Avon Belden Rd., N. Ridgeville, OH 44039
W. Atlee Burpee Co.	300 Park Ave., Warminster, PA 18974
D. V. Burrell Seed Growers Co.	Box 150-A, Rocky Ford, CO 81067
H. P. Cannon & Son, Inc.	Bridgeville, DE 19933
Alf Christianson Seed Co.	Box 98, Mt. Vernon, WA 98273
Daehnfeldt, Inc.	PO Box 947, Albany, OR 97321
Farmer Seed & Nursery Co.	2207 E. Oakland Ave., Bloomington, IL 95023
Ferry-Morse Co.	Box 4938, Modesto, CA 95354
FMC Corp., Seed Department	Box 3091, Modesto, CA 95353
Germain's Seeds, Inc.	Box 12447, Fresno, CA 93777
H. G. German Seeds, Inc.	Box 398, Smethport, PA 16749
Germania Seed Co.	5952 N. Milwaukee Ave., Chicago, IL 60646
Gleckers Seedsmen	Metamora, OH 43540
Gurney Seed & Nursery Co.	Yankton, SD 57079
Harris Moran Seed Co.	1155 Harkins Rd., Salinas, CA 93901
Harnish-Brinker Seed Co.	8539 W. California Ave., Fresno, CA 93706
Herbst Bros. Seedsmen, Inc.	1000 N. Main St., Brewster, NY 10509
Hollar & Co., Inc.	Box 106, Rocky Ford, CO 81067
Holmes Seed Co.	2125 46th St., N.W., Canton, OH 44709
Johnny's Selected Seeds	Foss Hill Road, Albion, ME 04910
Kilgore Seed Co.	1400 W. First St., Sanford, FL 32771
Letherman's, Inc.	1221 E. Tuscarawas St., Canton, OH 44707

SOME SOURCES OF VEGETABLE SEED[1]—Continued

Company	Address
Livingstone Seed Co.	880 Kinnear Rd., Columbus, OH 43216
Meyer Seed Co.	600 S. Caroline St., Baltimore, MD 21231
Henry F. Mitchell Co.	Box 160, King of Prussia, PA 19406
Midwest Seed Growers	505 Walnut, Kansas City, MO 64106
Neuman Seed Co.	PO Box 1530, El Centro, CA 93344
Nickerson-Zwaan	Box 19 2990 AA, Barendrecht, Holland
Northrup King & Co.	Box 1827, Gilroy, CA 95021
Geo. W. Park Seed Co.	Cokesbury Rd., Greenwood, SC 29647
Penn State Seed Co.	Box 390, Rt. 309, Dallas, PA 18612
Petoseed Co., Inc.	PO Box 4206, Saticoy, CA 93004
Quali-Sel, Inc.	1143 Madison Lane, Salinas, CA 93907
Reed's, Seeds	RD #2 Cortland, NY 13045 (cabbage seeds only)
Robson Seed Farms Corp.	Hall, NY 14463
Rogers Brothers Seed, Inc.	PO Box 1647, Idaho Falls, ID 83401
Royal Sluis, Inc.	1293 Harkins Road, Salinas, CA 93901
Seedway, Inc.	Hall, NY 14463
Shamrock Seed Co.	PO Box 3011, Lantana, FL 33465
R. H. Shumway	Box 1, Graniteville, SC 29829
Sluis & Groot of America, Inc.	124A Griffin St., Salinas, CA 93901
Stokes Seed, Inc.	5008 Stokes Bldg., Buffalo, NY 14240
Sunseeds	2320 Technology Pkwy, Hollister, CA 95024
Twilley Seed Co.	Box 65, Trevose, PA 19047
The Vaughn-Jacklin Corp.	5300 Katrine Ave., Downers Grove, IL 60515
Vesey's Seed, Ltd.	PO Box 9000, Houlton, ME 04730
Willhite Seed Co.	Box 23, Poolville, TX 76076
Yates and Co.	244 Horsley Rd., Milperra NSW 2214, Australia

[1]This partial list is presented with the understanding that no discrimination is intended and no guarantee of reliability implied.

Length

1 foot	=	12 inches
1 yard	=	3 feet
1 yard	=	36 inches
1 rod	=	16.5 feet
1 mile	=	5280 feet

Area

1 acre	=	43,560 square feet
1 section	=	640 acres
1 section	=	1 square mile

Volume

1 liquid pint	=	16 liquid ounces
1 liquid quart	=	2 liquid pints
1 liquid quart	=	32 liquid ounces
1 gallon	=	8 liquid pints
1 gallon	=	4 liquid quarts
1 gallon	=	128 liquid ounces
1 peck	=	16 pints (dry)
1 peck	=	8 quarts (dry)
1 bushel	=	4 pecks
1 bushel	=	64 pints (dry)
1 bushel	=	32 quarts (dry)

Mass or Weight

1 pound	=	16 ounces
1 hundredweight	=	100 pounds
1 ton	=	20 hundredweight
1 ton	=	2000 pounds

CONVERSION FACTORS FOR U.S. UNITS

Multiply	By	To Obtain
	Length	
feet	12.	inches
feet	0.33333	yards
inches	0.08333	feet
inches	0.02778	yards
miles	5,280.	feet
miles	63,360.	inches
miles	1,760.	yards
rods	16.5	feet
yards	3.	feet
yards	36.	inches
yards	0.000568	miles
	Area	
acres	43,560.	square feet
acres	160.	square rods
acres	4,840.	square yards
square feet	144.	square inches
square feet	0.11111	square yards
square inches	0.00694	square feet
square miles	640.	acres
square miles	27,878,400.	square feet
square miles	3,097,600.	square yards
square yards	0.0002066	acres
square yards	9.	square feet
square yards	1,296.	square inches
	Volume	
bushels	2,150.42	cubic inches
bushels	4.	pecks
bushels	64.	pints
bushels	32.	quarts
cubic feet	1,728.	cubic inches
cubic feet	0.03704	cubic yards
cubic feet	7.4805	gallons
cubic feet	59.84	pints (liquid)
cubic feet	29.92	quarts (liquid)

Multiply	By	To Obtain
	Volume	
cubic yards	27.	cubic feet
cubic yards	46,656.	cubic inches
cubic yards	202.	gallons
cubic yards	1,616.	pints (liquid)
cubic yards	807.9	quarts (liquid)
gallons	0.1337	cubic feet
gallons	231.	cubic inches
gallons	128.	ounces (liquid)
gallons	8.	pints (liquid)
gallons	4.	quarts (liquid)
gallons of water	8.3453	pounds of water
pecks	0.25	bushels
pecks	537.605	cubic inches
pecks	16.	pints (dry)
pecks	8.	quarts (dry)
pints (dry)	0.015625	bushels
pints (dry)	33.6003	cubic inches
pints (dry)	0.0625	pecks
pints (dry)	0.5	quarts (dry)
pints (liquid)	28.875	cubic inches
pints (liquid)	0.125	gallons
pints (liquid)	16.	ounces (liquid)
pints (liquid)	0.5	quarts (liquid)
quarts (dry)	0.03125	bushels
quarts (dry)	67.20	cubic inches
quarts (dry)	2.	pints (dry)
quarts (liquid)	57.75	cubic inches
quarts (liquid)	0.25	gallons
quarts (liquid)	32.	ounces (liquid)
quarts (liquid)	2.	pints (liquid)
	Mass or Weight	
ounces (dry)	0.0625	pounds
ounces (liquid)	1.805	cubic inches
ounces (liquid)	0.0078125	gallons
ounces (liquid)	0.0625	pints (liquid)
ounces (liquid)	0.03125	quarts (liquid)

Multiply	By	To Obtain
	Mass or Weight (Continued)	
pounds	16.	ounces
pounds	0.0005	tons
pounds of water	0.01602	cubic feet
pounds of water	27.68	cubic inches
pounds of water	0.1198	gallons
tons	32,000.	ounces
tons	20.	hundredweight
tons	2,000.	pounds
	Rate	
feet per minute	0.01667	feet per second
feet per minute	0.01136	miles per hour
miles per hour	88.	feet per minute
miles per hour	1.467	feet per second

METRIC UNITS OF MEASUREMENT

Length

1 millimeter	= 1000 microns
1 centimeter	= 10 millimeters
1 meter	= 100 centimeters
1 meter	= 1000 millimeters
1 kilometer	= 1000 meters

Area

1 hectare	= 10,000 square meters

Volume

1 liter	= 1000 milliliters

Mass or Weight

1 gram	= 1000 milligrams
1 kilogram	= 1000 grams
1 quintal	= 100 kilograms
1 metric ton	= 1000 kilograms
1 metric ton	= 10 quintals

CONVERSION FACTORS FOR U.S. AND METRIC UNITS

To Convert Column 1 into Column 2 Multiply by:	Column 1	Column 2	To Convert Column 2 into Column 1 Multiply By:
		Length	
0.621	kilometer (km)	mile (mi)	1.609
1.094	meter (m)	yard (yd)	0.914
0.394	centimeter (cm)	inch (in)	2.54
		Area	
0.386	square kilometer	square mile	2.59
247.1	square kilometer	acre	0.00405
2.471	hectare (ha)	acre	0.405
		Volume	
0.00973	cubic meter	acre-inch	102.8
3.532	hectoliter (hl)	cubic foot	0.2832
2.838	hectoliter	bushel (bu)	0.352
0.0284	liter	bushel	35.24
1.057	liter	quart (qt)	0.946

CONVERSION FACTORS FOR U.S. AND METRIC UNITS—Continued

To Convert Column 1 into Column 2 Multiply by:	Column 1	Column 2	To Convert Column 2 into Column 1 Multiply By:
		Mass	
1.102	metric ton (MT)	ton	0.9072
2.205	quintal (q)	hundredweight (cwt)	0.454
2.205	kilogram (kg)	pound (lb)	0.454
0.035	gram (g)	ounce (oz)	28.35
		Pressure	
14.22	kilograms per square centimeter	pounds per square inch (psi)	0.0703
14.50	bar	pounds per square inch	0.06895
0.9869	bar	atmosphere (atm)	1.013
0.9678	kilograms per square centimeter	atmosphere	1.033
14.70	atmosphere	pounds per square inch	0.06805
0.01450	kilopascal (KPa)	pounds per square inch	6.895
0.00987	kilopascal	atmosphere (atm)	101.30
10.0	megapascal (MPa)	atmosphere	0.101
10.0	megapascal	bar	0.1

	Yield or Rate		
0.446	metric tons per hectare	tons per acre	2.24
0.892	kilograms per hectare	pounds per acre	1.12
0.892	quintals per hectare	hundredweight per acre (cwt/acre)	1.12
	Temperature		
$\frac{9}{5}$ (°C) + 32	Celsius	Fahrenheit	$\frac{5}{9}$ (°F − 32)
	−17.8°C	0°F	
	0°C	32°F	
	20°C	68°F	
	100°C	212°F	
	Water Measurement		
8.108	hectare-meters	acre-feet	0.1233
97.29	hectare-meters	acre-inches	0.01028
0.08108	hectare-centimeters	acre-feet	12.33
0.973	hectare-centimeters	acre-inches	1.028
0.00973	cubic meters	acre-inches	102.8
0.981	hectare-centimeters per hour	cubic feet per second	1.0194
440.3	hectare-centimeters per hour	gallons per minute	0.00227
0.00981	cubic meters per hour	cubic feet per second	101.94
4.403	cubic meters per hour	gallons per minute	0.227
	Light		
0.0929	lux	footcandle (ft-c)	10.764

USEFUL CONVERSIONS FOR RATES OF APPLICATION

1 ton per acre = 20.8 grams per square foot
1 ton per acre = 1 pound per 21.78 square feet
1 ton per acre furrow slice (6-inch depth) = 1 gram per 1000 grams soil
1 gram per square foot = 96 pounds per acre
1 pound per acre = 0.0104 grams per square foot
1 pound per acre = 1.12 kilograms per hectare
100 pounds per acre = 0.2296 pounds per 100 square feet
grams per square foot × 96 = pounds per acre
kilograms per 48 square feet = tons per acre
pounds per square feet × 21.78 = tons per acre

INDEX